collections

Close Reader
TEACHER'S GUIDE

GRADE 11

Program Consultants:

Kylene Beers

Martha Hougen

Carol Jago

William L. McBride

Erik Palmer

Lydia Stack

HISTORY

ISBN 978-0-544-09122-1

4 5 6 7 8 9 10   1420   22 21 20 19 18 17 16 15 14

4500470058   B C D E F G

Close Reading— It's a Habit of Mind

By Carol Jago

You read closely every day. Each time you open a bank statement, mull over a new poem in the *New Yorker*, or grade a student paper, you perform a close reading. Often what appears on the page doesn't at first quite make sense. So what do you do? You read the text again, paying attention to places where comprehension broke down, focusing on unfamiliar words or familiar words used in unfamiliar ways. Sometimes you ask a friend for help when the meaning continues to elude you. Close reading isn't a strategy; it's a habit of mind.

In the past we protected students from texts they might find difficult, offering them only "considerate text" that made clear what the main ideas were and simplified dense passages. Unfortunately, college and career-readiness, not to mention the demands of citizenship, requires that students master the art of negotiating a great many inconsiderate texts. We thought we were helping students—trust me, no one has spent more time looking for shorter, easier, funnier things for kids to read than me—but we only succeeded in making the transition to college more difficult. The *Close Reader* offers students various protocols that, once internalized, will allow them to read independently with comprehension the complex texts called for in the Common Core State Standards.

Fortunately, many of these seemingly "inconsiderate" texts are also some of the finest literature ever written. The works of William Shakespeare, Homer, and Ralph Waldo Emerson as well as those of Isabelle Allende, Gwendolyn Brooks, and Ray Bradbury repay the investment of time and trouble taken to read them closely many times over. (So does an accurately read bank statement.)

Cognitive neuroscientist Maryanne Wolf, director of the Center for Reading and Language Research at Tufts University, warns that much of the reading today's young people are doing on the Internet develops a habit of what she calls a state of "continuous partial attention." In *Proust and the Squid: The Story and Science of the Reading Brain* (2007), Wolf describes how the time children spend daily processing a steady stream of online information is actually reshaping the architecture of their brains. As an English teacher, my concern is that while skimming and scanning may be an efficient and effective way to read a Twitter or Facebook feed, it's a very poor way to read poetry. I need my students to develop the ability to read profoundly and introspectively. And independently!

Common Core Anchor Standard #10 for reading states that students must "Read and comprehend complex literary and informational texts independently and proficiently." Working through this *Close Reader* will help your students perform proficiently by developing their independence as readers. As they practice unpacking challenging text for themselves, getting into the habit of rereading, slowing down when the going gets tough, knowing what to do when they meet a new word, students become more confident readers. We can't do the reading for them, not now or later. The *Close Reader* will give you ideas for what to do instead.

Let's make this a nation of close readers.

How to Use the Close Reader   vii

COLLECTION 1

Coming to America

HISTORICAL NARRATIVE
from The General History of Virginia   John Smith   2

ESSAY
Mother Tongue   Amy Tan   8

POEM
Indian Boy Love Song (#2)   Sherman Alexie   14

COLLECTION 2

Building a Democracy

PUBLIC DOCUMENT
from The United States Constitution   20

PUBLIC DOCUMENT
Petition to the Massachusetts General
Assembly   Prince Hall   24

HISTORY WRITING
Abigail Adams' Last Act of Defiance   Woody Holton   28

COLLECTION **3**
The Individual and Society

Poems by Walt Whitman   36

   POEM
   I Hear America Singing   Walt Whitman

   POEM
   A Noiseless Patient Spider   Walt Whitman

Essays by Ralph Waldo Emerson   40

   ESSAY
   from Nature   Ralph Waldo Emerson

   ESSAY
   from Self-Reliance   Ralph Waldo Emerson

   ESSAY
   Spoiling Walden: Or, How I Learned to
   Stop Worrying and Love Cape Wind   David Gessner   46

COLLECTION **4**
A New Birth of Freedom

LEGAL DOCUMENT
The Emancipation Proclamation   Abraham Lincoln   54

PUBLIC DOCUMENT
from The Iroquois Constitution   Dekanawida   58

NEWSPAPER ARTICLE
Bonding Over a Mascot   Joe Lapointe   62

COLLECTION 5
An Age of Realism

SHORT STORY
The Men in the Storm — Stephen Crane — 70

SCIENCE WRITING
The Yuckiest Food in the Amazon — Mary Roach — 78

SHORT STORY
A Journey — Edith Wharton — 84

POEM
Ode to a Large Tuna in the Market — Pablo Neruda — 94

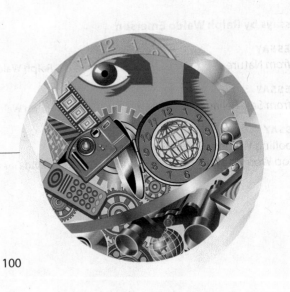

COLLECTION 6
The Modern World

SHORT STORY
Ambush — Tim O'Brien — 100

Selections from the Harlem Renaissance — 104

  ESSAY
  How It Feels to Be Colored Me — Zora Neale Hurston

  POEM
  The Weary Blues — Langston Hughes

DRAMA
from The Crucible — Arthur Miller — 110

ESSAY
Science, Guided by Ethics — Freeman Dyson — 124

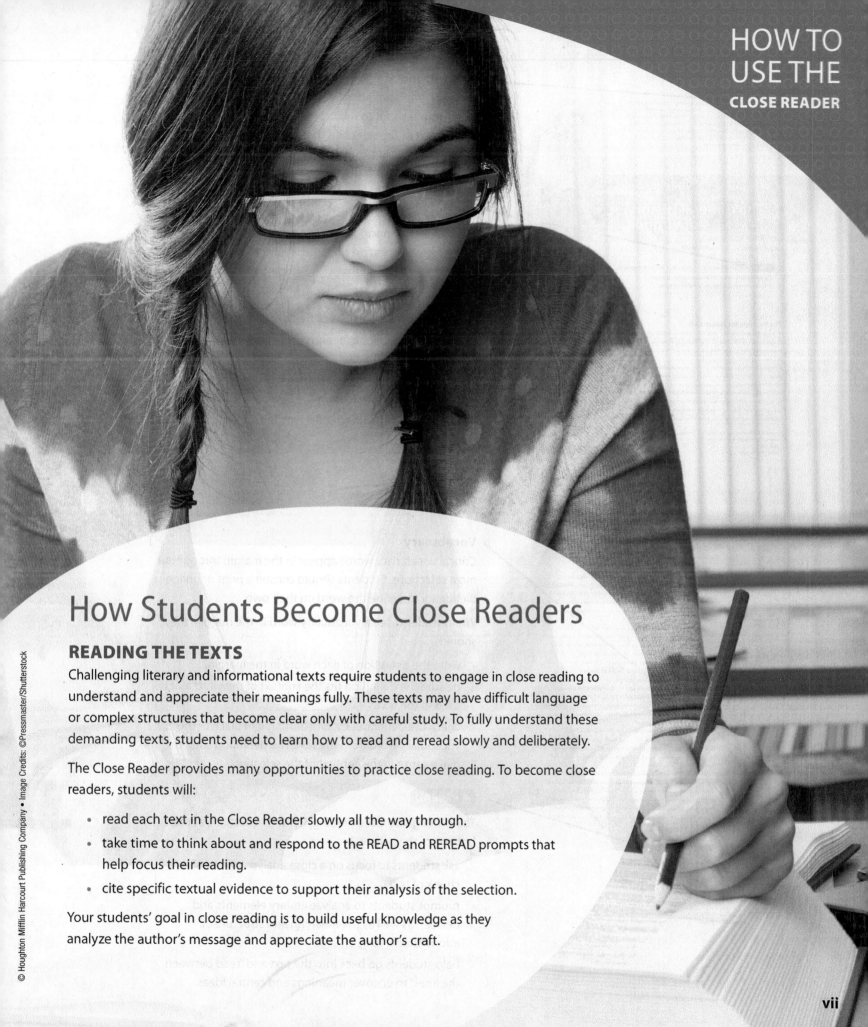

How Students Become Close Readers

READING THE TEXTS

Challenging literary and informational texts require students to engage in close reading to understand and appreciate their meanings fully. These texts may have difficult language or complex structures that become clear only with careful study. To fully understand these demanding texts, students need to learn how to read and reread slowly and deliberately.

The Close Reader provides many opportunities to practice close reading. To become close readers, students will:

- read each text in the Close Reader slowly all the way through.
- take time to think about and respond to the READ and REREAD prompts that help focus their reading.
- cite specific textual evidence to support their analysis of the selection.

Your students' goal in close reading is to build useful knowledge as they analyze the author's message and appreciate the author's craft.

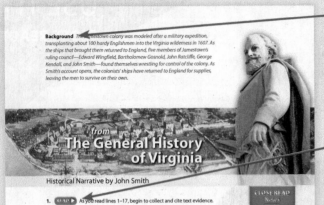

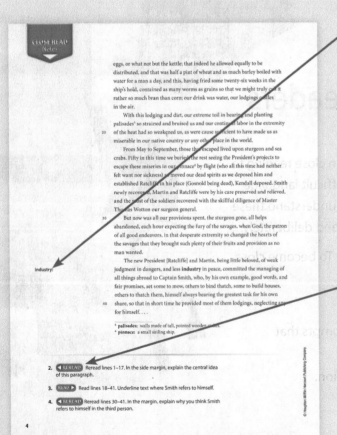

Background

This paragraph provides information about the text students are about to read. It helps them understand the context of the selection through additional information about the author, the subject, or the time period in which the text was written.

READ ▶

Questions and specific instructions at the beginning of the selection and on the bottom of the pages will guide students through a close reading of each text.

These questions and instructions:

- refer to specific sections of the text.

- ask students to look for and mark up specific information in the text.

- prompt students to record inferences and text analysis in the side margins.

- help students begin to collect and cite text evidence.

Vocabulary

Critical vocabulary words appear in the margin throughout most selections. Students should consult a print or online dictionary to define the word on their own.

When students see a vocabulary word in the margin, they should:

- write the definition of each word in the margin.

- be sure the definition fits the context of the word as it is used in the text.

- check the definition by substituting it in place of the vocabulary word from the text. The definition should make sense in the context of the selection.

◀ REREAD

To further guide close reading, REREAD questions at the bottom of the page will:

- ask students to focus on a close analysis of a smaller chunk of text.

- prompt students to analyze literary elements and devices, as well as the meaning and structure of informational text.

- help students go back into the text and "read between the lines" to uncover meanings and central ideas.

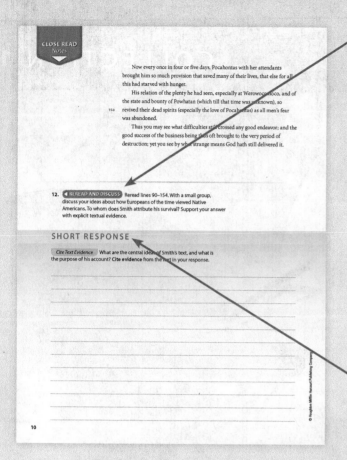

These prompts encourage students to work with a partner or in a small group to discuss specific events, details, statements, and evidence from the text. These discussions will allow students to acquire and share knowledge about the texts they are reading.

As they engage in these discussions, students should:

- be sure to cite specific text evidence in support of their statements.
- pose questions and integrate their ideas with the ideas of others.
- collaborate to reach a consensus or call attention to evidence that might have been missed or misinterpreted.
- acknowledge the views of others and be ready to modify their own thinking.

SHORT RESPONSE

At the end of each text, students will have an opportunity to sum up their thinking by completing a Short Response. The Short Response represents a place to convey some of the ideas they have developed through close reading of the text.

When students write the Short Response, they should:

- review all margin notes and REREAD responses.
- circle or highlight evidence from the notes that supports their position or point of view.
- clearly state a point of view and support it with reasons.
- cite specific text evidence to support their reasons.

Coming to America

COLLECTION 1

Coming to America

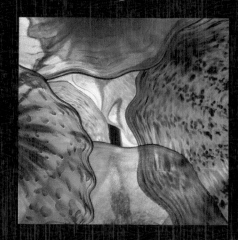

"[In America] individuals of all nations are melted into a new race . . . whose labors . . . will one day cause great changes in the world."

—Michel-Guillaume Jean de Crèvecoeur

HISTORICAL NARRATIVE

from The General History of Virginia

John Smith

ESSAY

Mother Tongue

Amy Tan

POEM

Indian Boy Love Song (#2)

Sherman Alexie

from **The General History of Virginia**

Historical Narrative by John Smith

Why This Text

This excerpt from "The General History of Virginia" provides an opportunity to analyze a historical narrative, a primary source with great significance in U.S. history. Students sometimes find it difficult to read older texts. They may also find it difficult to determine the author's purpose for writing. With the help of the close-reading questions, students will support their conclusions about the central ideas with strong and thorough textual evidence. This close reading will lead students to determine the central ideas of "The General History of Virginia."

Background Have students read the background and the information about the author. John Smith is well known as an American hero who was quick to boast about his accomplishments. Fact is often difficult to separate from fiction in his writing. Introduce the selection by explaining that the colonists were delivered to Virginia as employees of the *Virginia Company* with the purpose of profiting the company. The ships that brought the colonists returned to England, leaving the colonists to fend for themselves.

AS YOU READ Ask students to pay attention to clues that reveal Smith's central ideas and overall purpose. Remind them that this is an autobiography, and ask, "How does Smith present himself?"

Common Core Support

- cite strong and thorough textual evidence
- determine the central ideas of a text
- determine an author's purpose in a text
- analyze seventeenth-century foundational U.S. documents of historical and literary significance

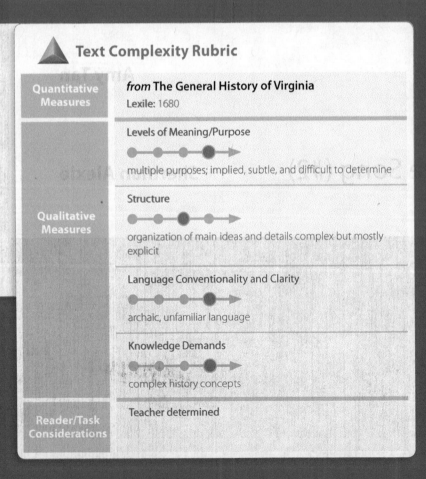

Text Complexity Rubric

Quantitative Measures

from **The General History of Virginia**
Lexile: 1680

Qualitative Measures

Levels of Meaning/Purpose

multiple purposes; implied, subtle, and difficult to determine

Structure

organization of main ideas and details complex but mostly explicit

Language Conventionality and Clarity

archaic, unfamiliar language

Knowledge Demands

complex history concepts

Reader/Task Considerations

Teacher determined

Strategies for CLOSE READING

Determine Central Ideas

Students should read this text carefully all the way through. Close-reading questions at the bottom of the page will help them focus on a thorough analysis of the text. As they read, students should jot down comments or questions about the text in the side margins.

WHEN STUDENTS STRUGGLE . . .

To help students determine the central ideas of the text, have them work in a small group to fill out a chart, such as the one shown below, as they analyze the text.

CITE TEXT EVIDENCE For practice in determining the central ideas of this excerpt from "The General History of Virginia," ask students to cite four important details from which they will determine two central ideas and one purpose. In filling out this chart, they should work from the bottom to the top.

Smith's Purpose: Smith tells the story of a colony saved by a single exceptional person—himself.

Central Idea: Smith was the one person responsible for overcoming the arduous and dangerous conditions at Jamestown.

Central Idea: Smith accepts no blame for charges brought against him, and draws attention to his leadership and courage.

Detail: "such extreme weakness and sickness oppressed us"

Detail: the President "committed the managing of all things" to Smith

Detail: Smith was "always bearing the greatest task for his own share"

Detail: Smith faced hundreds of "grim courtiers" and Powhatan "more like a devil"

Background *The Jamestown colony was modeled after a military expedition, transplanting about 100 hardy Englishmen into the Virginia wilderness in 1607. As the ships that brought them returned to England, five members of Jamestown's ruling council—Edward Wingfield, Bartholomew Gosnold, John Ratcliffe, George Kendall, and John Smith—found themselves wrestling for control of the colony. As Smith's account opens, the colonists' ships have returned to England for supplies, leaving the men to survive on their own.*

from The General History of Virginia

Historical Narrative by John Smith

1. **READ ▷** As you read lines 1–17, begin to collect and cite text evidence.
   - Circle the main problem described in the first paragraph.
   - Underline phrases that describe Wingfield's behavior.

CLOSE READ
Notes

The Struggle for Jamestown

A Being thus left to our fortunes, it fortuned that within ten days, scarce ten amongst us could either go or well stand, such extreme weakness and sickness oppressed us. And thereat none need marvel if they consider the cause and reason which was this: While the ships stayed, our allowance was somewhat bettered by a daily proportion of biscuit which the sailors would **pilfer** to sell, give, or exchange with us for money, sassafras, furs, or love. But when they departed, there remained neither tavern, beer-house, nor place of relief but the common kettle.[1] Had we been as free from all sins as [we were free from] gluttony and drunkenness we might have been canonized for saints,

B 10 but our President [Edward Wingfield] would never have been admitted [to sainthood] for engrossing to his private,[2] oatmeal, sack,[3] oil, aqua vitae,[4] beef,

pilfer:
steal articles of small value

[1] **common kettle:** food that was available to everyone.
[2] **engrossing to his private:** taking for his private use.
[3] **sack:** wine.
[4] **aqua vitae:** brandy.

3

---

1. **READ AND CITE TEXT EVIDENCE** Point out that Smith describes challenges faced by the colonists.

   A **ASK STUDENTS** to cite evidence that the colony faces both physical and interpersonal challenges. *Students should cite lines 1–3 as evidence of physical challenges, and lines 10–12 as evidence of a problem with Wingfield's behavior.*

   Critical Vocabulary: pilfer (line 6) Have students share their definitions of *pilfer*. Ask students to explain the exchange between the sailors and the colonists in their own words, and to use *pilfer* in their explanation.

Wingfield kept food and drink for himself; most other food was rotten.

eggs, or what not but the kettle; that indeed he allowed to be distributed, and that was half a pint of wheat and as much barley boiled with water for a man a day, and this, having fried some twenty-six weeks in the ship's hold, contained as many worms as grains so that we might truly call it rather so much bran than corn; our drink was water, our lodgings castles in the air.

With this lodging and diet, our extreme toil in bearing and planting
20   palisades⁵ so strained and bruised us and our continual labor in the extremity of the heat had so weakened us, as were cause sufficient to have made us as miserable in our native country or any other place in the world.

From May to September, those that escaped lived upon sturgeon and sea crabs. Fifty in this time we buried; the rest seeing the President's projects to escape these miseries in our pinnace⁶ by flight (who all this time had neither felt want nor sickness) so moved our dead spirits as we deposed him and

(C) established Ratcliffe in his place (Gosnold being dead), Kendall deposed. Smith newly recovered, Martin and Ratcliffe were by his care preserved and relieved, and the most of the soldiers recovered with the skillful diligence of Master
30   Thomas Wotton our surgeon general.

But now was all our provisions spent, the sturgeon gone, all helps abandoned, each hour expecting the fury of the savages, when God, the patron of all good endeavors, in that desperate extremity so changed the hearts of the savages that they brought such plenty of their fruits and provision as no man wanted.

(D) The new President [Ratcliffe] and Martin, being little beloved, of weak judgment in dangers, and less **industry** in peace, committed the managing of all things abroad to Captain Smith, who, by his own example, good words, and fair promises, set some to mow, others to bind thatch, some to build houses,
40   others to thatch them, himself always bearing the greatest task for his own share, so that in short time he provided most of them lodgings, neglecting any for himself. . . .

Smith probably refers to himself in the third person to make his account more believable.

industry: hard work; diligence

⁵ **palisades:** walls made of tall, pointed wooden stakes.
⁶ **pinnace:** a small sailing ship.

2. ◀ REREAD Reread lines 1–17. In the side margin, explain the central idea of this paragraph.

3. READ ▶ Read lines 18–41. Underline text where Smith refers to himself.

4. ◀ REREAD Reread lines 30–41. In the margin, explain why you think Smith refers to himself in the third person.

4

---

*"*But now was all our provisions spent, the sturgeon gone, all helps abandoned, each hour expecting the fury of the savages . . . *"*

A Surprise Attack

Smith, perceiving (notwithstanding their late misery) not any regarded but from hand to mouth, (the company being well recovered) caused the pinnace to be provided with things fitting to get provision for the year following, but in the **interim** he made three or four journeys and discovered the people of

(F) Chickahominy,⁷ yet what he carefully provided the rest carelessly spent.

(E) Wingfield and Kendall, living in disgrace strengthened themselves with the sailors and other confederates to regain their former credit and authority,
50   or at least such means aboard the pinnace (being fitted to sail as Smith had appointed for trade), to alter her course and to go for England.

Smith, unexpectedly returning, had the plot discovered to him, much trouble he had to prevent it, till with the store of saker⁸ and musket shot he forced them [to] stay or sink in the river: which action cost the life of Captain Kendall.⁹

These brawls are so disgustful, as some will say they are better forgotten, yet all men of good judgment will conclude it were better their **baseness** should be manifest to the world, than the business bear the scorn and shame of their excused disorders.

interim: period in between

baseness: lack of honor or morality

⁷ **Chickahominy:** a river in Virginia.
⁸ **saker:** canon shot.
⁹ **Captain Kendall:** Kendall was executed for mutiny in 1607.

5. READ ▶ As you read lines 42–62, continue to cite textual evidence. Paraphrase Wingfield and Kendall's plan in the margin on the next page. Explain what Smith does upon hearing about it.

5

---

2. REREAD AND CITE TEXT EVIDENCE

(B) ASK STUDENTS to cite evidence that supports their explanations. *Lines 10–16 show that President Wingfield kept the good food and drink for himself and left rotten food for others to eat.*

3. READ AND CITE TEXT EVIDENCE

(C) ASK STUDENTS to cite text evidence showing how Smith refers to himself. *Students should cite "Smith" in line 26, and "Captain Smith" in line 37.*

4. REREAD AND CITE TEXT EVIDENCE

(D) ASK STUDENTS what impression Smith would give if he had written lines 35–41 referring to himself in the first person. *He would sound self-opinionated and boastful.*

Critical Vocabulary: industry (line 36) Have students share their definitions of *industry*, and explain how it is used here.

5. READ AND CITE TEXT EVIDENCE

(E) ASK STUDENTS to cite textual evidence to support their paraphrase of Wingfield and Kendall's plan and Smith's intervention. *Students should cite text from lines 48–55.*

Critical Vocabulary: interim (line 45) Ask students to share definitions of *interim*. Ask them to paraphrase lines 44–47, using *interim* in context.

Critical Vocabulary: baseness (line 57) Ask students to share definitions of *baseness*. Then ask students to infer a reason that Smith would choose this word. *Students might say that Smith is disparaging Wingfield and Kendall to justify the actions he took that led to Kendall's death.*

FOR ELL STUDENTS Clarify the meaning of the preposition *notwithstanding*, which in this context means "in spite of."

Wingfield and Kendall plan to take over the ship and sail back to England. Smith puts an end to the plot, causing the death of Captain Kendall.

The Council accuses Smith of making little progress in finding the head of the Chickahominy river.

60   The President and Captain Archer[10] not long after intended also to have abandoned the country, which project also was curbed and suppressed by Smith.

    The Spaniard never more greedily desired gold than he [Smith] victual,[11] nor his soldiers more to abandon the country than he to keep it. But [he found] plenty of corn in the river of Chickahominy, where hundreds of savages in divers places stood with baskets expecting his coming. And now the winter approaching, the rivers became so covered with swans, geese, ducks, and cranes that we daily feasted with good bread, Virginia peas, pumpkins, and putchamins,[12] fish, fowl, and divers sort of wild beasts as fast as we could eat 70 them, so that none of our tuftaffety humorists[13] desired to go for England.

(G) (H)   But our comedies never endured long without a tragedy, some idle exceptions being muttered against Captain Smith for not discovering the head of Chickahominy river and [he being] taxed by the Council to be too slow in so worthy an attempt. The next voyage he proceeded so far that with much labor by cutting of trees asunder he made his passage, but when his barge could pass no farther, he left her in a broad bay of danger of shot, commanding none should go ashore till his return, himself with two English and two savages went up higher in a canoe, but he was not long absent but his men went ashore, whose want of government gave both occasion and opportunity to the savages 80 to surprise one George Cassen whom they slew and much failed not to have cut off the boat and all the rest.

    Smith little dreaming of that accident, being got to the marshes at the river's head twenty miles in the desert,[14] had his two men [Robinson and Emry] slain (as is supposed) sleeping by the canoe, while himself by fowling[15] sought

[10]**Captain Archer:** Gabriel Archer had abandoned the colony and then returned. He did not support Smith.
[11]**victual:** food.
[12]**putchamins:** persimmons.
[13]**tuftaffety humorists:** unreliable lace-wearers.
[14]**desert:** wilderness.
[15]**fowling:** hunting for birds.

6. ◀ REREAD AND DISCUSS   Reread lines 42–62. With a small group, discuss the extent to which Smith's account seems credible. To what extent is this a factual narrative?

7. READ ▶   As you read lines 63–89, continue to cite textual evidence.
   • Underline the details that make Smith seem like a hero.
   • In the margin, explain the Council's complaint against Smith (lines 71–74).

6

them victual, who finding he was beset with 200 savages, two of them he slew, still defending himself with the aid of the savage his guide, whom he bound to his arms with his garters[16] and used him as a buckler,[17] yet he was shot in his thigh a little, and had many arrows that stuck in his clothes but no great hurt, till at last they took him prisoner. . . .

At Powhatan's Court

90   At last they brought him to Werowocomoco, where was Powhatan, their Emperor. Here more than two hundred of those grim courtiers stood wondering at him, as [if] he had been a monster, till Powhatan and his train had put themselves in their greatest braveries.[18] Before a fire upon a seat like a bedstead, he sat covered with a great robe made of raccoon skins and all the tails hanging by. On either hand did sit a young wench of sixteen or eighteen years and along on each side [of] the house, two rows of men and behind them as many women, with all their heads and shoulders painted red, many of their heads bedecked with the white down of birds, but every one with something, and a great chain of white beads around their necks.

[16]**garters:** shirtlaces.
[17]**buckler:** shield.
[18]**braveries:** clothes.

8. ◀ REREAD   Reread lines 63–89. What explanations does Smith give for the loss of men, and his own capture? Why does he include these explanations? Support your answer with textual evidence.

He blames the Council for pushing him too hard. He blames the colonists who did not obey him. He blames two colonists who fell asleep in the canoe while he was getting food. Finally, he blames being outnumbered 200 to 1 by so-called "savages." He wants to show that it is not his fault that members of his party died and that he was captured. He is trying to remain blameless of all wrongdoing.

9. READ ▶   As you read lines 90–135, continue to cite textual evidence.
   • Underline language Smith uses to describe Powhatan.
   • In the margin, explain what happens in lines 100–112.

7

---

6. **REREAD AND DISCUSS USING TEXT EVIDENCE**

(F) **ASK STUDENTS** to cite specific textual evidence to support their conclusion about the degree to which Smith's account seems credible. *Students may cite evidence that shows that Smith takes credit for saving the colony and foiling plots of those who try to escape. They can cite lines 46–47 and lines 61–62.*

7. **READ AND CITE TEXT EVIDENCE**

(G) **ASK STUDENTS** to give the actual words in the text that Smith uses to describe the Council's claims against him. *Smith writes that he was charged for "not discovering the head of Chickahominy river" and for being "too slow in so worthy an attempt."*

8. **REREAD AND CITE TEXT EVIDENCE**

(H) **ASK STUDENTS** to read their answers to a partner, discuss the explanations Smith gives for the loss of men and his own capture, and revise their answers. *Students should cite evidence from lines 73–75 to show that Smith blames the Council for pushing him too hard, lines 83–84 to show that Smith blames his men for sleeping, and lines 85–89 to show that Smith blames the 200 savages for the losses incurred on his journey.*

9. **READ AND CITE TEXT EVIDENCE**

(I) **ASK STUDENTS** to cite text evidence to support their explanations of what happens in lines 100–112. *Students should cite evidence that shows that Smith was brought before the King (line 100), was about to be executed (lines 106–107), and was saved by Pocahontas (lines 107–109).*

CLOSE READ Notes

Smith was brought before the King, and was about to be executed. Pocahontas, the King's daughter, intervened and the King lets him live.

mollified: soothed; calmed

I 100 At his entrance before the King, all the people gave a great shout. The Queen of Appomattoc[19] was appointed to bring him water to wash his hands, and another brought him a bunch of feathers, instead of a towel, to dry them; having feasted him after their best barbarous manner they could, a long consultation was held, but the conclusion was, two great stones were brought before Powhatan; then as many as could, laid hands on him, dragged him to them, and thereon laid his head and being ready with their clubs to beat out his brains, Pocahontas, the King's dearest daughter, when no entreaty could prevail, got his head in her arms and laid her own upon his to save him from death, whereat the Emperor was contended he should live to make him 110 hatchets, and her bells, beads, and copper, for they thought him as well of all occupations as themselves. For the King himself will make his own robes, shoes, bows, arrows, pots; plant, hunt, or do anything so well as the rest.

J Two days after, Powhatan, having disguised himself in the most fearfulest manner he could, caused Captain Smith to be brought forth to a great house in the woods and there upon a mat by the fire to be left alone. Not long after, from behind a mat that divided the house, was made the most dolefulest noise he **L** ever heard; then Powhatan more like a devil than a man, with some two hundred more as black as himself, came unto him and told him now that they were friends, and presently he should go to Jamestown to send him two great 120 guns and a grindstone for which he would give him the country of Capahowasic and forever esteem him as his son Nantaquoud.

So to Jamestown with twelve guides Powhatan sent him. That night they quartered in the woods, he still expecting (as he had done all this long time of his imprisonment) every hour to be put to one death or other, for all their feasting. But almighty God (by His divine providence) had **mollified** the hearts of those stern barbarians with compassion. The next morning betimes they came to the fort, where Smith having used the savages with what kindness he could, he showed Rawhunt, Powhatan's trusty servant, two demi-culverins[20] and a millstone to carry [to] Powhatan; they found them somewhat too heavy, 130 but when they did see him discharge them, being loaded with stones, among the boughs of a great tree loaded with icicles, the ice and branches came so tumbling down that the poor savages ran away half dead with fear. But at last we regained some conference with them and gave them such toys and sent to Powhatan, his women, and children such presents as gave them in general full content.

[19]**Appomattoc:** a nearby village.
[20]**demi-culverins:** large cannons.

CLOSE READ Notes

Pocahontas appeals to Powhatan to spare John Smith.

K Now in Jamestown they were all combustion, the strongest preparing once more to run away with the pinnace; which, with the hazard of his life, with saker falcon and musket shot, Smith forced now the third time to stay or sink.

140 Some, no better than they should be, had plotted with the President the next day to have him put to death by the Levitical law,[21] for the lives of Robinson and Emry; pretending the fault was his that had led them to their ends; but he quickly took such order with such lawyers that he laid them by the heels[22] till he sent some of them prisoners for England.

[21]**Levitical law:** laws, ascribed to Moses, from the Book of Leviticus in the Old Testament.
[22]**laid them by the heels:** put them in prison.

10. **◀ REREAD AND DISCUSS** Reread lines 90–135. With a small group, discuss why Smith included an account of his time with Powhatan.

11. **READ ▶** As you read lines 136–154, continue to cite textual evidence.
   - Underline language that hints at Smith's attitude towards the "strongest" in Jamestown.
   - In the margin, explain how Pocahontas again helped Smith.

Critical Vocabulary: mollified (line 125) Have students explain the meaning of *mollified* as it is used here. Ask them to explain the significance of lines 122–126 using the word *mollified*.

FOR ELL STUDENTS Review the use of the suffix *-est* for superlatives. Point out the words *fearfulest* and *dolefulest* on this page. Ask students to provide the base word for each, *fearful* and *doleful*, and then guess what meaning the word takes with the suffix *-est*. You may have volunteers give examples of other words with the suffix *-est*.

10. **REREAD AND DISCUSS USING TEXT EVIDENCE**

J **ASK STUDENTS** to cite textual evidence to support their conclusions about why Smith included an account of his time with Powhatan. *Students should cite evidence showing that Smith characterizes the Native Americans as "fearful" (line 113), and inhuman (line 117, "like a devil"; line 127, "the savages") and characterizes himself as a hero with God on his side (lines 125–126).*

11. **READ AND CITE TEXT EVIDENCE**

K **ASK STUDENTS** to infer Smith's attitude towards the "strongest" using text they underlined as evidence. *Students should cite lines 136–137 to show that Smith has contempt for the leaders who repeatedly attempt to leave with the colony's ship. They should cite text from lines 140–142 to show that Smith claims to be falsely accused of causing the deaths of Robinson and Emry.*

Pocahontas brings food to Smith and his men.

Now every once in four or five days, Pocahontas with her attendants brought him so much provision that saved many of their lives, that else for all this had starved with hunger.

His relation of the plenty he had seen, especially at Werowocomoco, and of the state and bounty of Powhatan (which till that time was unknown), so
150 revived their dead spirits (especially the love of Pocahontas) as all men's fear was abandoned.

Thus you may see what difficulties still crossed any good endeavor; and the good success of the business being thus oft brought to the very period of destruction; yet you see by what strange means God hath still delivered it.

12. **◄ REREAD AND DISCUSS** Reread lines 90–154. With a small group, discuss your ideas about how Europeans of the time viewed Native Americans. To whom does Smith attribute his survival? Support your answer with explicit textual evidence.

SHORT RESPONSE

Cite Text Evidence What are the central ideas of Smith's text, and what is the purpose of his account? **Cite evidence** from the text in your response.

Smith presents details of the arduous and dangerous conditions at Jamestown; he also promotes himself as the one person responsible for overcoming each event that might have brought ruin to the colony. He writes that the President "committed the managing of all things" to Smith, who was "always bearing the greatest task for his own share." He defends himself against charges, accepting no blame, and goes on to explain how courageous he was in the face of hundreds of "grim courtiers" and Powhatan himself, "more like a devil." Smith tells the story of a colony saved by a single exceptional person—himself.

10

TO CHALLENGE STUDENTS . . .

To give students more background for this selection, have them research John Smith and the Jamestown colony online.

ASK STUDENTS to share the results of their research with the class. Encourage students to research Smith's credibility as an author. How do historians regard his account today?

DIG DEEPER

With the class, return to Question 6, Reread and Discuss. Have students share the results of their discussions.

ASK STUDENTS whether they were satisfied with the outcome of their small-group discussions. Have each group share their conclusions about the extent to which Smith's account seems credible, and the extent to which this is a factual narrative. What textual evidence did students find to support their conclusions?

- Guide each group to share whether they came to a unanimous conclusion about the degree to which Smith seems credible and the narrative seems factual. If not, have groups share the variety of conclusions that emerged from their discussion.
- Ask groups to share the textual evidence that seemed the most compelling. Discuss evidence that Smith is credible and that he is not credible.
- After groups have shared the results of their discussion, ask whether another group shared any ideas they wish they had thought of.

ASK STUDENTS to return to their Short Response answer and revise it based on the class discussion.

12. **REREAD AND DISCUSS USING TEXT EVIDENCE**

Ⓛ **ASK STUDENTS** to cite explicit textual evidence to support their conclusions about how Europeans of the time viewed Native Americans. *Students should cite evidence that shows that Europeans had a negative view of Native Americans, as evidenced in line 117 "like a devil" and line 127 "the savages." They should point out that Smith credits "God" (line 154) with saving the colony despite all the evidence that points to Native Americans having saved the lives of the colonists (lines 145–151).*

SHORT RESPONSE

Cite Text Evidence Students should:

- explain the central idea that life in Jamestown was difficult and dangerous.
- analyze the central idea that Smith defended himself against charges brought against him.
- infer Smith's purpose—to tell a story in which he is the heroic savior of the colony.

Mother Tongue

Essay by Amy Tan

Why This Text

Students often read an essay without evaluating its structure or understanding the author's purpose. In "Mother Tongue," Amy Tan argues that "nonstandard" English is not necessarily "broken." She illustrates her points with examples from her personal and professional life. With the help of the close-reading questions, students will an analyze how Tan structures her essay. This close reading will lead students to develop a coherent understanding of Tan's purpose.

Background Have students read the background and the information about the author. Tan earned a Master's Degree in Linguistics in 1974, but in the opening of her essay, she makes clear that her point of view is not that of a scholar. Introduce the selection by telling students that Tan is best known for her novel *The Joy Luck Club*, a collection of related stories about mothers and daughters. She also wrote the screenplay when the novel was turned into a film. As the daughter of Chinese immigrants, Tan grew up speaking Chinese English at home, and standard American English at school.

AS YOU READ Ask students to take notes on the structure of Tan's essay, both its organization, and its methods of making and supporting claims. How does Tan support her claims?

Common Core Support

- cite strong and thorough textual evidence
- determine the central ideas of a text
- determine an author's purpose
- analyze the effectiveness of the structure an author uses

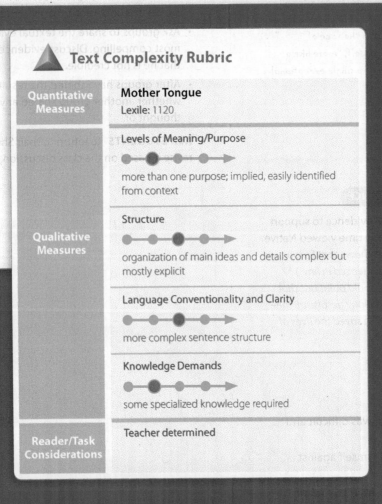

Text Complexity Rubric

Quantitative Measures	**Mother Tongue**
	Lexile: 1120

Levels of Meaning/Purpose

more than one purpose; implied, easily identified from context

Structure

organization of main ideas and details complex but mostly explicit

Language Conventionality and Clarity

more complex sentence structure

Knowledge Demands

some specialized knowledge required

Reader/Task Considerations	Teacher determined

8

Strategies for CLOSE READING

Analyze Structure: Essays

Students should read this essay carefully all the way through. Close-reading questions at the bottom of the page will help them focus on a thorough analysis of the essay. As they read, students should jot down comments or questions about the text in the side margins.

WHEN STUDENTS STRUGGLE . . .

To help students analyze the structure of Tan's essay, have them work in a small group to fill out a chart, such as the one shown below.

CITE TEXT EVIDENCE For practice analyzing the structure of "Mother Tongue," ask students to identify Tan's purpose in each of the following sections:

	TAN'S MAIN PURPOSE
Lines 1–49	Tan introduces the different Englishes her family speaks.
Lines 50–97	Tan defends her mother's speech, explaining that while others might call it "broken," she understands it perfectly, and calls it "mother tongue."
Lines 98–169	Tan shows that the concepts of "broken" or "limited" English can have serious negative consequences.
Lines 170–191	Tan closes by restating her thesis that her "mother tongue" is not "broken."

Background *Although her mother wanted her to be a neurosurgeon and a concert pianist,* **Amy Tan** *found her own road to success by becoming a writer. Her first novel,* The Joy Luck Club, *is a collection of related stories told by four mothers and four daughters and was later turned into a film. Tan was born in Oakland, California, two and a half years after her parents fled China's Communist revolution and settled in the United States. As the daughter of immigrant parents, Tan says she grew up with two Englishes—American English and Chinese English.*

Mother Tongue

Essay by Amy Tan

CLOSE READ
Notes

1. **READD▶** As you read lines 1–30, begin to collect and cite text evidence.
   - Underline text Tan uses that explains what Tan is not.
   - Circle words that explain how Tan describes herself.
   - In the margin, make a running list of the types of English Tan describes and how she describes them.

I am not a scholar of English or literature. I cannot give you much more than personal opinions on the English language and its variations in this country or others.

I am a writer. And by that definition, I am someone who has always loved language. I am fascinated by language in daily life. I spend a great deal of my time thinking about the power of language—the way it can evoke an emotion, a visual image, a complex idea, or a simple truth. Language is the tool of my trade. And I use them all—all the Englishes I grew up with.

Recently, I was made keenly aware of the different Englishes I do use. I was giving a talk to a large group of people, the same talk I had already given to half a dozen other groups. The talk was about my writing, my life, and my book *The Joy Luck Club*, and it was going along well enough, until I remembered one major difference that made the whole talk sound wrong. My mother was in the room. And it was perhaps the first time she had heard me give a lengthy speech, using the kind of English I have never used with her. I was saying things like "the intersection of memory and imagination" and "There is an aspect of my fiction that relates to thus-and-thus"—a speech filled with

B

10

11

1. **READ AND CITE TEXT EVIDENCE**

   A **ASK STUDENTS** to identify two types of English Tan describes, and to describe them using words and phrases taken directly from the text. *Students should identify that Tan describes "standard English" (line 20) as "carefully wrought" and "burdened" (line 18). She describes "family talk" as a "language of intimacy" (line 29).*

standard
English—
carefully
wrought,
burdened

family talk—
language of
intimacy

Tan's mother
speaks in
clipped, lyrical
phrases that
are incomplete
sentences and
have atypical
verb tenses.

A carefully wrought grammatical phrases, burdened, it suddenly seemed to me, with nominalized[1] forms, past perfect tenses, conditional phrases, forms of
20 standard English that I had learned in school and through books, the forms of English I did not use at home with my mother.

Just last week, as I was walking down the street with her, I again found myself conscious of the English I was using, the English I do use with her. We were talking about the price of new and used furniture, and I heard myself saying this: "Not waste money that way." My husband was with us as well, and he didn't notice any switch in my English. And then I realized why. It's because over the twenty years we've been together I've often used the same kind of English with him, and sometimes he even uses it with me. It has become our language of intimacy, a different sort of English that relates to family talk, the
30 language I grew up with.

So that you'll have some idea of what this family talk sounds like, I'll quote what my mother said during a conversation that I videotaped and then transcribed. During this conversation, she was talking about a political gangster in Shanghai who had the same last name as her family's, Du, and how in his early years the gangster wanted to be adopted by her family, who were rich by comparison. Later, the gangster became more powerful, far richer than my mother's family, and he showed up at my mother's wedding to pay his respects. Here's what she said in part:

C D "Du Yusong having business like fruit stand. Like off-the-street kind. He is
40 Du like Du Zong—but not Tsung-ming Island people. The local people call *putong*. The river east side, he belong to that side local people. That man want to ask Du Zong father take him in like become own family. Du Zong father wasn't look down on him, but didn't take seriously, until that man big like become a mafia. Now important person, very hard to inviting him. Chinese way, came only to show respect, don't stay for dinner. Respect for making big celebration, he shows up. Mean gives lot of respect. Chinese custom. Chinese

[1] **nominalized:** in grammar or linguistics, converted into a noun.

2. **◀ REREAD** Reread lines 9–21. Explain what Tan realized during her talk. Support your answer with explicit textual evidence.

Tan realized that the language she used in her talk was very different from the language she uses with her mother and her family.

3. **READ ▶** Read lines 31–49. In the margin, describe in your own words the English spoken by Tan's mother.

12

> **"** But to me, my mother's English is perfectly clear, perfectly natural. It's my mother tongue. **"**

social life that way. If too important won't have to stay too long. He come to my wedding. I didn't see, I heard it. I gone to boy's side, they have YMCA dinner. Chinese age I was nineteen."

E 50 You should know that my mother's expressive command of English **belies** how much she actually understands. She reads the *Forbes* report, listens to *Wall Street Week*, converses daily with her stockbroker, reads Shirley MacLaine's books with ease—all kinds of things I can't begin to understand. Yet some of my friends tell me they understand fifty percent of what my mother says. Some say they understand eighty to ninety percent. Some say they understand none of it, as if she were speaking pure Chinese.

But to me, my mother's English is perfectly clear, perfectly natural. It's my mother tongue. Her language, as I hear it, is vivid, direct, full of observation and imagery. That was the language that helped shape the way I saw things,
60 expressed things, made sense of the world.

F Lately I've been giving more thought to the kind of English my mother speaks. Like others, I have described it to people as "broken" or "fractured" English. But I wince when I say that. It has always bothered me that I can

belies:
gives a false
idea of

Tan doesn't
like the term
"broken"
English
because it
sounds like
it's damaged,
and lacks
clarity.

4. **◀ REREAD AND DISCUSS** Reread lines 9–49. With a small group, discuss Tan's use of personal anecdotes. What does including her mother's story add to the essay?

5. **READ ▶** As you read lines 50–68, continue to cite textual evidence.
   - Underline text that Tan uses to describe her mother's English.
   - Circle text that shows how others perceive Tan's mother's English.

6. **◀ REREAD** Reread lines 61–68. In the margin, explain Tan's position on "broken" English. Support your answer with explicit textual evidence.

13

---

2. **REREAD AND CITE TEXT EVIDENCE**

B **ASK STUDENTS** to cite explicit textual evidence to support their explanations of what Tan realized. *Students should cite text from lines 13–15, or lines 19–21.*

3. **READ AND CITE TEXT EVIDENCE**

C **ASK STUDENTS** to cite explicit textual evidence to support their descriptions of the English spoken by Tan's mother. *Students might describe her English as clipped ("Chinese custom," line 46) and lyrical ("Du Yusong having business like fruit stand. Like off-the-street kind," line 39). They might point out that her sentences are incomplete ("Chinese social life that way," lines 46–47) and that the verb tenses are atypical ("very hard to inviting him," line 44).*

FOR ELL STUDENTS Make sure that students understand that sentences such as "Not waste money that way" are grammatically incorrect. Invite a volunteer to share the correct form of this sentence ("Do not waste money that way").

4. **REREAD AND DISCUSS USING TEXT EVIDENCE**

D **ASK STUDENTS** to discuss how Tan's use of personal anecdotes adds to her essay. *Students might comment on the story as an engaging means of illustrating clearly what she means when she talks about "Englishes."*

5. **READ AND CITE TEXT EVIDENCE**

E **ASK STUDENTS** to contrast Tan's perceptions with the perceptions of others using the text evidence they have identified.

6. **REREAD AND CITE TEXT EVIDENCE**

F **ASK STUDENTS** to cite evidence to support their explanations. *Students should cite evidence from lines 63–65.*

Critical Vocabulary: belies (line 50) Have students compare definitions for *belies*.

think of no way to describe it other than "broken," as if it were damaged and needed to be fixed, as if it lacked a certain wholeness and soundness. I've heard other terms used, "limited English," for example. But they seem just as bad, as if everything is limited, including people's perceptions of the limited-English speaker.

70   I know this for a fact, because when I was growing up, my mother's "limited" English limited my perception of her. I was ashamed of her English. I believed that her English reflected the quality of what she had to say. That is, because she expressed them imperfectly, her thoughts were imperfect. And I had plenty of **empirical** evidence to support me: the fact that people in department stores, at banks, and in restaurants did not take her seriously, did not give her good service, pretended not to understand her, or even acted as if they did not hear her.

    My mother has long realized the limitations of her English as well. When I was a teenager, she used to have me call people on the phone and pretend I was she. In this **guise,** I was forced to ask for information or even to complain and

80 yell at people who had been rude to her. One time it was a call to her stockbroker in New York. She had cashed out her small portfolio, and it just so happened we were going to New York the next week, our first trip outside California. I had to get on the phone and say in an adolescent voice that was not very convincing, "This is Mrs. Tan."

    My mother was standing in the back whispering loudly, "Why he don't send me check, already two weeks late. So mad he lie to me, losing me money."

    And then I said in perfect English on the phone, "Yes, I'm getting rather concerned. You had agreed to send the check two weeks ago, but it hasn't arrived."

90   Then she began to talk more loudly. "What he want, I come to New York tell him front of his boss, you cheating me?" And I was trying to calm her down, make her be quiet, while telling the stockbroker, "I can't tolerate any more excuses. If I don't receive the check immediately, I am going to have to speak to your manager when I'm in New York next week." And sure enough, the following week, there we were in front of this astonished stockbroker, and I was sitting there red-faced and quiet, and my mother, the real Mrs. Tan, was shouting at his boss in her impeccable broken English.

empirical:
based on observation or experience

guise:
outer or disguised appearance

Tan uses this story to show how her mother's English is quite effective.

---

7. **READ ▶** Read lines 69–97. Underline the evidence Tan uses to support her ideas about the limitations of her mother's English.

8. **◀ REREAD** Reread lines 77–97. In the margin, explain Tan's purpose for telling this story about her mother and the stockbroker.

14

    We used a similar routine more recently, for a situation that was far less humorous. My mother had gone to the hospital for an appointment to find out

100 about a CAT scan she had had a month earlier. She said she had spoken very good English, her best English, no mistakes. Still, she said, the hospital staff did not apologize when they informed her they had lost the CAT scan and she had come for nothing. She said they did not seem to have any sympathy when she told them she was anxious to know the exact diagnosis, since both her husband and her son had died of brain tumors. She said they would not give her any more information until the next time and she would have to make another appointment for that. So she said she would not leave until the doctor called her daughter. She wouldn't budge. And when the doctor finally called her daughter, me, who spoke in perfect English—lo and behold—we had

110 assurances the CAT scan would be found, promises that a conference call on Monday would be held, and apologies for any suffering my mother had gone through for a most regrettable mistake.

    I think my mother's English almost had an effect on limiting my possibilities in life as well. Sociologists and linguists probably will tell you that a person's developing language skills are more influenced by peers than by family. But I do think that the language spoken in the family, especially in immigrant families which are more insular, plays a large role in shaping the language of the child. And I believe that it affected my results on achievement tests, IQ tests, and the SAT. While my English skills were never judged poor,

120 compared with math, English could not be considered my strong suit. In grade school I did moderately well, getting perhaps B's, sometimes B-pluses, in English and scoring perhaps in the sixtieth or seventieth percentile on achievement tests. But those scores were not good enough to override the opinion that my true abilities lay in math and science, because in those areas I achieved A's and scored in the ninetieth percentile or higher.

    This was understandable. Math is precise; there is only one correct answer. Whereas, for me at least, the answers on English tests were always a judgment call, a matter of opinion and personal experience. Those tests were constructed around items like fill-in-the-blank sentence completion, such as "Even though

She did poorly on tests.

Her teachers thought she was better in math and science.

---

9. **READ ▶** As you read lines 98–152, continue to cite textual evidence.

- Underline text that explains how Tan's mother's English "almost had an effect on limiting [Tan's] possibilities in life."
- In the margin, briefly note the examples Tan uses to support her position.

15

---

7. **READ AND CITE TEXT EVIDENCE**

G **ASK STUDENTS** to evaluate the effectiveness of Tan's evidence. *Students might point out that Tan was in a position to make repeated, firsthand observations, making her evidence strong (lines 72–76).*

8. **REREAD AND CITE TEXT EVIDENCE**

H **ASK STUDENTS** to cite textual evidence to support their explanations. *Students should cite evidence from lines 94–97.*

Critical Vocabulary: empirical (line 73) Have students share their definitions for *empirical*.

Critical Vocabulary: guise (line 79) Have students explain the meaning of *guise* as it is used here. *On the phone, Tan speaks to the family stockbroker pretending to be her mother—in her mother's guise.*

9. **READ AND CITE TEXT EVIDENCE**

I **ASK STUDENTS** to cite textual evidence that explains the effect of her mother's English on Tan. *Students should cite evidence of the effect on test results (lines 118–119, lines 136–137, and lines 142–144) and on her teachers' perceptions of her abilities (lines 123–124).*

FOR ELL STUDENTS You may wish to explain to your ELL students the meanings of the acronyms *IQ (intelligence quotient)* and *SAT (Scholastic Assessment Test)*.

> *I began to write stories using all the Englishes I grew up with.*

bland:

dull, boring

130 Tom was _____ Mary thought he was _____." And the correct answer always seemed to be the most **bland** combinations, for example, "Even though Tom was shy, Mary thought he was charming," with the grammatical structure "even though" limiting the correct answer to some sort of opposites, so you wouldn't get answers like "Even though Tom was foolish, Mary thought he was ridiculous." Well, according to my mother, there were very few limitations as to what Tom could have been and what Mary might have thought of him. So I never did well on tests like that.

The same was true with word analogies, pairs of words for which you were supposed to find some logical semantic² relationship, for instance, "Sunset is to

140 nightfall as _____ is to _____." And here you would be presented with a list of four possible pairs, one of which showed the same kind of relationship: *red* is to *stoplight*, *bus* is to *arrival*, *chills* is to *fever*, *yawn* is to *boring*. Well, I could never think that way. I knew what the tests were asking, but I could not block out of my mind the images already created by the first pair, *sunset* is to *nightfall*—and I would see a burst of colors against a darkening sky, the moon rising, the lowering of a curtain of stars. And all the other pairs of words—*red, bus, stoplight, boring*—just threw up a mass of confusing images, making it impossible for me to see that saying "A sunset precedes nightfall" was as logical as saying "A chill precedes a fever." The only way I would have gotten that

150 answer right was to imagine an associative situation, such as my being

² **semantic:** of or relating to language

16

disobedient and staying out past sunset, catching a chill at night, which turned into feverish pneumonia as punishment—which indeed did happen to me.

(K) I have been thinking about all this lately, about my mother's English, about achievement tests. Because lately I've been asked, as a writer, why there are not more Asian-Americans represented in American literature. Why are there few Asian-Americans enrolled in creative writing programs? Why do so many Chinese students go into engineering? Well, these are broad sociological questions I can't begin to answer. But I have noticed in surveys—in fact, just last week—that Asian-American students, as a whole, do significantly better on

160 math achievement tests than on English tests. And this makes me think that there are other Asian-American students whose English spoken in the home might also be described as "broken" or "limited." And perhaps they also have teachers who are steering them away from writing and into math and science, which is what happened to me.

Fortunately, I happen to be rebellious and enjoy the challenge of disproving assumptions made about me. I became an English major my first year in college, after being enrolled as pre-med. I started writing nonfiction as

(J) a freelancer the week after I was told by my boss at the time that writing was my worst skill and I should hone my talents toward account management.

170 But it wasn't until 1985 that I began to write fiction. At first I wrote what I thought to be wittily crafted sentences, sentences that would finally prove I had mastery over the English language. Here's an example from the first draft of a story that later made its way into *The Joy Luck Club*, but without this line: "That was my mental quandary in its nascent state." A terrible line, which I can barely pronounce.

(L) Fortunately, for reasons I won't get into here, I later decided I should envision a reader for the stories I would write. And the reader I decided on was my mother, because these were stories about mothers. So with this reader in mind—and in fact she did read my early drafts—I began to write stories using

180 all the Englishes I grew up with: the English I spoke to my mother, which for lack of a better term might he described as "simple"; the English she used with me, which for lack of a better term might be described as "broken"; my translation of her Chinese, which could certainly be described as "watered

10. **READ ▶** Read lines 153–169. Underline how other people reacted to Tan's English.

11. **◀ REREAD** Reread lines 153–164. In the margin, summarize Tan's main purpose in this paragraph. Support your answer with explicit textual evidence.

17

Here, Tan's purpose is to explain that the lack of Asian Americans represented in American literature might be due to misconceptions about the abilities of Asian Americans.

Critical Vocabulary: bland (line 131) Have students share their definitions of *bland*. Ask how Tan's choice of the word *bland* supports her purpose in this paragraph. *Tan is challenged by the limitations of standard ways of thinking about English word meanings and relationships, calling the correct answers on tests "bland" interpretations. Her mother did not follow these limitations (line 135, "according to my mother…").*

FOR ELL STUDENTS Practice the use and meaning of the prefix *dis-* with students. Point out examples on the next page (*disobedient, disproving*). Have volunteers provide the opposite of these words (*obedient, proving*). Then encourage students to give more examples of words with the same prefix.

10. **READ AND CITE TEXT EVIDENCE**

(J) **ASK STUDENTS** to cite textual evidence of her boss's reaction to Tan's English. *Students should cite "I was told by my boss at the time that writing was my worst skill," in lines 168–169.*

11. **REREAD AND CITE TEXT EVIDENCE**

(K) **ASK STUDENTS** to cite textual evidence to support their summaries of Tan's main purpose. *Students should cite evidence from lines 154–157 to show that Tan is answering a question about the lack of Asian Americans represented in American literature. They should cite evidence from lines 161–164 to show that Tan's theory is that there are misconceptions about the abilities of Asian Americans.*

CLOSE READ
Notes

Tan envisioned her ideal reader—her mother. When her mother approved of her stories, Tan knew she had done her job well.

down"; and what I imagined to be her translation of her Chinese if she could speak in perfect English, her internal language, and for that I sought to preserve the essence, but neither an English nor a Chinese structure. I wanted to capture what language ability tests could never reveal: her intent, her passion, her imagery, the rhythms of her speech and the nature of her thoughts.

190   Apart from what any critic had to say about my writing, I knew I had succeeded where it counted when my mother finished reading my book and gave me her verdict: "So easy to read."

12. **READ ▶** Read lines 170–191. Underline the four types of English Tan describes. In the margin, explain why Tan finally felt she had succeeded.

SHORT RESPONSE

Cite Text Evidence Trace the structure of Tan's essay, describing both its organization and its methods. How does the structure of her essay support her purpose? **Cite evidence** from the text to support your response.

Tan has divided her essay into sections, explaining her understanding of different types of English. She describes these different languages and also shows how they are effective, rather than "broken." She shows the negative impact on her mother of limited perceptions of her and then explains how those perceptions nearly limited Tan's own life. Her conclusion is a vindication of her mother tongue: "So easy to read." Tan's purpose is to educate readers about limited-English speakers. The use of personal anecdotes and the description of her own journey learning about English is effective because it helps us understand her own revelations.

18

12. ╱READ AND CITE TEXT EVIDENCE╲

Ⓛ ASK STUDENTS to cite textual evidence to support their explanation of why Tan felt she had succeeded. *Students should cite evidence from lines 176–178 showing that Tan's ideal reader is her mother, and from lines 189–191 showing that her mother found the writing "easy to read."*

SHORT RESPONSE

Cite Text Evidence Student responses will vary, but they should cite evidence from the text to support their explanations and descriptions. Students should:

• explain Tan's organization.

• describe Tan's methods.

• evaluate the effectiveness of Tan's structure in supporting her purpose.

TO CHALLENGE STUDENTS . . .

For more context, have students research how the English language evolves, changes, and incorporates new words, even today. Recent additions to *The Merriam-Webster Dictionary* include *aha moment* and *man cave*. The Chinese language has enriched English with words such as *kumquat* (1699), *gung ho* (1941), and *wok* (1952).

ASK STUDENTS to research some aspect of the continuing evolution of English. Each student should identify an area of research such as how words are added to dictionaries, how rules of syntax change over time, or words that come to English from other languages. Have students share the results of their research with the class, and discuss how Englishes like Tan's mother tongue influence what Tan calls standard English.

DIG DEEPER

With the class, return to Question 4, Reread and Discuss. Have students share the results of their discussion.

ASK STUDENTS whether they were satisfied with the outcome of their small-group discussions. Have each group share their conclusions about Tan's use of personal anecdotes. Ask groups to share the textual evidence that supports their conclusions.

• In lines 9–21, what does the story about Tan's mother add to the essay? *Students may conclude that the anecdote about her mother helps to establish Tan's point of view, her credentials, and/or her purpose in an engaging way.*

• In lines 31–38, how does Tan establish the authenticity of her illustration "of what this family talk sounds like"? *Students should point out that Tan is quoting a transcribed videotape.*

• In lines 39–49, how does the quotation support Tan's purpose? *Students should explain that the anecdote is a clear illustration of Tan's "mother tongue."*

ASK STUDENTS to return to their Short Response answer and to revise it based on the class discussion.

Indian Boy Love Song (#2)

Poem by Sherman Alexie

Why This Text

Alexie compresses thoughts and emotions in this short poem. The poem is written in free verse, so there is little to draw attention to the deeper meaning, especially if students read it quickly (which is easy to do). The concise thoughts—making use of deliberately "friendly" vocabulary—present a larger theme. With the help of the close-reading questions, students will be able to infer the theme. This close reading will lead students to a deeper understanding of a powerful poem.

Background Have students read the background and information about the author. Tell students that Sherman Alexie decided to attend a high school 30 miles away from the Spokane Indian Reservation, before he went to college. Much of Alexie's early work tries to reconcile his desire to improve himself with his feeling of having abandoned his people. His work also explores the many problems plaguing contemporary American Indian society, including poverty and alcoholism.

AS YOU READ Ask students to pay attention to the author's choice of words, and how they affect the tone. The poem's tone helps the reader infer the theme of the poem.

Common Core Support

- cite strong and thorough textual evidence
- determine a theme of a text
- determine figurative and connotative meanings of words and phrases

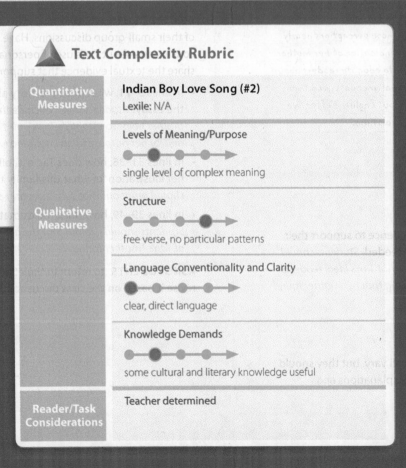

Text Complexity Rubric

Quantitative Measures

Indian Boy Love Song (#2)
Lexile: N/A

Qualitative Measures

Levels of Meaning/Purpose
single level of complex meaning

Structure
free verse, no particular patterns

Language Conventionality and Clarity
clear, direct language

Knowledge Demands
some cultural and literary knowledge useful

Reader/Task Considerations
Teacher determined

Strategies for CLOSE READING

Analyze Language

Students should read this poem carefully all the way through. Close-reading questions at the bottom of the page will help them draw inferences from the poet's language about the poem's deeper message. As they read, students should jot down comments or questions about the text in the margins.

WHEN STUDENTS STRUGGLE . . .

To help students analyze the language in "Indian Boy Love Song (#2)," have them work in small groups to fill out a chart like the one shown below.

CITE TEXT EVIDENCE For practice in analyzing language, ask students to explain the impact of each text example.

Text Example	Impact
"I never spoke . . . I never held my head . . ." (lines 1 and 8)	Repeating the words "I never" adds weight to the lines. The word never is a powerful word.
". . . in winters so cold they could freeze the tongue whole." (lines 5–7)	The imagery gives an immediate understanding of the physical effects of the cold.
". . . believing in the heart." (line 10)	The heart is usually a symbol of something important and essential.
". . . and always afraid." (line 13)	The use of always contrasts with the previous use of never. Perhaps never doing the things mentioned resulted in always feeling afraid.

Background Sherman Alexie *is a poet, writer, and filmmaker who was raised on the Spokane Indian Reservation in Wellpinit, Washington. His work—which includes the acclaimed short story collection* The Lone Ranger and Tonto Fistfight in Heaven—*is largely inspired by his American Indian heritage and experiences. One of Alexie's recurring themes is the powerlessness many American Indians feel in contemporary society.*

Indian Boy Love Song (#2)

Poem by Sherman Alexie

CLOSE READ
Notes

1. **READ ▷** As you read lines 1–13, begin to collect and cite evidence.
   - Underline text describing what the speaker never did.
   - Circle adjectives describing people.

A B
I never spoke
the language
of the old women

5 visiting my mother
in winters so cold
they could freeze
the tongue whole.

I never held my head
to their thin chests
10 believing in the heart.

Indian women, forgive me.
I grew up distant
and always afraid.

19

1. **READ AND CITE TEXT EVIDENCE** Remind students that an author's word choice can set the tone of a poem.

A ASK STUDENTS what the word *distant* implies in the poem. *Students may suggest that the word implies that the speaker was distant not only in terms of proximity but also in terms of his emotions and allegiances.*

FOR ELL STUDENTS Explain that poets sometimes take "poetic license" by using a different syntax, or order of words, than is used in standard English. In this case, the poet uses the adjective *whole* after the noun. Remind your students that in English adjectives precede the nouns they refer to.

15

2. **◄ REREAD** Reread the poem. How would you describe the tone of the poem? Cite textual evidence in your response.

The tone of the poem is reverential and solemn. The speaker seems repentant ("Indian women, forgive me") and almost ashamed because of actions he never took.

SHORT RESPONSE

Cite Text Evidence What do you think is the theme of "Indian Boy Love Song (#2)"? What is the central idea about life or human nature that Alexie wants to communicate to his readers? **Cite textual evidence** in your response.

The theme is the loss of culture and the responsibility the speaker feels for failing to listen and believe "in the heart." Alexie hints at the fragility of American Indian culture with images of the cold winters and "their thin chests." The speaker also expresses remorse at his lack of connection to the culture: "I grew up distant / and always afraid." Perhaps this poem is an apology and a promise to set things right by addressing this in verse.

20

TO CHALLENGE STUDENTS . . .

Sherman Alexie's poems often have similar themes. Have students read "Sonnet, Without Salmon." (They can find this poem online at *Orion* magazine.)

ASK STUDENTS why the speaker compares his grandmother to a salmon. *The grandmother and salmon both swam in water, but are no longer there. The water itself has been dammed.* Ask students to compare the themes of "Sonnet, Without Salmon" and "Indian Boy Love Song (#2)." *Students will probably suggest that in these poems, Alexie writes about the loss of culture, and not feeling at home any more. The river in "Sonnet, Without Salmon" has been dammed to generate electricity to power appliances that take us further from nature.*

---

2. **REREAD AND CITE TEXT EVIDENCE** Remind students that word choice often sets the tone. This poem is short and its tone is consistent.

B ASK STUDENTS to cite text evidence that supports their interpretation of the poem's tone. *The tone is respectful and humble. The use of the word* never *lets the reader know that the speaker had the opportunity to learn "the language of the old women," and to believe "in the heart." He is repentant ("forgive me") and sad that he was "distant and always afraid."*

SHORT RESPONSE

Cite Text Evidence Students' responses should:

- determine the poem's theme.
- describe the poem's central idea about life or human nature.
- support their response with specific text evidence.

DIG DEEPER

1. With the class, return to Question 1, Read. Have students read the poem.

   ASK STUDENTS to cite the text evidence that they use to interpret the poem.

   - Have students explain who the "old women" in line 3 are. *They are the "Indian women" mentioned in line 11. They are the women the speaker grew up with: his mother and her friends and relatives.*

   - Have students describe in their own words why the speaker wants the Indian women's forgiveness. *Students should point out that the Indian women offered the speaker opportunities to speak their language and to follow their beliefs, but he "never" took advantage of these opportunities.*

   - Ask students to infer why the speaker was "always afraid." *Students may infer that the speaker had not followed his own culture, and so was always "distant." Not having a place in the world left him afraid.*

2. With the class, return to Question 2, Reread. Have students share their responses.

   ASK STUDENTS how the poet creates the tone of the poem.

   - Have students determine what purpose the repetition in the poem serves. *Students may suggest that the repetitive use of the words "I never" strengthens the poet's point; he sets up a pattern.*

   - Have students infer what the words "believing in the heart" mean to the poet. *Students may infer that the women in the poem place a higher value on what is in their hearts than what shows outwardly. The poet seems to accept (as he writes the poem) that the women were wiser than he, and that he could have learned from them.*

   - Have students explain the impact of the final two lines of the poem, and how they resonate with the reader. *Students may suggest that the lines express a powerful emotion in very few words. The emotion is one that is easy to understand; everyone in their youth has felt alienated and scared.*

   ASK STUDENTS to return to their Short Response answer and revise it based on the class discussion.

CLOSE READING NOTES

Building a Democracy

Building a Democracy

"A nation is formed by the willingness of each of us to share the responsibility for upholding the common good."

—Barbara Jordan

PUBLIC DOCUMENT

from The United States Constitution

PUBLIC DOCUMENT

Petition to the Massachusetts General Assembly

Prince Hall

HISTORY WRITING

Abigail Adams' Last Act of Defiance

Woody Holton

from **The United States Constitution**

For additional background, students can view the video "America Gets a Constitution" in their eBooks.

Public Document

Why This Text

Students reading foundational U.S. documents for the first time may find them difficult to comprehend. The authors of these documents employed language, syntax, and structure that students rarely encounter today. With the help of the close-reading questions, students will identify and analyze key provisions of Article II of the U.S. Constitution. This close reading will lead students to understand the meaning behind this foundational document.

Background Have students read the background and information about the U.S. Constitution. Alternatively, students can watch the video "America Gets a Constitution" in their eBooks. Remind students that the Constitution begins with the Preamble, which is followed by Articles I through VII (the body of the Constitution), and ends with the Bill of Rights and later Amendments.

AS YOU READ Ask students to pay attention to the organization of the Sections. How does this structure help readers understand the purpose of Article II?

Common Core Support

- cite strong and thorough textual evidence
- analyze and evaluate the structure of a text
- analyze foundational U.S. documents

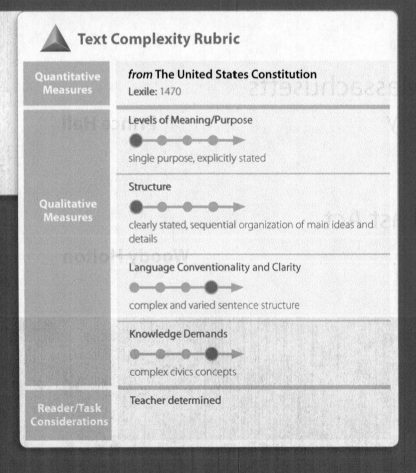

▲ Text Complexity Rubric

Quantitative Measures

from **The United States Constitution**
Lexile: 1470

Qualitative Measures

Levels of Meaning/Purpose

single purpose, explicitly stated

Structure

clearly stated, sequential organization of main ideas and details

Language Conventionality and Clarity

complex and varied sentence structure

Knowledge Demands

complex civics concepts

Reader/Task Considerations

Teacher determined

Analyze Foundational Documents

Students should read this document carefully all the way through. Close-reading questions at the bottom of the page will help them focus on a thorough analysis of the text. As they read, students should jot down comments or questions about the text in the margins.

WHEN STUDENTS STRUGGLE . . .

To help students analyze the structure of this excerpt of the U.S. Constitution, have them work in small groups to fill out a chart like the one shown below.

CITE TEXT EVIDENCE For practice in analyzing a foundational document, ask students to summarize key provisions of each section of Article II.

Section 1	Section 2
President has executive power.	President is in charge of the Army and Navy.
There are limits on who can become President.	President makes treaties—with the advice and consent of the Senate.
President must swear an oath.	President appoints judges to the Supreme Court—with the advice and consent of the Senate.
Section 3	**Section 4**
President can make recommendations to Congress.	President, Vice President, and other government officials can be impeached.
President can convene and adjourn Congress.	
President makes sure laws are carried out.	

Background *The Constitution of the United States was written in September 1787 by a group of 55 men now known as the Framers of the Constitution, including George Washington and Benjamin Franklin. The document was written to replace the old Articles of Confederation and to establish the three branches of the federal government. The Constitution went into effect in 1789 and is considered the supreme law of the United States.*

from
The United States Constitution
Public Document

CLOSE READ
Notes

1. **READ** ▶ As you read lines 1–16, begin to collect and cite text evidence.
   - Circle the length of a presidential term.
   - Underline those who may *not* be appointed an Elector.
   - Make notes in the margin about who can hold the office of President.

ARTICLE. II.
Section. 1.

The executive Power shall be vested in a President of the United States of America. He shall hold his Office during the Term of ⟨four Years⟩, and, together with the Vice President, chosen for the same Term, be elected, as follows:

Each State shall appoint, in such Manner as the Legislature thereof may direct, a Number of Electors, equal to the whole Number of Senators and Representatives to which the State may be entitled in the Congress: but no Senator or Representative, or Person holding an Office of Trust or Profit under the United States, shall be appointed an Elector.

10 The Congress may determine the Time of chusing the Electors, and the Day on which they shall give their Votes; which Day shall be the same throughout the United States.

Ⓐ
Ⓑ No Person except a natural born Citizen, or a Citizen of the United States, at the time of the Adoption of this Constitution, shall be eligible to the Office of President; neither shall any Person be eligible to that Office who shall not have attained to the Age of thirty five Years, and been fourteen Years a Resident within the United States.

Only a natural-born citizen who has been a U.S. resident for 14 years and who is older than the age of 35 can become President.

23

1. **READ AND CITE TEXT EVIDENCE** Section 1 of Article II of the Constitution lays the foundation for the office of the presidency, establishing who can become President and how the President will be elected.

Ⓐ ASK STUDENTS to discuss the text that outlines who can become President (lines 12–16). Have them cite examples of language, grammar, and syntax that would be uncommon in a modern document. *The entire paragraph is one long sentence. The order and structure of clauses seems complicated. Most of the nouns are capitalized. Phrases such as "attained to the Age of thirty five Years" are no longer used.*

The President shall, at stated Times, receive for his Services, a
Compensation, which shall neither be increased nor diminished during the
Period for which he shall have been elected, and he shall not receive within that
20　Period any other **Emolument** from the United States, or any of them.

emolument:
payment

Before he enter on the Execution of his Office, he shall take the following
Oath or Affirmation:—"I do solemnly swear (or affirm) that I will faithfully
execute the Office of President of the United States, and will to the best of my
Ability, preserve, protect and defend the Constitution of the United States."

Section. 2.

The President shall be Commander in Chief of the Army and Navy of the
United States, and of the Militia of the several States, when called into the
actual Service of the United States; he may require the Opinion, in writing, of
the principal Officer in each of the executive Departments, upon any Subject
relating to the Duties of their respective Offices, and he shall have Power to
C 30　grant Reprieves and Pardons for Offences against the United States, except in
Cases of **Impeachment**.

D　He shall have Power, by and with the Advice and Consent of the Senate, to

impeachment:
*the charge
against a
public official
of a crime or
misconduct*

make Treaties, provided two thirds of the Senators present concur; and he shall
nominate, and by and with the Advice and Consent of the Senate, shall appoint
Ambassadors, other public Ministers and Consuls, Judges of the supreme

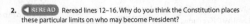

The United States Capitol, which houses Congress, is located on Capitol Hill, at
the eastern end of the National Mall in Washington, DC.

Court, and all other Officers of the United States, whose Appointments are
not herein otherwise provided for, and which shall be established by Law: but
the Congress may by Law vest the Appointment of such inferior Officers, as
they think proper, in the President alone, in the Courts of Law, or in the Heads
40　of Departments.

The President shall have Power to fill up all Vacancies that may happen
during the Recess of the Senate, by granting Commissions which shall expire at
the End of their next Session.

Section. 3.

He shall from time to time give to the Congress Information of the State of
the Union, and recommend to their Consideration such Measures as he shall
judge necessary and expedient; he may, on extraordinary Occasions, convene
both Houses, or either of them, and in Case of Disagreement between them,
with Respect to the Time of Adjournment, he may adjourn them to such Time
as he shall think proper; he shall receive Ambassadors and other public
50　Ministers; he shall take Care that the Laws be faithfully executed, and shall
Commission all the Officers of the United States.

---

2. ◀**REREAD**　Reread lines 12–16. Why do you think the Constitution places
these particular limits on who may become President?

*The Framers of the Constitution did not want a foreign ruler. The
President should be old enough to be a mature ruler and should have
lived in the United States long enough to understand the nation.*

3. **READ** ▶　As you read lines 17–54, continue to cite text evidence.

• Underline text that describes the President's executive power.
• Circle reasons for impeachment.

---

2. **REREAD AND CITE TEXT EVIDENCE**

B **ASK STUDENTS** why there is an exception to the rule that
only a "natural born Citizen" may become President. *Perhaps they
include this exception because some important political leaders were
born in other countries.*

3. **READ AND CITE TEXT EVIDENCE**

C **ASK STUDENTS** about the limit on the President's authority
to grant reprieves and pardons. *The President cannot pardon public
officials who have been impeached.* Why might this limit be
included? *Section 4 states that the reasons for impeaching a public
official are serious—treason, bribery, and other "high Crimes."*

Critical Vocabulary: emolument (line 20) Have students
identify the synonym for *emolument* in the same paragraph
(*compensation*).

Critical Vocabulary: impeachment (line 31) Have students
contrast *impeachment* and *charging a person with a crime.*

FOR ELL STUDENTS Your students may be familiar with the
term *recess* in a school context. Clarify that in the context of the
Constitution it means a brief period in which the activity in a
branch of government or in a court stops.

CLOSE READ
Notes

Section. 4.

The President, Vice President and all civil Officers of the United States, shall be removed from Office on Impeachment for, and Conviction of, Treason, Bribery, or other high Crimes and Misdemeanors.

4. ◀ **REREAD AND DISCUSS** In a small group, discuss the Presidential powers that you underlined in lines 17–54. For every executive power that the President has, discuss the Senate's role in the decision-making process.

SHORT RESPONSE

Cite Text Evidence Analyze how the authors structured this part of the Constitution. How does this part of the Constitution uphold the principles of a respresentative democracy, a separation of powers, and a system of checks and balances? Review your reading notes. Be sure to **cite text evidence** in your response.

The authors first address who can become President. There are specific requirements that must be met before someone can be considered for the office. The authors then lay out the President's responsibilities and what he has the power to do. He can make many decisions, but in some cases only with the "Advice and Consent of the Senate," so the President does not have sole authority. The authors also include reasons setting out why the President may be removed from office.

26

4. REREAD AND DISCUSS USING TEXT EVIDENCE

D **ASK STUDENTS** in each group to identify the executive powers that are limited by the Senate. Then assign one of these executive powers to each group and have the members of the group discuss the importance of the Senate's role. Describe how these executive powers have made the news in recent years. *Students should be able to recount the appointment of Supreme Court justices and/or the adoption of trade treaties.*

SHORT RESPONSE

Cite Text Evidence Students' responses should include text evidence that supports their positions. They should:

- describe how Article II is organized.
- explain that some of the President's executive powers are limited by the Senate.
- state that the President can be removed from office.

TO CHALLENGE STUDENTS . . .

To gain a deeper understanding of the U.S. Constitution, students can read the 22nd Amendment, ratified in 1951.

ASK STUDENTS what the 22nd Amendment put into law. *It limited to two terms the time a person could serve as President.* What did the Constitution say about limits for the President's office? *It only included limits on power and on eligibility for the office.* Ask students which U.S. Presidents would have been in office for a shorter time had this amendment existed, and whether there are people alive today who are affected. *The only President who would have been in office for a shorter time is Franklin D. Roosevelt. Bill Clinton, George W. Bush, and Barack Obama cannot run again for President.*

DIG DEEPER

With the class, return to Question 3, Read. Have students share their responses to the question.

ASK STUDENTS about other executive powers mentioned in Article II.

- How can the President influence the work of Congress? *The President can give Congress "Information of the State of the Union." This occurs each January, when the President gives a speech to Congress, trying to convince legislators to follow his agenda.*

- What oversight of the legislative process does the President have? *Once Congress passes laws, it is the President's duty to insure that they are "faithfully executed."*

- Under what circumstances can the President convene or adjourn Congress? *He can convene or adjourn both Houses of Congress "on extraordinary Occasions." This would usually only happen when the country is at war or has been attacked.*

ASK STUDENTS to return to their Short Response answer and revise it based on the class discussion.

Petition to the Massachusetts General Assembly

Public Document by Prince Hall

Why This Text

Students may not grasp the premises and purposes of historical documents, which were written in periods distant from students' lives. Yet the authors employed similar techniques in their arguments as we do today. With the help of the close-reading questions, students will analyze Hall's petition. This close reading will lead them to more fully understand how Hall presents his premises and how they support the purpose of the petition.

Background Have students read the background and information about Prince Hall. When he wrote the petition, Hall had been a free man for six or seven years. Importantly, he had witnessed the gradual breakdown in relations between the thirteen colonies and Great Britain. Rebelling at their perceived lack of freedom and rights under the British crown, colonists declared their independence the summer before Hall made his petition.

AS YOU READ Ask students to pay attention to the themes in the petition. How does Hall use these themes to try to persuade Massachusetts' representatives of the merits of his petition?

Common Core Support

- cite strong and thorough textual evidence
- determine the central ideas of a text
- evaluate the reasoning and the premises, purposes, and arguments in a text

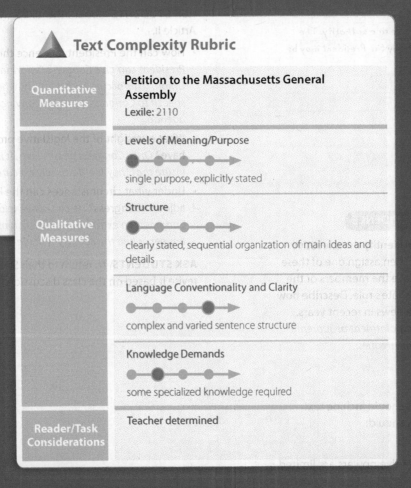

Text Complexity Rubric

Quantitative Measures

Petition to the Massachusetts General Assembly

Lexile: 2110

Qualitative Measures

Levels of Meaning/Purpose

single purpose, explicitly stated

Structure

clearly stated, sequential organization of main ideas and details

Language Conventionality and Clarity

complex and varied sentence structure

Knowledge Demands

some specialized knowledge required

Reader/Task Considerations

Teacher determined

Strategies for CLOSE READING

Analyze Purpose and Premises of an Argument

Students should read this document carefully all the way through. Close-reading questions at the bottom of the page will help them focus on a thorough analysis of the author's purpose and premises. As they read, students should jot down comments or questions about the text in the margins.

WHEN STUDENTS STRUGGLE . . .

To help students analyze the "Petition to the Massachusetts General Assembly," have them work in small groups to fill out a chart like the one shown below.

CITE TEXT EVIDENCE For practice in analyzing the purpose and premises of an argument, ask students to cite the premises Hall gives and the purpose of his petition.

Purpose
To persuade the State of Massachusetts to free all slaves
Premises
". . . in common with all other men a natural and unalienable right to that freedom which the Great Parent of the Universe bestowed equally on all mankind . . ."
". . . a life of slavery . . . is far worse than nonexistence."
. . . every principle from which America has acted . . . pleads stronger than a thousand arguments in favor of your petitioners."
"So may the inhabitants of this State no longer be guilty of the inconsistency of acting in ways that they condemn and oppose in others."

Background Prince Hall (1735–1807) was held as a slave by William Hall, in Boston until the age of 35, when he was freed. Hall used his freedom to become an advocate for African Americans. Hall made many petitions on behalf of free blacks and successfully petitioned for the release of three Boston African Americans who had been kidnapped into slavery. For years, Hall protested that African American children did not have public schools, and eventually he started a school of his own for them.

Petition to the Massachusetts General Assembly

Public Document by Prince Hall

CLOSE READ
Notes

1. **READ ▷** As you read the petition, begin to collect and cite text evidence.
   - In the margin, paraphrase the first sentence (lines 3–10).
   - Underline three of Hall's premises that support his argument against slavery.
   - In the margin on the next page, analyze what Hall means by "the natural right of all men" (line 30).

(A) To the Honorable Counsel and House of Representatives for the State of Massachusetts Bay in General Court assembled, January 13, 1777:

The petition of a great number of blacks detained in a state of slavery in a free and Christian county humbly points out that your petitioners understand that they have in common with all other men a natural and unalienable right to that freedom which the Great Parent of the Universe bestowed equally on all mankind, and which they have never forfeited by any compact or agreement whatever, but that they were unjustly dragged by the hand of cruel power along with their dearest friends, and some of them even torn from the embraces of

10 their tender parents, from a populous, pleasant, and plentiful country. In violation of Laws of Nature and of Nations and in defiance of all the tender feelings of humanity, they were brought here to be sold like beasts of burden, and like them condemned to slavery for life among a people professing the mild religion of Jesus—a people not insensible of the secrets of rational being nor without spirit to resent the unjust endeavors of others to reduce *them* to a state of bondage and **subjugation**. Your Honors need not to be informed that a life of slavery like that of your petitioners, deprived of every social

Blacks, like all other humans, are entitled to freedom, and their enslavement is an unjust abuse of power.

subjugation: *suppression*

27

---

1. **READ AND CITE TEXT EVIDENCE** The first sentence of Hall's petition is a masterpiece of rhetoric. Here he manages to eloquently set forth his purpose of his petition.

(A) **ASK STUDENTS** to discuss Hall's purpose that he explains in the petition's first sentence. *Hall's purpose is to point out the inconsistencies of a nation that claims to be founded on the "unalienable right to freedom" while still holding "blacks detained in a state of slavery."*

Critical Vocabulary: subjugation (line 16) Have students share their definitions of *subjugation*. Ask volunteers to use the noun in a sentence.

The "natural right" is freedom. This is what the petitioners have in common with all other men, the right to freedom.

privilege and of every thing requisite to render life tolerable, is far worse than nonexistence.

20   In imitation of the laudable example of the good people of these states, your petitioners have long and patiently waited the outcome of petition after petition presented by them to the Legislative Body of this state, and with grief reflect that their lack of success has been similar each time. They cannot but express their astonishment that it has never been considered that every principle from which America has acted in the course of their unhappy difficulties with Great Britain pleads stronger than a thousand arguments in favor of your petitioners. They therefore humbly beseech Your Honors to give this petition its due weight and consideration and cause an act of the legislature to be passed whereby they may be restored to the enjoyments which is the
30 natural right of all men and that their children, who were born in this Land of
B Liberty, may not be held as slaves after they arrive at the age of twenty-one years. So may the inhabitants of this State no longer be guilty of the inconsistency of acting in ways that they condemn and oppose in others. May they prosper in their present glorious struggle for Liberty and have those blessings to them.

2. ◀ REREAD AND DISCUSS Reread the petition. Circle Hall's purpose for this petition. Explain the three main premises that support his reasoning.

Slavery is contrary to people's professed faith; it is worse than death; it is un-American.

SHORT RESPONSE

Cite Text Evidence Summarize the purpose and premises of Hall's argument. Review your reading notes, and be sure to **cite text evidence** in your response.

Hall's purpose is to convince the State of Massachusetts to free all slaves. His premises are general principles that he presents as self-evident. First, "the Great Parent of the Universe bestowed [the right to freedom] equally on all mankind." Second, a life of slavery is intolerable and "far worse than nonexistence." And finally, slavery is inconsistent with American values, because America is the "Land of Liberty."

28

TO CHALLENGE STUDENTS . . .

To gain a deeper understanding of the social context of Hall's petition, students can research the role of slaves in colonial America and in the American Revolution.

ASK STUDENTS to compare the role of slavery in the economies of northern colonies, such as Massachusetts, and southern colonies, such as Virginia. *Students should recognize that slavery was an important institution throughout the colonies, but that slaves were used differently in the south and north. In the south, landholdings were large, and slave labor was crucial for export crops like tobacco. Farms were also important in the north, but they were smaller and generally did not rely on slave labor. In the north, slaves were more frequently found in the cities, where they worked in households and manufacturing establishments.*

ASK STUDENTS how the newly-formed American government and the British government dealt with the issue of slavery during the Revolution. *Students should understand that the American government confirmed its commitment to slavery, thus protecting the interests of slave owners, who were key backers of the Revolution. The British government saw the American position as an opportunity—and offered freedom to runaway slaves.*

---

2. **REREAD AND DISCUSS USING TEXT EVIDENCE**

B **ASK STUDENTS** to explain the apparent contradiction Hall proposes and why he might have included it. *Slaves were valuable pieces of property, so their emancipation would hurt owners' fortunes. By allowing slaves' children to remain slaves until age 21, Hall's proposal would soften this economic blow, perhaps making it more politically palatable.*

FOR ELL STUDENTS Explain that the word *weight* in line 28 does not refer to "heaviness" in this context, but to "importance."

SHORT RESPONSE

Cite Text Evidence Students should:

- note that Hall wants the legislature to pass an act to free slaves.
- explain that slaves, as members of mankind, have unalienable rights.
- clearly state the other premises found in Hall's petition.

DIG DEEPER

1. With the class, return to Question 1, Read. Have students share their paraphrases of the first sentence. Point out that one of Hall's purposes in the petition is to expose the inconsistencies that allow slavery to exist in the United States. Hall's language describing these inconsistencies aims to make his audience hear the petition with the insight of the kinds of men they profess to be.

   ASK STUDENTS to focus on the rhetorical device of repeating the idea of inconsistency.

   - What other examples of the theme of inconsistency did Hall include in his petition? *Students should note the following examples: "condemned to slavery . . . among a people professing the mild religion of Jesus" (lines 13–14), "to resent the unjust endeavors of others to reduce them to a state of bondage and subjugation" (lines 15–16), "every principle from which America has acted . . . pleads stronger than a thousand arguments in favor of your petitioners" (lines 25–27), "may the inhabitants of this State no longer be guilty of the inconsistency of acting in ways that they condemn and oppose in others" (lines 32–33).*

   - Why might this rhetorical device resonate with Hall's audience? *Students should recognize that the members of the Assembly were then engaged in a great fight for their own freedom and rights, as the colonies battled Great Britain for independence. Hall hoped that the representatives' experience with tyranny would make them more sympathetic to the plight of slaves.*

2. With the class, return to Question 2, Reread and Discuss. Have students share their three main premises.

   - What is another premise that Hall used to support his petition? Cite text evidence. *Students should note the premise that all people, including blacks, have an unalienable right to freedom, citing the explicit statement in the first sentence, (lines 5–6), "In violation of Laws of Nature and of Nations" (lines 10–11), and "the enjoyments which is the natural right of all men" (lines 29–30).*

   - How did Hall use language to evince sympathy from his audience? *Students should recognize that Hall frequently returned to the theme of compassion: "even torn from the embraces of their tender parents" (lines 9–10), "in defiance of all the tender feelings of humanity" (lines 11–12), and "deprived of every social privilege and of every thing requisite to render life tolerable" (lines 17–18).*

   ASK STUDENTS to return to their Short Response answer and revise it based on the class discussion.

CLOSE READING NOTES

Abigail Adams' Last Act of Defiance

History Writing by Woody Holton

Why This Text

Articles that examine the lives of important historical people often attempt to clarify some aspect of the person's life that previous historians may have ignored. "Abigail Adams' Last Act of Defiance" is such a text. Some students may have difficulty understanding the author's central idea. With the help of the close-reading questions, students will determine the author's central idea and cite specific supporting details. This close reading will lead students to develop a deeper understanding of the topic and the evidence presented by the author.

Background Have students read the background information about Abigail Smith Adams, paying special attention to her intelligence and passion for the cause of women's rights. Tell students that as a diplomat in France and later in England, John Adams was often away from their home. He and Abigail communicated extensively by letter. These letters provide valuable information not only about Abigail's influence on her husband and the couple's marriage, but also about a crucial period in American history.

AS YOU READ Ask students to pay attention to the information given in the text about women's rights during the period and Abigail Adams's reaction to those limited rights.

Common Core Support

- cite multiple pieces of evidence from the text
- determine central ideas
- make inferences and draw conclusions

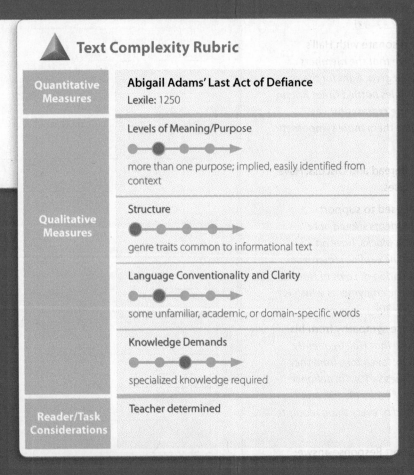

Text Complexity Rubric

Quantitative Measures

Abigail Adams' Last Act of Defiance
Lexile: 1250

Qualitative Measures

Levels of Meaning/Purpose

more than one purpose; implied, easily identified from context

Structure

genre traits common to informational text

Language Conventionality and Clarity

some unfamiliar, academic, or domain-specific words

Knowledge Demands

specialized knowledge required

Reader/Task Considerations

Teacher determined

Strategies for CLOSE READING

Determine Central Ideas

Students should read this article carefully all the way through. Close-reading questions at the bottom of the page will help them determine the central ideas of the text. As they read, students should jot down comments or questions about the text in the margins.

WHEN STUDENTS STRUGGLE . . .

To help students determine central ideas in "Abigail Adams' Last Act of Defiance," have them work in small groups to fill out a chart like the one shown below.

CITE TEXT EVIDENCE For practice in determining central ideas, ask students to cite text evidence that supports the main facts given by the author.

Central Idea
Abigail Adams "did not simply complain about the government's denial of married women's property rights. She defied it." (lines 18–19)

Text Evidence
"As the Revolutionary War drew to a close, Adams started setting aside a portion of her husband's property and declaring it her own." (lines 20–21)
"She added more and more to this stash over the ensuing decades." (lines 21–22)
She wrote her own will and left almost all of "her" money and property to women. (lines 26–32)

Background Abigail Smith Adams *(1744–1818) was the daughter of liberal Congregational minister, William Smith. She was considered too sickly for formal education, but was taught at home and had access to her father's library. She was embarrassed by her poor spelling and punctuation, yet was known for her intelligence and passion for the cause of women's rights. The Adams family was the first one to live in the White House. Abigail was nicknamed "Her Majesty" because of her perceived influence over her husband.*

Abigail Adams' Last
Act of Defiance

History Writing by Woody Holton

CLOSE READ
Notes

1. **READ ▶** As you read lines 1–19, begin to cite and collect text evidence.
   - Underline references to dates and events that orient the reader and provide historical context.
   - Circle the main idea in lines 1–9 and in lines 10–19.
   - In the margin, summarize the situation that concerns Adams.

Weeks before the Continental Congress issued the Declaration of Independence in 1776, Abigail Adams penned a now famous letter to her husband, John, admonishing him to "Remember the Ladies" when drawing up a new code of laws. "If perticular care and attention is not paid to the Laidies," she wrote, "we are determined to **foment** a Rebellion, and will not hold ourselves bound by any Laws in which we have no voice, or Representation." Within a few years of writing these words, Adams did something that has never been revealed until now. She carried out a mini-revolution in the arena that mattered to her the most: her own household.

10   Of all the means by which the Founding Fathers and other men lorded it over women, none annoyed Adams more than the legal degradation that women had to submit to the moment they got married. Single women, including widows, were allowed to own and control property. Yet as Adams

foment:
to stir up

29

---

1. **READ AND CITE TEXT EVIDENCE** The author quotes Abigail Adams in a letter to her husband asking him to "Remember the Ladies" when he served as a delegate to the Continental Congress.

A **ASK STUDENTS** which law most annoyed Adams. *Adams was annoyed by the law that said that married women did not have the right to own and control property.*

Critical Vocabulary: foment (line 5) Have students share their definitions of *foment*. Ask why an angry and frustrated Abigail Adams might want women to foment a rebellion. *A rebellion would be a way for women to fight unjust laws.*

> " ... scratching out the four-page document was the ultimate act of rebellion. "

Married women were not allowed to have control over their own possessions.

complained to her husband in a June 1782 letter, wives' property was "subject to the controul and disposal of our partners, to whom the Laws have given a sovereign Authority." Historians have studied Abigail Adams' denunciations of married women's inability to control property for decades. But what they have overlooked is that she did not simply complain about the government's denial of married women's property rights. She defied it.

B 20 As the Revolutionary War drew to a close, Adams started setting aside a portion of her husband's property and declaring it her own. She added more and more to this stash over the ensuing decades, and she invested it wisely. By the end of 1815 her "pocket money," as she sometimes called it, had grown to more than $5,000—which would be about $100,000 today.

C Finally in 1816, racked with pain and convinced she was dying, Adams delivered the parting shot in her household revolution. On January 18, she sat down to write a will. Since she had no legal right as a married woman to own property in her name and her husband was still very much alive, scratching out the four-page document was the ultimate act of rebellion. Moreover, a close

---

2. **REREAD** Reread lines 10–19. In what way did the laws for single women and married women differ? Support your answer with explicit textual evidence.

Single women (and widowed women) were allowed to own and control property, but married women had to give control of their property to their husbands.

---

3. **READ** As you read lines 20–55, continue to cite text evidence.

- Circle actions of Adams that were caused by the government's denial of property rights for married women.
- Underline references to dates that show the order in which events occurred.

This portrait of Adams was painted by Benjamin Blythe in 1766, when she was 22 years old.

D 30 look at the will reveals a curious fact that historians have mostly ignored. Apart from a couple of token gifts to her two sons, all the people Adams chose to bequeath money to were women. And many of those women were married.

Adams' personal property rights revolution had its roots in her struggle to shield her family from the financial destruction that accompanied the Revolutionary War. Of all the patriot soldiers and statesmen who were forced to abandon their families for long periods, few stayed away as long as John Adams, who saw very little of his Braintree, Mass., farm from 1774 to 1784. John put Abigail in charge of all of the Adams family finances, and she ended up handling her husband's money much better than he ever had, primarily 40 because she was more open to risk. During the course of the war she became an

---

4. **REREAD** Reread lines 25–32. Why does Holton call writing a will "the ultimate act of rebellion"? Support your answer with explicit textual evidence.

As a married woman, Abigail Adams " had no legal right" to own property. All property legally belonged to her husband, so only her husband could legally write a will to bequeath his property.

---

2. **REREAD AND CITE TEXT EVIDENCE**

B **ASK STUDENTS** what effect the property laws had on Abigail Adams. *She was not allowed control over her own possessions.*

3. **READ AND CITE TEXT EVIDENCE** Before she died, Adams "delivered the parting shot in her household revolution."

C **ASK STUDENTS** to use context clues to interpret the meaning of "parting shot." *Writing her will was something Abigail Adams did just before she died. "Parting shot" probably means something like "last words" or "something you do or say just before you're about to leave."*

FOR ELL STUDENTS Review the prefix *in-*. Point out the word *inability* (line 17). Ask a volunteer to identify the base word (*ability*) and its meaning. Then ask another volunteer to guess the meaning of *inability*. Ask students to provide other words with the prefix *in-*.

4. **REREAD AND CITE TEXT EVIDENCE** The text explains that most historians have ignored the fact that Adams left the bulk of her money to women, many of whom were married.

D **ASK STUDENTS** What is the significance of the fact that Adams left the bulk of her money to women? *Students should understand that since married women technically were not able to own property, it was unusual for women to receive any money from a will.*

FOR ELL STUDENTS The use of the expression *very little* (line 37) can be confusing to ELL students, who might be more familiar with using *little* referring to quantities. Explain that in this context, it doesn't mean that John saw a small part of his farm, but that he rarely was at the farm.

depreciate:

lower in price or value

envoy:

a diplomatic representative sent by one government to another

import merchant and then a speculator in **depreciated** government securities and Vermont land titles. And as she repeatedly reinvested her profits, she increasingly thought of the money she earned as her own.

Abigail lived by the credo "nothing venture nothing have"—a notion that John found somewhat alarming. While he was an **envoy** in France, the couple confronted a seemingly mundane problem. How could he remit a portion of his salary home? Her solution was audacious. If he shipped her trunkloads of merchandise from Europe, she could extract the few items her family needed and arrange to sell the rest to New England shopkeepers whose shelves were
50 nearly empty because of the war. She convinced John the scheme would allow her to avoid having to "pay extravagant prices" for basic necessities, downplaying that she could also turn a healthy profit by selling the imported goods at an enormous markup. When some of these shipments were captured by the British, John wanted to abandon the whole thing, but she wrote back, "If one in 3 arrives I should be a gainer."

Nearly all of Abigail Adams' biographers mention her will, but they usually move on, overlooking not only the remarkable fact of its existence but its contents. In it, she made token gifts to her two surviving sons, but she gave nothing to her grandsons, nephews or male servants. Everything went to her
60 granddaughters, nieces, female servants and daughters-in-law. In addition to gowns and small sums of cash to pay for mourning rings, Abigail handed out more than $4,000 worth of bank stock, a $1,200 IOU and a total of seven shares of stock in the companies managing the Weymouth and Haverhill toll bridges.

Adams not only ignored the law by writing her will, but left property to married women.

5. (READ ▶) As you read lines 56–96, continue to cite text evidence.

- In the margin of lines 56–63 explain Adams's solution to the problem regarding women's property rights.
- Circle evidence that shows that Adams's family supported her "mini-revolution."
- In the lines below, analyze the structure of lines 70–85. How does the author organize the facts he presents in these lines?

The author presents the facts in chronological order. He explains who carried out the specific duties as written in the will and explains how her relatives honored Adams's requests.

32

> **Louisa acknowledged what the law of the land denied and Abigail had always affirmed: that the money was hers to give.**

There is no indication that Adams had any **animus** against her male relatives. So why did she exclude all but two of them from her will? Having spent three decades asserting control over land and ownership of personal property despite being married, Adams now bequeathed the bulk of her estate to her granddaughters, nieces, daughters-in-law and female servants in order to enable them, as far as lay in her power, to make the same claim.
70 To her own surprise, Abigail held on for another year and a half after writing her will. She died about 1 p.m. on October 28, 1818, a few weeks shy of her 74th birthday. Abigail's will was not a legal document that any court was bound to respect, and John would have been within his rights in throwing it in the fire. But he honored it to the letter. Abigail had assigned her son Thomas the responsibility of supervising the distribution of her property. Thomas' brother, John Quincy Adams, and their father assisted him in carrying out Abigail's wishes. On November 9, less than two weeks after her death, John transferred the $1,200 promissory note to Louisa Smith [Abigail's niece and steadfast companion], just as Abigail had
80 directed. The former president's compliance with the provisions of his wife's will transformed it into a legally valid document. In the eyes of the law, she had acted as his agent and distributed property that belonged to him. In 1819 John Quincy replaced the promissory note he had given his mother years earlier with a new one made out to Louisa herself. No one could ever challenge his cousin's legal right to recover these funds, for she had never married.

animus:

hostility or ill feeling

33

---

5. (READ AND CITE TEXT EVIDENCE)

E **ASK STUDENTS** which members of Adams's family who could have contested her will actually honored her directions. *John Adams, Thomas Adams, and John Quincy Adams—all men—made sure her will was followed (lines 74–84).*

Critical Vocabulary: depreciate (line 41) Have students share their definitions of *depreciate*. Ask students: *If you discovered that something you owned that you had thought was very valuable had depreciated, how would you feel?* *very disappointed*

Critical Vocabulary: envoy (line 45) The text says that John Adams was an envoy in France. Ask students: *What might a prominent American citizen, like John Adams, be doing in France?* Then, have students share their definitions of *envoy*.

Critical Vocabulary: animus (line 64) Have students share their definitions of *animus*. Ask students to think of a situation in which you might feel animus against another person. *Answers will vary. Students should cite a situation in which they feel angry at, or hostile toward, another person.*

FOR ELL STUDENTS Clarify the meaning of *shy of* (line 71). Explain that in the text it doesn't refer to someone's character; in this context it means "before."

CLOSE READ
Notes

bequest:
something given or left by a will

In January 1819, when Louisa Catherine Adams, John Quincy's wife, learned that Abigail had left her an inheritance of $150, she set aside half of the **bequest** to be divided equally among her three sons, who seemed "to have a better title to it than I could boast." By passing this money on to Abigail's grandsons, Louisa may have indicated disapproval of her mother-in-law's 90 decision to exclude all male descendants other than her own sons from her will. Yet it seems unlikely that Abigail would have considered the younger woman's gift a defeat. After all, by deciding on her own authority to present the money to her children instead of her husband, Louisa acknowledged what the law of the land denied and Abigail had always affirmed: that the money was hers to give.

F

6. ◀ **REREAD** Reread lines 86–96. Explain the author's assertion that Adams would not consider it a defeat that Louisa Catherine Adams bequeathed part of her inheritance to her sons.

As long as Louisa was the one to decide what would be done with the money she was acting as the owner of the property. Abigail only wanted her female relatives to have the power to do with their money what they wished.

SHORT RESPONSE

Cite Text Evidence What problem did Adams confront and what was her solution? Review your reading notes, and be sure to **cite text evidence** in your response.

Adams was upset by the injustice of laws that made married women's property "subject to the controul and disposal" of their husbands. She addressed this problem in her own household by "setting aside a portion of her husband's property and declaring it her own." Over time, what she called her "pocket money" grew to more than $5,000. She finally wrote a will, leaving what was legally her husband's money to her female relatives and companions. Although it was not a legal document, John honored his wife's will.

34

6. **REREAD AND CITE TEXT EVIDENCE**

F **ASK STUDENTS** why some people might consider Louisa's gift to her sons a defeat. *They might think that Louisa was going against Adams's wishes by giving the money to men, thereby endorsing the property laws.*

Critical Vocabulary: bequest (line 88) Have students share their definitions of *bequest*. Ask students: *What might you bequest in a will to someone you cared about? Answers will vary. Students should name something that means a great deal to them.*

SHORT RESPONSE

Cite Text Evidence Students should:

- explain the problem that Adams confronts.
- describe her solution.
- cite text evidence.

TO CHALLENGE STUDENTS . . .

For more context about Abigail Adams personally, and her marriage to John Adams, have students view the video "The Romance of John and Abigail Adams" in their eBooks.

ASK STUDENTS to integrate what they have learned about Abigail Adams and the times in which she lived with what they learn about her and her marriage in this video. What attracted the couple to each other? *John Adams loved her combination of beauty and brains, and Abigail Adams loved the fact that he treated her as an intellectual equal and that they could talk together for hours.* How would you describe their marriage? *Answers will vary, but students should mention that they were deeply in love with each other, that they respected each other, and that they were equal partners in the marriage.* How do you think the marriage of Abigail and John Adams was different from other marriages of the period? *Answers will vary, but students should mention that most couples of the period probably did not treat each other as equals and that most husbands probably did not respect their wives' intelligence as much as John respected Abigail's.*

DIG DEEPER

With the class, return to Question 2, Reread. Have students share and discuss their responses.

ASK STUDENTS what additional information they have learned about Abigail Adams's defiance of the law, in particular her decision to write a will and the significance of that decision, the people she bequeathed her property to and why, her adeptness at handling her husband's financial affairs, and her husband's decision to honor the provisions of her will. Remind students to cite text evidence that supports what they have learned.

- Have students explain the significance of Adams's decision to write a will. *Because married women were not allowed to own personal property, Adams's decision to write a will stating to whom "her" property was to go defied the law of the day.*

- Have students explain Adams's choices regarding to whom she would leave her considerable property. *Adams left the bulk of her estate to her granddaughters, nieces, daughters-in-law, and female servants. She gave very little to her male relatives. She did this in the hope that her female relatives might someday be able to make the same claim: that they owned property.*

- Ask students to give examples of Adams's skill at handling her husband's financial affairs. *During the ten-year period that her husband was away, Adams invested her husband's money wisely, while putting away a portion of the money she had made for herself. By the end of 1815, the money she had made for herself was more than $5,000—or about $100,000 today. Adams handled her husband's money much better than he would have, primarily because she was willing to take risks.*

- Have students infer why John Adams chose to honor all of the provisions of his wife's will, even though he was not legally bound to do so. *Answers will vary. Students may infer that Adams loved and respected his wife and so honored her wishes, or that he agreed with her that married women ought to be able to own their own property.*

ASK STUDENTS to return to their Short Response answer and revise it based on their discussion.

CLOSE READING NOTES

The Individual and Society

The Individual and Society

"Trust thyself: every heart vibrates to that iron string."

—Ralph Waldo Emerson

Poems by Walt Whitman

POEMS

I Hear America Singing	**Walt Whitman**
A Noiseless Patient Spider	**Walt Whitman**

Essays by Ralph Waldo Emerson

ESSAYS

from Nature	**Ralph Waldo Emerson**
from Self-Reliance	**Ralph Waldo Emerson**

ESSAY

Spoiling Walden: Or, How I Learned to Stop Worrying and Love Cape Wind	**David Gessner**

Poems by Walt Whitman

I Hear America Singing

A Noiseless Patient Spider

Why These Texts

Students may have difficulty determining themes of poems. A close reading of the text and an analysis of the poem's details wll help provide clues to the theme. Students may also have difficulty understanding details particular to nineteenth-century city life. This may be especially applicable to "I Hear America Singing," in which various tradespeople are mentioned. With the help of the close-reading questions, students will identify and analyze details that contribute to the clear understanding of each poem and its theme.

Background Have students read the background information and the biographical information about Walt Whitman. Tell students that Ralph Waldo Emerson (1803–1882) was an important essayist and poet from New England. He wrote about the power of nature, the need for individualism, and the relationship of the individual to the world in general. All of these themes attracted the young Walt Whitman, who once said, "Let your soul stand cool and composed before a million universes."

AS YOU READ Ask students to read each poem closely, paying special attention to the details in each line. Encourage students to think about how the details in one line relate to details in the lines that follow and, thereby, create the meaning of the poem.

Common Core Support

- cite evidence from the text
- determine two or more themes of a text
- determine the meaning of words and phrases in a text
- analyze how an author's choices concerning how to structure a text contribute to its overall meaning

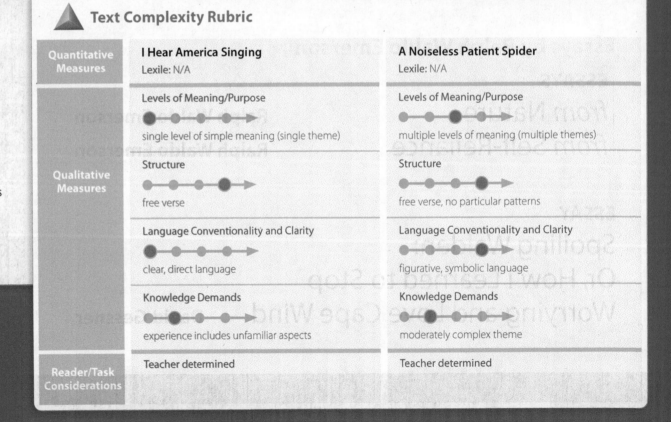

Text Complexity Rubric

	I Hear America Singing	A Noiseless Patient Spider
Quantitative Measures	Lexile: N/A	Lexile: N/A
Qualitative Measures	Levels of Meaning/Purpose — single level of simple meaning (single theme)	Levels of Meaning/Purpose — multiple levels of meaning (multiple themes)
	Structure — free verse	Structure — free verse, no particular patterns
	Language Conventionality and Clarity — clear, direct language	Language Conventionality and Clarity — figurative, symbolic language
	Knowledge Demands — experience includes unfamiliar aspects	Knowledge Demands — moderately complex theme
Reader/Task Considerations	Teacher determined	Teacher determined

Strategies for CLOSE READING

Determine Themes

Students should read each poem slowly, paying attention to specific details throughout each. Close-reading questions at the bottom of the page will help them collect and cite text evidence to understand the theme of each poem. As they read, students should jot down comments or questions about the text in the margins.

WHEN STUDENTS STRUGGLE . . .

To help students understand the overall theme of each poem, have them work in small groups or with a partner to fill out charts for each poem like the one shown below.

CITE TEXT EVIDENCE Encourage students to identify both general statements and specific details in the poem that support the theme of each poem.

I Hear America Singing		
Theme	**General Statements**	**Specific Details**
The poet praises and expresses his admiration for American workers.	"I hear America singing, the varied carols I hear"	"Those of mechanics"
	"Each singing what belongs to him or her . . ."	"The carpenter singing"
	". . . their strong melodious songs"	"The mason singing"
		"The boatman . . . the deckhand"
		"The shoemaker . . . the hatter"
		"The wood-cutter's song . . . the ploughboy's"
		"The delicious singing of the mother"

Background *Less than a hundred years after the United States was founded, the new nation discovered its voice in a poet who spoke to all the world. His name was **Walt Whitman**, and he struck a note in literature that was as forthright, as original, and as deeply charged with democracy's energies as the land that produced him.*

Poems by
Walt Whitman

I Hear America Singing . . . . .Walt Whitman
A Noiseless Patient Spider . . . . .Walt Whitman

Walt Whitman *(1819–1892) grew up in rural Long Island and crowded Brooklyn. He held a series of jobs including typesetter, printer, newspaper editor, school teacher, carpenter, and journalist. In the 1840s, Whitman published a number of poems and short stories—and even a fairly successful novel—but these were conventional efforts. Whitman was just waiting for the proper inspiration. Upon reading Ralph Waldo Emerson, he realized that he could celebrate all aspects of nature and humanity by using spiritual language. "I was simmering, simmering, simmering," he once declared. "Emerson brought me to a boil."*

In the early 1850s, Whitman quit his job as a journalist and worked on a book of poems called Leaves of Grass. Many people were shocked by its controversial content and revolutionary form. Of the 800 copies printed, most were eventually thrown away. However, a few readers recognized the poet's genius. In a letter to Whitman, Emerson called Leaves of Grass "the most extraordinary piece of wit and wisdom that America has yet contributed."

37

1. **READ ▶** As you read lines 1–11, begin to collect and cite text evidence.

   • Underline the different kinds of workers the poem catalogs.
   • Circle the word that refers to the collective group of singers.
   • In the margin, note the type of people the speaker "hears."

I Hear America Singing

A I hear America singing, the varied carols I hear,
   Those of mechanics, each one singing his as it should be blithe
      and strong,
   The carpenter singing his as he measures his plank or beam,
   The mason singing his as he makes ready for work, or leaves off
      work,
5 The boatman singing what belongs to him in his boat, the
      deckhand singing on the steamboat deck,
   The shoemaker singing as he sits on his bench, the hatter singing
      as he stands,
   The wood-cutter's song, the ploughboy's on his way in the
      morning, or at noon intermission or at sundown,
   The delicious singing of the mother, or of the young wife at work,
      or of the girl sewing or washing,
   Each singing what belongs to him or her and to none else,
B 10 The day what belongs to the day—at night the party of young
      fellows, robust, friendly,
   Singing with open mouths their strong melodious songs.

The speaker refers to working people.

2. **◀ REREAD** Reread lines 10–11. What attitude does the speaker express toward the young men? Cite evidence from the text in your response.

The speaker expresses an admiring, grateful, friendly attitude. Words that convey this attitude include "party," "robust," "friendly," "strong," and "melodious."

SHORT RESPONSE

Cite Text Evidence What is the theme of this poem—what is the author revealing about America? **Cite text evidence** in your response.

Even though all of the people are working, their "strong melodious songs" reflect that they are happy—the author feels that America is full of hard-working but happy people. Although each person sings their own song "which belongs to him or her and to none else," when all of these songs combine into "varied carols," they reflect the spirit and vast diversity of America.

---

1. **READ AND CITE TEXT EVIDENCE** Point out to students that the general declaration the speaker makes in the first line ("I hear America singing, the varied carols I hear") is a good clue toward understanding the theme of the poem.

   A **ASK STUDENTS** to cite specific details that support this first general statement. *Students should cite as examples the various kinds of working people the speaker describes in lines 2–8.*

2. **REREAD AND CITE TEXT EVIDENCE** Explain to students that the last two lines of the poem contain several words and phrases that have positive connotations.

   B **ASK STUDENTS** to identify the words in lines 10–11 that portray the workers in a positive way. *Students should cite party, robust, friendly, strong and melodious.*

   FOR ELL STUDENTS Many students may identify carols with songs that are sung at Christmas. Clarify for them that they can also be songs of joy, in general.

SHORT RESPONSE

Cite Text Evidence The exact wording of students' responses will vary, but students should:

• express that the theme of the poem is a celebration of American workers.
• include descriptions of the workers as varied, hard working, and optimistic.
• cite specific evidence in the form of words, phrases, and lines from the poem to support their idea of the poem's theme.

1. **READ** As you read lines 1–10, begin to collect and cite text evidence.

    • Underline the two subjects the speaker observes.
    • Circle references to web-making.
    • In the margin, explain what surrounds the "noiseless patient spider" and "you O my soul."

A Noiseless Patient Spider

The spider and "you" are surrounded by vast amounts of space.

A noiseless patient spider,
I mark'd where on a little promontory[1] it stood isolated,
Mark'd how to explore the vacant vast surrounding,
It launch'd forth filament, filament, filament, out of itself,
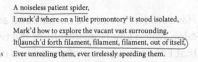 5 Ever unreeling them, ever tirelessly speeding them.

And you O my soul where you stand,
Surrounded, detached, in measureless oceans of space,
Ceaselessly musing, venturing, throwing, seeking the spheres to
   connect them,
Till the bridge you will need be form'd, till the ductile[2] anchor
   hold,
10 Till the gossamer[3] thread you fling catch somewhere, O my soul.

[1] **promontory:** a ridge of land or rock jutting out over water or land.
[2] **ductile:** capable of being drawn or stretched out.
[3] **gossamer:** extremely light or fine.

2. **REREAD AND DISCUSS** Reread lines 1–10. With a small group, discuss the use of parallelism in lines 5 and 8. What do these parallel elements suggest about the relationship between the spider and the speaker?

SHORT RESPONSE

Cite Text Evidence What is the theme of the poem? What details communicate that theme? **Cite text evidence** in your response.

The poem draws a comparison between a spider making a web and the speaker's desire to make a connection with the universe. The speaker's soul launches filaments seeking connections just as the spider launches physical filaments to connect with the solid ground.

40

---

1. READ AND CITE TEXT EVIDENCE

C ASK STUDENTS to cite evidence in the text that explains what the speaker of the poem does that is similar to the action of the spider. *Students should cite lines 8–10.*

2. REREAD AND DISCUSS USING TEXT EVIDENCE

D ASK STUDENTS to identify the words in lines 5 and 8 that create the parallel structure. *The words* unreeling *and* speeding *in line 5 and* musing, venturing, throwing, *and* seeking *in line 8.*

SHORT RESPONSE

Cite Text Evidence Students should:

• include a general statement about the importance of making connections with the world, both physical and mental.

• compare the actions of the spider with those of the speaker.

• include text evidence that supports the theme of the poem.

TO CHALLENGE STUDENTS . . .

Walt Whitman worked most of his adult life on the volume of poetry that he called *Leaves of Grass*. Among the more famous poems in the long volume are "I Sing the Body Electric," and two poems about President Abraham Lincoln: "When Lilacs Last in the Dooryard Bloom'd" and "O Captain! My Captain!" Students can also view a short biography of Whitman online.

ASK STUDENTS to research Whitman's *Leaves of Grass*, specifically the aforementioned poems. Small groups could prepare a brief presentation, giving some background about a poem and the circumstances under which it was written, followed by a dramatic reading of parts of the poem. Students might also find it interesting to read more recent essays about Whitman and his contribution to American poetry. Some twentieth century critics, such as John Berryman, have praised Whitman's poems. Other critics, such as Yvor Winters, have been far less flattering.

DIG DEEPER

With the class, return to Question 2, Reread, on page 38. Have students share their responses.

ASK STUDENTS to cite the text evidence that helped them understand the speaker's attitude toward the young male and female workers he invokes and describes throughout the poem.

• Have students cite specific workers mentioned and details that inform the reader about their jobs.

• Encourage students to discuss the particular jobs of the workers, some of which, like the hatter's or mason's, may be unfamiliar to them. Should that be the case, encourage students to briefly research the job and what it might have entailed in the mid-19th century in New York City.

• Finally, have students identify other details in the poem that are evidence of the speaker's enthusiasm for the workers, and for America in general.

ASK STUDENTS to return to their Short Response answer on page 39 and revise it based on the class discussion.

Essays by Ralph Waldo Emerson

from Nature

Why These Texts

Students may leave the text of an essay without a complete understanding of the author's central ideas. Essays such as these by the great American writer, lecturer, philosopher, and poet Ralph Waldo Emerson include difficult language, an ornate prose style, and complex ideas that are clarified only with careful study. With the help of the close-reading questions, students will determine the central ideas by examining specific textual evidence, guiding them to develop a coherent understanding of each of the essays.

from Self-Reliance

Background Have students read the background and biography of Ralph Waldo Emerson. Introduce the two essays by explaining that Emerson was one of the editors of the *Dial*, which was the chief literary publication of the transcendentalists, promoting the talents of many young writers, such as Henry David Thoreau. When the original *Dial* ceased publication in 1844, Horace Greeley, the most influential newspaper editor of the time, reported it as an end to the "most original and thoughtful periodical ever published in this country."

AS YOU READ Ask students to pay close attention to the central ideas in each essay and to the details that support these ideas. How soon into each essay does Emerson present his first central idea?

Common Core Support

- cite multiple pieces of evidence
- determine two or more central ideas developed over the course of a text
- provide an objective summary of a text

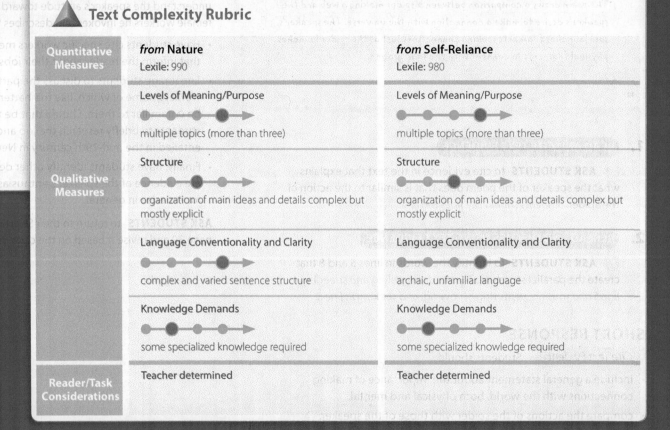

Text Complexity Rubric

	from Nature	*from* Self-Reliance
Quantitative Measures	Lexile: 990	Lexile: 980
Qualitative Measures	**Levels of Meaning/Purpose** multiple topics (more than three)	**Levels of Meaning/Purpose** multiple topics (more than three)
	Structure organization of main ideas and details complex but mostly explicit	**Structure** organization of main ideas and details complex but mostly explicit
	Language Conventionality and Clarity complex and varied sentence structure	**Language Conventionality and Clarity** archaic, unfamiliar language
	Knowledge Demands some specialized knowledge required	**Knowledge Demands** some specialized knowledge required
Reader/Task Considerations	Teacher determined	Teacher determined

Strategies for CLOSE READING

Determine Central Ideas

Students should read each of these essays carefully all the way through. Close-reading questions at the bottom of the page will help them focus on a thorough analysis of the central ideas of each essay and the evidence, including facts, details, and examples, that support these key ideas. As they read, students should record comments or questions about the text in the side margins.

WHEN STUDENTS STRUGGLE . . .

To help students follow the central ideas of each essay, students should work in a small group to fill out a chart such as the one shown below as they provide an analysis of each essay.

CITE TEXT EVIDENCE For practice in finding the central ideas of each essay, ask students to cite details and evidence that support each central idea.

"Nature"

Central Idea: One feels perpetually young in the woods.
Detail 1: One casts off one's years in the woods as a snake sloughs off its skin.
Detail 2: One is always a child when in the woods.
Detail 3: One returns to reason and faith in the woods, fundamental ways of thinking.

"Self-Reliance"

Central Idea: One needs to rely on oneself.
Detail 1: One must accept oneself for better or worse.
Detail 2: One must rely on one's own capabilities and hard work.
Detail 3: One must trust oneself.

Background *As the acknowledged leader of the transcendentalists, Ralph Waldo Emerson (1803–1882) was a towering figure in the 19th-century literary world. He helped shape a new, uniquely American body of literature and is often cited as one of the most significant writers in American history. "All life is an experiment," the radical thinker and writer once said. "The more experiments you make, the better."*

Essays by
Ralph Waldo Emerson

from **Nature** . . . . Ralph Waldo Emerson

from **Self-Reliance** . . . . Ralph Waldo Emerson

Ralph Waldo Emerson *was born in Boston, Massachusetts, in 1803. He attended Harvard and was ordained as a Unitarian minister in 1829. Just over a year later, his beloved wife, Ellen, died of tuberculosis. Ellen's death threw Emerson into a state of spiritual crisis. In 1832, after much consideration, Emerson resigned his post. He settled in Concord, Massachusetts, and devoted himself to the study of philosophy, religion, and literature.*

In 1836 Emerson published Nature, in which he eloquently articulated his transcendental philosophy, an outgrowth of European romanticism. That same year, Emerson formed the Transcendental Club with a group of like-minded friends, including Henry David Thoreau and Margaret Fuller. Nature, with its emphasis on self-reliance and individuality, became the group's unofficial manifesto. He elaborated upon his ideas in essays and a series of popular lectures. By the 1840s, the Sage of Concord, as he was known, had become a major literary force whose influence is still evident in American culture today.

41

1. READ ▶ As you read lines 1–20, begin to collect and cite evidence.

• Underline metaphorical phrases.
• Circle language that Emerson uses to describe the woods.
• In the margin, explain what event causes the author "perfect exhilaration" (lines 2–5).

He feels exhilarated from a walk across a common in winter.

from Nature

Ⓐ Nature is a setting that fits equally well a comic or a mourning piece. In good health, the air is a cordial of incredible virtue. Crossing a bare common, in snow puddles, at twilight, under a clouded sky, without having in my thoughts any occurrence of special good fortune, I have enjoyed a perfect exhilaration. I am glad to the brink of fear. In the woods too, a man casts off his years, as the snake his slough,[1] and at what period soever of life, is always a
Ⓑ child. In the woods, is perpetual youth. Within these plantations of God, a decorum and sanctity reign, a perennial festival is dressed, and the guest sees not how he should tire of them in a thousand years. In the woods, we return to
10 reason and faith. There I feel that nothing can befall me in life,—no disgrace, no calamity, (leaving me my eyes,) which nature cannot repair. Standing on the bare ground,—my head bathed by the blithe air, and uplifted into infinite space,—all mean egotism vanishes. I become a transparent eye-ball; I am nothing; I see all; the currents of the Universal Being circulate through me; I am part or particle of God. The name of the nearest friend sounds then foreign and accidental: to be brothers, to be acquaintances,—master or servant, is then a trifle and a disturbance. I am the lover of uncontained and immortal

decorum:
good taste in conduct or appearance

[1] **slough:** the cast-off skin of a snake.

2. ◀ REREAD Reread lines 5–15. How is a man "always a child" in the woods? Which sentence acts as a central idea and best supports this metaphor?

A man is always a child in the woods because in the woods, we "return to reason and faith," which is the fundamental way a child thinks. "In the woods, is perpetual youth" best supports the metaphor of a man being a child and acts as a central idea.

3. READ ▶ As you read lines 21–35, continue to cite textual evidence.

• Underline the topic sentence Emerson uses to introduce each paragraph.
• In the margin, explain what the "colors of the spirit" refers to (line 32).
• Circle examples of personification.

42

---

beauty. In the wilderness, I find something more dear and connate[2] than in streets or villages. In the tranquil landscape, and especially in the distant line
20 of the horizon, man beholds somewhat as beautiful as his own nature.
Ⓓ The greatest delight which the fields and woods minister, is the suggestion of an **occult** relation between man and the vegetable. I am not alone and unacknowledged. They nod to me and I to them. The waving of the boughs in the storm, is new to me and old. It takes me by surprise, and yet it is not unknown. Its effect is like that of a higher thought or a better emotion coming over me, when I deemed I was thinking justly or doing right.
Yet it is certain that the power to produce this delight, does not reside in nature, but in man, or in a harmony of both. It is necessary to use these pleasures with great temperance. For, nature is not always tricked[3] in holiday
30 attire, but the same scene which yesterday breathed perfume and glittered as
Ⓒ for the frolic of the nymphs, is overspread with melancholy today. Nature always wears the colors of the spirit. To a man laboring under calamity, the heat of his own fire hath sadness in it. Then, there is a kind of contempt of the landscape felt by him who has just lost by death a dear friend. The sky is less grand as it shuts down over less worth in the population.

occult:
secret or hidden from view

The "colors of the spirit" refers to one's feelings and emotions.

[2] **connate:** agreeable; able to be related to.
[3] **tricked:** dressed.

4. ◀ REREAD AND DISCUSS Reread lines 21–35. With a small group, discuss what Emerson is referring to when he alludes to the relationship between "man and the vegetable."

SHORT RESPONSE

Cite Text Evidence Write an objective summary of the piece by restating the central ideas in your own words. Be sure that your objective summary is free from personal opinions and **cite text evidence** in your response.

Nature provides an escape for man where he can become like a child again and be overwhelmed by nature's beauty. There is a secret relationship between man and nature, almost as if nature communicates to man in its actions. This relationship is heavily dictated by one's own feelings, because what was beautiful when one feels optimistic may be dreary when one is feeling melancholy.

43

---

1. READ AND CITE TEXT EVIDENCE

Ⓐ **ASK STUDENTS** why Emerson feels elated. *He feels "perfect exhilaration" from a walk outside in winter (lines 2–5).*

2. REREAD AND CITE TEXT EVIDENCE

Ⓑ **ASK STUDENTS** to cite the sentence that states the key idea of the first paragraph and compares man to a child in the woods. *The central idea is that "In the woods, is perpetual youth" (line 7).*

3. READ AND CITE TEXT EVIDENCE

Ⓒ **ASK STUDENTS** to explain how "Nature always wears the colors of the spirit" supports the central idea in lines 27–35. *One's perception of nature is guided by one's emotions. The power of nature to delight rests more with man than with nature.*

Critical Vocabulary: decorum (line 8) Have students share their definitions.

4. REREAD AND DISCUSS USING TEXT EVIDENCE

Ⓓ **ASK STUDENTS** to appoint a reporter for each group to cite textual evidence to support their opinion about the meaning of the hidden relationship "between man and the vegetable" (line 22). *Students should cite "the waving of the boughs" (line 23), which suggests trees and an unknown, unspoken connection between man and nature.*

Critical Vocabulary: occult (line 22) Have students explain *occult*. Why does Emerson use the word in this context? *He wants to suggest the hidden relation between man and nature.*

SHORT RESPONSE

Cite Text Evidence Students should:

• restate the central ideas of this part of essay.
• use the central ideas to write an objective summary.
• cite text evidence in their response.

CLOSE READ
Notes

1. **READ** ▷ As you read lines 1–24, begin to collect and cite evidence.

   • Underline the topic sentence in each paragraph.
   • In the margin, explain the central idea of lines 1–11.
   • Circle the response of the "valued adviser."

People should rely upon their own capabilities and instincts.

from Self-Reliance

(A) There is a time in every man's education when he arrives at the conviction that envy is ignorance; that imitation is suicide; that he must take himself for better for worse as his portion; that though the wide universe is full of good, no kernel of nourishing corn can come to him but through his toil bestowed on that plot of ground which is given to him to till. . . .

Trust thyself: every heart vibrates to that iron string. Accept the place the divine providence has found for you, the society of your contemporaries, the connection of events. Great men have always done so, and confided themselves childlike to the genius of their age, betraying their perception that the
10 absolutely trustworthy was seated at their heart, working through their hands, predominating in all their being . . . .

nonconformist:
one who does not follow generally accepted beliefs or customs

(B) Whoso would be a man, must be a **nonconformist**. He who would gather immortal palms[1] must not be hindered by the name of goodness, but must explore if it be goodness. Nothing is at last sacred but the integrity of your own mind. Absolve you to yourself, and you shall have the suffrage[2] of the world. I remember an answer which when quite young I was prompted to make to a valued adviser who was wont to importune[3] me with the dear old doctrines of the church. On my saying, "What have I to do with the sacredness of traditions, if I live wholly from within?" my friend suggested—"But these impulses may be
20 from below, not from above." I replied, "They do not seem to me to be such; but

[1] **immortal palms:** everlasting triumph and honor. In ancient times, people carried palm leaves as a symbol of victory, success, or joy.
[2] **suffrage:** approval, support.
[3] **importune:** ask persistently.

2. **◄ REREAD** Reread lines 12–24 and restate the central idea.

Emerson believes that people should follow their own impulses and that what is sacred is what comes from one's nature.

---

if I am the Devil's child, I will live then from the Devil." No law can be sacred to me but that of my nature. Good and bad are but names very readily transferable to that or this; the only right is what is after my **constitution**; the only wrong is what is against it . . . .

(C) What I must do is all that concerns me, not what the people think. This rule, equally arduous in actual and in intellectual life, may serve for the whole distinction between greatness and **meanness**. It is the harder because you will always find those who think they know what is your duty better than you know it. It is easy in the world to live after the world's opinion; it is easy in solitude to
30 live after our own; but the great man is he who in the midst of the crowd keeps with perfect sweetness the independence of solitude . . . .

For nonconformity the world whips you with its displeasure. And therefore a man must know how to estimate a sour face. The by-standers look askance on him in the public street or in the friend's parlor. If this aversion had its origin in contempt and resistance like his own he might well go home with a sad countenance; but the sour faces of the multitude, like their sweet faces, have no deep cause, but are put on and off as the wind blows and a newspaper directs . . . .

(D) The other terror that scares us from self-trust is our consistency; a
40 reverence for our past act or word because the eyes of others have no other data for computing our orbit than our past acts, and we are loth to disappoint them . . . .

A foolish consistency is the hobgoblin of little minds, adored by little statesmen and philosophers and divines. With consistency a great soul has simply nothing to do. He may as well concern himself with his shadow on the wall. Speak what you think now in hard words and tomorrow speak what

constitution:
physical or mental condition

meanness:
being inferior in quality, character, or value

Nonconform-ists may be met with resis-tance.

3. **READ** ▷ As you read lines 25–38, continue to collect and cite evidence.

   • Underline the topic sentence in each paragraph.
   • In the margin, explain common reactions to nonconformists.

4. **READ** ▷ Read lines 39–51. Underline text that explains why we are reluctant to trust ourselves.

---

1. READ AND CITE TEXT EVIDENCE

(A) ASK STUDENTS to cite evidence from the text supporting their statement of the central idea of these lines. *Students may cite lines 3–6 as support for the idea that people should rely on themselves and their own hard work.*

2. REREAD AND CITE TEXT EVIDENCE

(B) ASK STUDENTS to cite textual evidence to paraphrase the central idea in lines 12–24, which is an extension of the idea "Trust thyself." *The central idea is that people need to follow their own mind, impulses, and nature—to be nonconformists (lines 12, 14–15, and 19–24).*

Critical Vocabulary: nonconformist (line 12) Have students explain the meaning and importance of the word.

FOR ELL STUDENTS Explain that a compound word may consist of two words that are joined together by a hyphen, as in *self-reliance*. Ask students to find other hyphenated compounds.

3. READ AND CITE TEXT EVIDENCE

(C) ASK STUDENTS to state the central idea of lines 25–38. *The central idea is that it does not matter what other people think of you, but nonconformists are viewed by others with displeasure and resistance because they do not follow the crowd.*

4. READ AND CITE TEXT EVIDENCE

(D) ASK STUDENTS to explain what Emerson calls our "other terror." *Emerson thinks we are scared by our own "reverence for our past": we think consistency is important when in fact it's useless. Students should cite specific textual evidence from lines 39–42 and 43–48.*

Critical Vocabulary: constitution (line 23) and **meanness** (line 27) Have students explain the words as Emerson uses them here.

CLOSE READ Notes

tomorrow thinks in hard words again, though it contradict everything you said today.—"Ah, so you shall be sure to be misunderstood."—Is it so bad then to be misunderstood? Pythagoras was misunderstood, and Socrates, and Jesus, and
50 Luther, and Copernicus, and Galileo, and Newton,[4] and every pure and wise
E spirit that ever took flesh. To be great is to be misunderstood.

> [4] **Pythagoras was misunderstood, and Socrates, and Jesus, and Luther, and Copernicus, and Galileo, and Newton:** great thinkers whose radical theories and viewpoints caused controversy.

5. **◄ REREAD** Reread lines 39–51. Which sentence best summarizes the central idea of this part of the essay?

The sentence "To be great is to be misunderstood" best summarizes this section of the text because it explains Emerson's opinion about self-reliance and self-worth. Rather than being worried by what other people think, Emerson wants us to ignore popular opinion and fulfill ourselves as individuals.

SHORT RESPONSE

Cite Text Evidence Write an objective summary of the piece by restating the central ideas in your own words. Be sure that your objective summary is free from personal opinions. **Cite text evidence.**

It is honorable, but difficult, to be self-reliant. Self-reliance requires one to use his or her mind and heart to make judgments of what is good and bad, not to rely on the judgments of others. A great person is able to maintain this manner of self-reliance even if others misunderstand him or her. However, being misunderstood is a sign of greatness.

46

5. **REREAD AND CITE TEXT EVIDENCE** Explain that sometimes the central idea comes at the end of a section.

E **ASK STUDENTS** to summarize lines 39–51. _The central idea is that "to be great is to be misunderstood" (line 51), supported by examples of famous thinkers, such as Galileo and Newton, whose views caused public distrust and disdain (lines 46–51). This statement explains Emerson's idea about eschewing public opinion._

SHORT RESPONSE

Cite Text Evidence Student responses will vary, but students should cite textual evidence to support their paraphrase of central ideas for their summary. Students should:

- restate the central ideas of this part of the essay.
- show the development and interactions of the central ideas.
- use the central ideas to write an objective summary.

TO CHALLENGE STUDENTS . . .

For more context about Emerson's time and beliefs, students can research a "protest" movement of that era, transcendentalism.

ASK STUDENTS to find out more about the transcendentalist movement and the people associated with it. (These include essayists such as Emerson and Thoreau, naturalist John Muir, novelist Louisa May Alcott, journalist and activist Margaret Fuller, and poets Emily Dickinson and Walt Whitman.) Have students report back to the class on their findings.

- What were transcendentalists protesting against? _Basically, they were against the organized religion and political parties of the time. They wanted to promote a style of literature that wasn't part of the European tradition._

- What did they believe in? _They were trying to become more in touch with their senses, to define spirituality, to be self-reliant, and to fulfill their human potential._

- Aside from literature, what did many transcendentalists have in common? _Many of them were involved in social reform: anti-slavery and women's rights._

Have each group plan, write, revise, and proofread its essay, publishing and sharing it in print or online.

DIG DEEPER

With the class, return to "*from* Nature," Question 4, Reread and Discuss. Have students share the results of their group discussion.

ASK STUDENTS whether they were satisfied with the outcome of their small-group discussions. Have each group share their explanation of Emerson's allusion to the relationship between "man and the vegetable." What text evidence did the group cite to support its explanation?

- Guide students to tell whether there was any convincing evidence cited by group members who did not agree with the explanation accepted by the majority. If so, why wasn't the evidence strong enough to sway the group's opinion?
- Have groups tell how they decided whether or not they had found sufficient textual evidence to support their explanation.
- Did everyone in the group agree as to what made the evidence sufficient? If not, how did the group resolve conflicts?
- After groups have stated their "findings," ask if another group shared evidence they wish they had thought of.

ASK STUDENTS to return to their Short Response answer on page 43 and to revise it based on the class discussion.

CLOSE READING NOTES

Spoiling Walden: Or, How I Learned to Stop Worrying and Love Cape Wind

Essay by David Gessner

Why This Text

Students may lose their way in argumentative essays, especially when the essay develops a complex set of ideas. If students don't understand the essay's structure, they may miss its argument altogether. With the help of the close-reading questions, students will analyze how David Gessner develops his central ideas in this essay. This close reading will lead students to understand how the essay's structure helps make the argument clear and engaging.

Background Have students read the background and information about the author and his essay. Introduce the essay by pointing out that people consume energy with practically every action they take and every product they use. In this essay, Gessner explores how his ideas regarding a "new" energy source—wind—evolved as he traveled around the country and talked to people.

AS YOU READ Ask students to pay attention to how the author organizes his essay. How does this structure help him make his argument?

Common Core Support

- cite strong and thorough textual evidence
- determine the central ideas of a text and analyze how they are developed
- analyze and evaluate the effectiveness of the structure an author uses in his or her argument
- determine an author's point of view

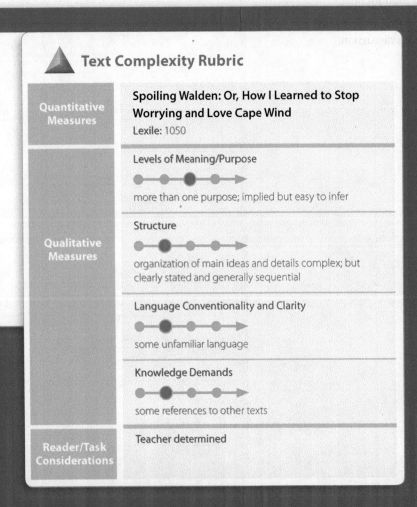

Text Complexity Rubric

Spoiling Walden: Or, How I Learned to Stop Worrying and Love Cape Wind
Lexile: 1050

Quantitative Measures

Qualitative Measures

Levels of Meaning/Purpose

more than one purpose; implied but easy to infer

Structure

organization of main ideas and details complex; but clearly stated and generally sequential

Language Conventionality and Clarity

some unfamiliar language

Knowledge Demands

some references to other texts

Reader/Task Considerations

Teacher determined

Strategies for CLOSE READING

Analyze the Structure of an Essay

Students should read this essay carefully all the way through. Close-reading questions at the bottom of the page will help them focus on a thorough analysis of the essay's structure. As they read, students should jot down comments or questions about the text in the margins.

WHEN STUDENTS STRUGGLE . . .

To help students analyze the structure of Gessner's essay, have them work in small groups to fill out a chart like the one shown below.

CITE TEXT EVIDENCE For practice in analyzing the structure of an essay, ask students to cite text evidence that helps explain each step in the author's "wind journey."

Step	Text Evidence
starting point	"love of a place" (Cape Cod) "love of a book" (Walden)
proposal for wind farm	"I react with outrage" "This is a sacred place"
moves away	"I start seeing the place . . . from a distance"
travels to Cape Breton	"I talk to a local man named Keith" "There were no jobs, you see."
travels to Gulf Coast	"The place was stunningly beautiful . . . it was also slathered in the substance that we all use to power our lives"
revisits Thoreau	"our patron saint of frugality"
recalls visit to Cape Cod	"this ain't the Grand Canyon" "We need to connect the dots." "if there are Waldens then they are all interconnected"

Background *The following article was written by* **David Gessner**, *a contributing editor to OnEarth magazine. In it, he explains his change of opinion about Cape Wind, the first federally approved offshore wind farm. The note accompanying the article, published in December 2011, reads: "It's been 10 years since a proposal was submitted to build America's first offshore wind farm in Nantucket Sound off Cape Cod. The federal government finally approved the project earlier this year, although court battles continue to delay construction. After a decade of division, our contributing editor [Gessner] shares his personal journey of acceptance."*

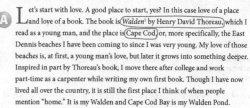

Spoiling Walden

Or, How I Learned to Stop Worrying and Love Cape Wind

Essay by David Gessner

CLOSE READ
Notes

1. **READ ▶** As you read lines 1–17, begin to collect and cite text evidence.

   • Circle the two things the author loves in lines 1–9.
   • Underline loaded language the author uses to describe his first reaction to the wind farm proposal.
   • In the margin, explain Gessner's initial opposition to the wind farm.

A   Let's start with love. A good place to start, yes? In this case love of a place and love of a book. The book is Walden[1] by Henry David Thoreau, which I read as a young man, and the place is Cape Cod, or, more specifically, the East Dennis beaches I have been coming to since I was very young. My love of those beaches is, at first, a young man's love, but later it grows into something deeper. Inspired in part by Thoreau's book, I move there after college and work part-time as a carpenter while writing my own first book. Though I have now lived all over the country, it is still the first place I think of when people mention "home." It is my Walden and Cape Cod Bay is my Walden Pond.

10   So of course when someone—a businessman no less—suggests that he wants to place 130 wind turbines—bird-killing turbines!—in Nantucket Sound off the shores of my Walden, I react with outrage. Not in my backyard? Not in my backyard! This is a sacred place, a place apart, and if this is a sacred place then these wind turbines are, as I tell anyone who will listen, a desecration.

[1] **Walden**: Thoreau's book about his time living simply and self-sufficiently in nature.

Margin note: He is against the wind farm because a businessman proposed it, turbines cause bird deaths, and the turbines will mess up the views on the beach.

47

---

1. **READ AND CITE TEXT EVIDENCE** Explain to students that Gessner opens the essay with a disarming appeal to love—specifically, love for a book and a place—to draw the reader in.

   A **ASK STUDENTS** to discuss *Walden* and Cape Cod and how they became the author's starting point. What does the author mean when he writes that Cape Cod "is my Walden and Cape Cod Bay is my Walden Pond"? *Students should understand that the author is speaking figuratively. Thoreau wrote memorably of his years at Walden Pond, where he lived close to nature. Walden Pond and the surrounding woods—to which Thoreau developed strong physical and spiritual connections—have come to symbolize the natural home that most city dwellers have lost. So when Gessner calls Cape Cod "my Walden," he means that it is a natural place of great physical and spiritual significance for him.*

I cling to this position for years, holding tight, but then, gradually, my grip starts to loosen. Some things happen, some things change. The story of those **(B)** things, those happenings and changes, is the story of my wind journey.

One thing I do is to move away from Cape Cod, and so I start seeing the **(C)** place I still consider home from a distance, from arm's length, while at the same time seeing how that place connects to others. Another thing I do is start to travel extensively, reporting for an environmental magazine. I visit Cape Breton in Nova Scotia, which seems like driving onto Cape Cod a hundred years ago, until I reach a city called Sydney Mines. The city looks like it has been cracked open and had its insides sucked out, which it turns out, is pretty much what happened. In Mike's Place Pub & Grill, I talk to a local man named Keith who tells me the story of the town's glory years, when it supplied coal for much of Canada, and of the depths to which the town fell after the coal was gone.

2. **◄ REREAD** Reread lines 15–17. What do these lines explain about Gessner's approach to the topic? Support your answer with explicit textual evidence.

These lines explain that Gessner has changed his position about the wind farm. He begins by explaining his initial opposition to Cape Wind and his reasons why, then states that the rest of the essay will trace his "wind journey"—the story of his change of heart.

3. **READ ▷** As you read lines 18–35, underline the first two things Gessner does on his "wind journey."

4. **◄ REREAD** Reread lines 21–35. What can you infer about the comment that the only jobs left in Sydney Mines were funeral directors? Why does Gessner include this conversation with Keith?

Because there was a need for funeral directors, you can infer that the coal industry affected the health of the people who worked in the mines. Gessner includes the conversation with Keith to show how learning about the devastation of one town starts to change his own thinking about natural resources.

"The coal was gone and they had taken everything out of the town. Where it had been wall-to-wall with people on a Saturday night you suddenly couldn't find anyone. Maybe a stray dog and a single taxi. A ghost town."

His eyes drooped as if in sympathy with the town. His voice sounded beautiful, his accent vaguely Irish.

(D) "There were no jobs, you see. Other than funeral directors. There was a big call for those."

The more I travelled, the more I found men like Keith and places like Sydney Mines. Places hollowed out and then deserted. I began to think more, not just about beautiful places, but about what we extract from them. This culminated last summer when I travelled along the Gulf Coast during the height, or depths, of the BP oil spill. There I found the most intense **juxtaposition** of beauty and energy as I spent mornings birdwatching—seeing roseate spoonbills and ibises—near Halliburton Road and oil refineries, or spent a night out in a fish camp, a few hundred yards from a fringe of marsh that appeared burned, but was, in fact, oiled.

juxtaposition:
contrast

5. **READ ▷** As you read lines 36–69, continue to cite textual evidence.
• Underline text that shows how Gessner connects Cape Cod and the Gulf Coast.
• In the margin of lines 45–62, explain how Gessner connects modern people to Thoreau and his personal math.

48

49

---

2. **REREAD AND CITE TEXT EVIDENCE**

(B) **ASK STUDENTS** to discuss the elements of a journey and how the author's "wind journey" might affect the essay's structure. *A journey has a beginning, a middle, and an end. The essay will be structured so that the author can describe the journey's key steps.*

3. **READ AND CITE TEXT EVIDENCE**

(C) **ASK STUDENTS** to discuss the first two steps of Gessner's journey. How would you describe the journey? *The journey is both physical and mental. The author travels across the country, and that movement opens his mind to new perspectives. He starts to see Cape Cod "from a distance" and how it "connects" to other places.*

4. **REREAD AND CITE TEXT EVIDENCE**

(D) **ASK STUDENTS** to cite evidence to support their inference. *Students should cite evidence from lines 27–28 about "the depths to which the town fell," and from lines 29–31.*

5. **READ AND CITE TEXT EVIDENCE** Birdwatchers are familiar with impressive examples of birds "doing the math of energy." For example, before migrating south across the Gulf of Mexico, tiny birds such as hummingbirds and warblers must bulk up, increasing their body fat by as much as 50 percent in order to have sufficient energy reserves to make the long flight.

(E) **ASK STUDENTS** to state some of the implications of Gessner's "math of energy." *There is something like a global "ledger sheet," showing how much energy is extracted from the planet and how much is used and squandered. Energy gains and losses have a "strict mathematical relationship," so we cannot ignore the "loss" side of the equation.*

Critical Vocabulary: juxtaposition (line 41) Have students share their definitions of *juxtaposition*. What things does the author find in juxtaposition on the Gulf Coast? *beauty and energy, spoonbills and oil refineries, fish camp and oiled marsh*

Thoreau's math explains that we are responsible for our own input and output. The energy we use has to be replaced, just as animals conserve energy. Today, we have to think about replacing the resources we use.

The place was stunningly beautiful, and for the Cajun fishermen I met, like Ryan Lambert, it was their Walden. But it was also slathered in the substance that we all use to power our lives. The Gulf has been called "a national sacrifice zone," and it seemed to have been sacrificed so that the rest of us could keep on living the way we live. I thought to myself: this place is connected to Cape Cod. Not metaphorically, but literally, by its waters.

And I thought, because I could not help but think of it, of energy. Where we get our energy from and how we pay for it, in the broadest sense. As a birdwatcher, I know that every animal is required to do the math of energy in its own way, and humans, whatever we may think, are not exempt. It was Thoreau, our patron saint of frugality, who created the initial ledger sheet, the personal math that many of us have begun to think about again during these difficult times, the calculus of our own input and output. In *Walden* he did his figuring right there on the page for us. *Here is how much I spent and here is what I gained.* It is the same math that animals rely on instinctively when they hunt. By Thoreau's reasoning, human lives, like the lives of other animals, require a strict mathematical relationship with energy, its gains and losses, its conservation and squandering.

Years ago, on Cape Cod, I had been quick to embrace, and mimic, Thoreau's love of nature but slow to hear his sterner message of personal responsibility. I rationalized this by saying that I preferred Thoreau the celebrator to Thoreau the preacher. But in the Gulf I found myself returning to the other, stricter Thoreau. His relationship with energy was simple but

6. **REREAD** Reread lines 51–69. Circle the three titles Gessner gives to Thoreau. Why does Gessner come to prefer the stricter Thoreau?

While Gessner has always appreciated Thoreau and his celebration of nature, he comes to prefer Thoreau the preacher, who was aware of what he was consuming and giving back. The "patron saint of frugality" focused on using less and "refining his output."

> *The place was stunningly beautiful . . . it was their Walden.*

profound: instead of just focusing on getting more, he limited his input and refined his output.

As I travelled through the Gulf, I also thought back to a meeting I'd had two summers before. A friend had put me in touch with Jim Gordon, the president of Cape Wind, and we met for lunch in Hyannis before driving out to one of the beaches that would face out toward the hundred-plus turbine towers that would make up the wind farm. The beach was crammed with people, umbrellas sprouting and kids running this way and that, and once we got to the shore we looked out past kids on inflatable rafts and roaring Jet Skis and powerboats to where the towers would stand on the horizon. One of the arguments that wind opponents have made is that putting wind turbines out in this water would be like putting them in the Grand Canyon. Jim, consciously or not, was using this beach as both prop and stage, and the message was clear: *this ain't the Grand Canyon.*

The question many have asked is: does having a wind farm out on the horizon detract from that elemental experience of the beach? The argument that Jim Gordon was making, without saying a word, was that this experience was already limited enough, and that the site of blades blowing in the breeze was not going to detract from it one iota.

Now Jim held up his thumb against the horizon.

The beach is a shared space, littered with people and their possessions. The wind farm would not take away from the scenery any more than these things.

7. **READ** As you read lines 70–111, continue to cite textual evidence.
- Underline what Gessner sees on the beach.
- In the margin of lines 70–86, explain why the beach is already "limited enough."
- Circle Jim Gordon's statements about why the turbines should be seen.

---

6. **REREAD AND CITE TEXT EVIDENCE**

F **ASK STUDENTS** how "Thoreau the preacher" lived. *Thoreau lived simply and close to nature; he kept a ledger of his inputs and outputs. He was frugal and believed in personal responsibility. He didn't try just to get more—he "limited his input and refined his output."*

FOR ELL STUDENTS Clarify the meaning of the expression *do the math* (line 53). Explain that it has a figurative meaning—"to reach your own conclusion."

7. **READ AND CITE TEXT EVIDENCE** Gessner alludes to one of the main arguments against wind farms—that they destroy the beauty of America's natural landscapes.

G **ASK STUDENTS** how Gessner's trip to the beach with Jim Gordon marks an important step in his journey. *Gordon helps Gessner see that the beach and bay are anything but pristine. This realization moves Gessner closer to accepting a wind farm there.*

CLOSE READ
Notes

CLOSE READ
Notes

"From here the turbines will be six or seven miles out. They'll be about as big as my thumbnail."

90 This, of course, was another big point of contention. How big would they really look from the shore? And what would it mean for Cape Codders to look out at their theoretically wild waters and see what would be, for all its techno grace, an industrial site? While I had deep sympathy with the **aesthetic** point of view, it was hard to argue that windmills that would appear a few inches tall on the horizon would ruin the place's wildness.

And with what Jim said next, he almost won me over entirely. "We need to connect the dots," he said.

Connect the dots. Wasn't that what Thoreau had tried to do? Wasn't that the definition of ecology?

100 "We would barely see the turbines from here, but maybe we should see them," he continued. "It's what we can't see that's killing us. Like the particle emissions from the power plant in Sandwich. And the oil being shipped to run that plant."

He shook his head and stared out at the horizon where his windmills would turn. "Maybe it's not such a bad idea for us to see just where our energy is coming from," he said.

I nodded. At the time my thoughts on wind power were still in flux. But with this I could not disagree. I still was, and still am, worried that migrating birds might run into the turbines. A million birds a night migrate over the
110 Cape during the fall migration, and I fret that by supporting wind I am becoming an avian Judas. But it is a time of tough choices.

aesthetic:
concerned with beauty

> ...if there are Waldens then they are all interconnected.

"Do you know the windfarms will kill more birds in a year than were killed during the whole Gulf disaster?" a wind opponent said to me recently. This "statistic," of course, hinges on a very narrow definition of bird fatalities. My accuser was not thinking of habitat destruction and warming, and the whole host of other consequences of the rabid pursuit of oil. Meanwhile, Jim Gordon's camp claims that the slow-moving and well-lit turbines should prove less of a threat to birds than most tall buildings.

I am not sure of that. What I am sure of is that there are no more Waldens,
120 or, more accurately, if there are Waldens then they are all interconnected. Cape Cod has been called "a place apart." I am writing this from Cape Cod right now, and I understand what the phrase means: the land of this fragile ex-peninsula is very specific to itself, and when you come here, and cross the bridge, you leave other places behind and enter a place like nowhere else.

But I can no longer use this term to describe the Cape. It is not apart from the fragile Louisiana fish camp where I spent the night, oil lapping nearby, and it is not apart from Sydney Mines. Each place in this threatened world, separate but connected, must now make an accounting, keep its own ledger sheet with a cold and honest eye. We hold onto our pristine place by sacrificing other places.
130 I hear that up in Nova Scotia, where I visited Sydney Mines, they are proposing power plants that will take advantage of the massive tides. I hope they do and I support it. I also support Jim Gordon and his wind farm. There is no place apart.

8. ◀ REREAD Reread lines 96–99. How does the point Jim Gordon makes in these lines influence Gessner?

Jim Gordon's comment about needing to "connect the dots" echoes Thoreau's beliefs, and Gessner's. Gessner points out that the "definition of ecology" is taking responsibility for the costs of energy.

9. READ ▶ As you read lines 112–133, continue to cite textual evidence.
  • Underline the conclusions that Gessner reaches about turbines on Cape Cod.
  • Circle text that discusses bird fatalities.

52

53

---

8. **REREAD AND CITE TEXT EVIDENCE**

Ⓗ **ASK STUDENTS** to compare what Jim Gordon means by "connect the dots" and what the author means. *Gordon wants consumers to start seeing the connections between energy sources and their invisible but harmful consequences. If consumers don't "connect the dots," they are likely to protest relatively clean wind energy. For the author, the phrase reminds him of Thoreau's ledger sheets and careful notes about inputs and outputs.*

Critical Vocabulary: aesthetic (line 93) Have students share their definitions of *aesthetic*, and ask volunteers to use the adjective in sentences about natural landscapes.

FOR ELL STUDENTS *Sympathy* is a term that can be confusing for Spanish speakers, since it has a false cognate, *simpática* (friendly, charming). Clarify that in English it means "a feeling of support or compassion for someone else's experience."

9. **READ AND CITE TEXT EVIDENCE**

Ⓘ **ASK STUDENTS** which lines discuss bird fatalities. *lines 112–118* Which lines include text about Gessner's conclusions? *lines 120, 127–129, 132–133* Then ask students to restate Gessner's conclusions in their own words. *Possible response: In any place, people should balance their own discomfort with the needs of the environment.*

10. ◀REREAD Reread lines 112–133. How does Gessner react to the "statistic" about wind farms and the Gulf oil spill? Why does he include this interaction in the piece?

Gessner questions his "accuser" because the opponent limits his statistic to wind farms alone and not to other considerations like habitat destruction and global warming, or tall buildings—all of which contribute to bird deaths. Gessner is not sure of either group's argument, perhaps because they are only claims and not backed by hard proof. Gessner includes this interaction because he's a bird lover and is concerned about bird fatalities.

SHORT RESPONSE

Cite Text Evidence In what ways does the structure of Gessner's essay help engage his reader? **Cite text evidence** in your response.

Gessner begins by saying how much he loves Cape Cod. He gives personal background for why the turbine issue matters to him. He then explains his journey (both physical and mental) that leads to his change of heart. By including the reader on this "journey," he effectively shows us the conversations and realizations that help change his mind. He provides evidence to show the disadvantages of using up natural resources and then moves on to show the seemingly minimal visual impact the turbines will have. His argument is convincing, because he shares his own process in coming to the decision, which makes it more engaging—because it's personal.

54

---

10. **REREAD AND CITE TEXT EVIDENCE** Gessner points out that one "wind opponent" says that wind farms on migration flyways or near important habitats kill large numbers of birds.

J **ASK STUDENTS** how the author "connects the dots" to rebut the wind opponent's argument about bird fatalities. *Gessner acknowledges that he is still worried about bird fatalities at the Cape Cod wind farm since a million birds might migrate over the Cape each fall. But, he argues, the wind opponent isn't weighing these fatalities against the potentially larger problems for birds caused by oil extraction and use: habitat destruction and global warming.*

SHORT RESPONSE

Cite Text Evidence Students should:

- note that the essay is structured around a journey.
- cite text evidence to show the journey on which the author embarks.
- explain how the author engages the reader.

TO CHALLENGE STUDENTS . . .

For more context on the wind energy debate, students can research modern wind farms online.

ASK STUDENTS to summarize the pros and cons of wind energy. *Students should understand that there are three main cons associated with modern wind farms: the aesthetic loss of natural landscapes, bird and bat fatalities, and the industry's continued reliance on government subsidies. The benefits of wind energy are also compelling: no greenhouse gas emissions, no possibility of large-scale pollution from spills, and relatively little habitat destruction (compared to that caused by oil, coal, and natural gas mining).*

DIG DEEPER

With the class, return to Question 7, Read. Have students share their responses to the question.

ASK STUDENTS to discuss Jim Gordon's suggestion that people *should* see the turbines off Cape Cod.

- Why does Gordon think people ought to see where their energy comes from? *He understands that every energy source has its drawbacks and wants people to be aware of them. If we can see where our energy comes from, it will be easier to be realistic about the drawbacks. When we can't see an energy source, we can forget or ignore the drawbacks.*

- How does Gordon's suggestion relate to Thoreau's ledger sheets? *Gordon wants people to see and think about their energy consumption and use, the same way that Thoreau kept track of how much he spent and gained on Walden Pond.*

- How does this interaction help move the author along his journey? *Gordon's statement about "connecting the dots" has resonance for the author, who now understands that keeping a wind farm away from Cape Cod would simply mean more reliance on coal or oil. The author is finally connecting the dots, which takes him back to his starting point.*

ASK STUDENTS to return to their Short Response answer and revise it based on the class discussion.

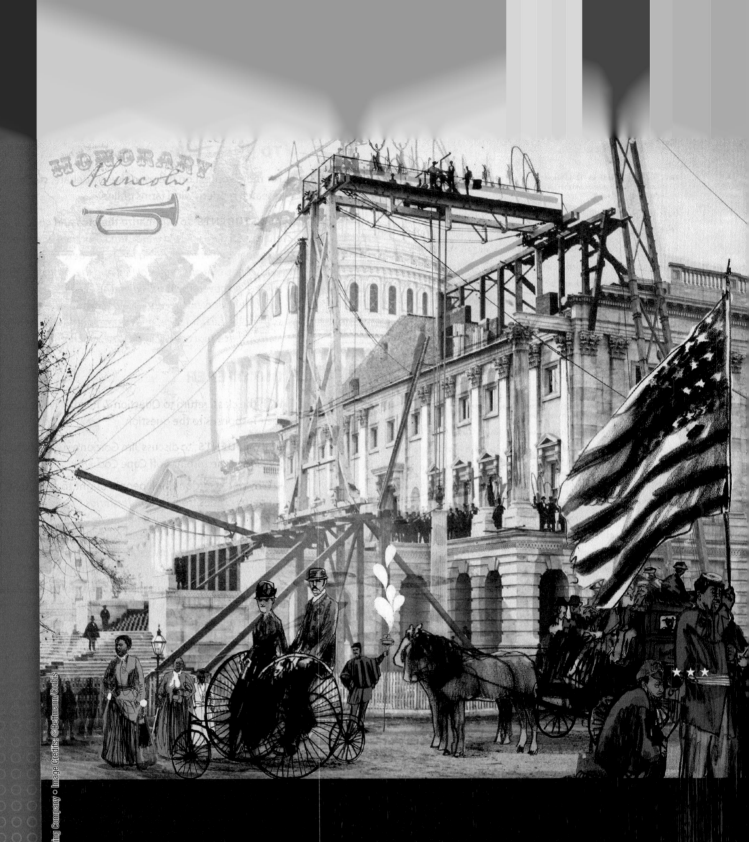

A New Birth of Freedom

A New Birth of Freedom

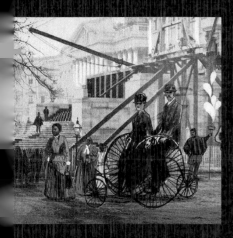

"My father was a slave and my people died to build this country, and I'm going to stay here and have a part of it."

—Paul Robeson

LEGAL DOCUMENT

Emancipation Proclamation   **Abraham Lincoln**

PUBLIC DOCUMENT

from The Iroquois Constitution   **Dekanawida**

NEWSPAPER ARTICLE

Bonding Over a Mascot   **Joe Lapointe**

The Emancipation Proclamation

For more context, students can view "The Story of Us: Abraham Lincoln" in their eBooks.

Legal Document by Abraham Lincoln

Why This Text

Students may have difficulty understanding nineteenth-century foundational U.S. documents. The Emancipation Proclamation is a significant historical document because it outlines a direct opposition to slavery. With the help of the close-reading questions, students will analyze Lincoln's purpose and central ideas. This close reading will lead students to explain Lincoln's argument that he is taking action that is of "military necessity."

Background Have students read the background and the information about Abraham Lincoln. Alternatively, they can watch the video "The Story of Us: Abraham Lincoln" in their eBooks. Tell students that the Emancipation Proclamation was not a law passed by Congress, and it did not abolish slavery. The Proclamation was issued under Lincoln's role as Commander-in-Chief. Slavery was not abolished until the adoption of the Thirteenth Amendment to the Constitution in 1865. Lincoln's home state of Illinois was first to ratify the Thirteenth Amendment.

AS YOU READ Ask students to pay attention to how Lincoln builds his argument.

Common Core Support

- cite strong and thorough textual evidence
- analyze the development of two or more central ideas
- delineate and evaluate the reasoning in seminal U.S. texts
- analyze nineteenth-century foundational U.S. documents

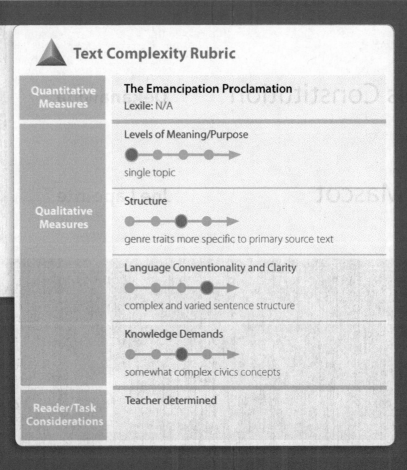

Text Complexity Rubric

Quantitative Measures

The Emancipation Proclamation
Lexile: N/A

Qualitative Measures

Levels of Meaning/Purpose
single topic

Structure
genre traits more specific to primary source text

Language Conventionality and Clarity
complex and varied sentence structure

Knowledge Demands
somewhat complex civics concepts

Reader/Task Considerations
Teacher determined

Strategies for CLOSE READING

Evaluate Seminal Texts: Premises, Purposes, and Arguments

Students should read this document carefully all the way through. Close-reading questions at the bottom of the page will help them focus on a thorough analysis of the text. As they read, students should jot down comments or questions about the proclamation in the side margins.

WHEN STUDENTS STRUGGLE . . .

To help students analyze Lincoln's argument, have them work in small groups to fill out a chart, such as the one shown below.

CITE TEXT EVIDENCE For practice in analyzing an argument, ask students to identify a claim Lincoln makes and show how he supports it.

> **CLAIM:**
>
> *The Emancipation Proclamation is a necessary war measure.*
>
> **SUPPORT:**
>
> *Reason 1: There are states and parts of states that are in rebellion.*
>
> *Reason 2: Rebel states are not represented in Congress.*
>
> *Reason 3: Lincoln is empowered as Commander-in-Chief to suppress the rebellion.*

Background Abraham Lincoln *(1809–1865) was elected president in 1860 and was clear in his opposition to expanding slavery to U.S. territories in the West. By the time of Lincoln's inauguration in March of 1861, seven slave states had formed the Confederacy and seceded from the Union. By April, the Union and the Confederacy were at war. After the Union victory at Antietam in September 1862, Lincoln issued a preliminary proclamation, stating that on January 1, 1863, slaves in rebel states would be declared free. Though more of a symbolic gesture than an enforceable law, the Emancipation Proclamation heartened abolitionists and African Americans and made the issue of slavery a central focus of the war.*

The Emancipation Proclamation

Legal Document by Abraham Lincoln

CLOSE READ
Notes

1. **READD** ▶ As you read lines 1–21, begin to cite text evidence.
   - Circle the three dates noted in these lines.
   - Underline the states affected by the proclamation, and in the margin explain which states this proclamation affects (lines 5–12).
   - Underline text that explains how the president will classify the states (lines 13–21).

A Transcription By the President of the United States of America: A Proclamation.

Ⓐ Whereas, on the twenty-second day of September, in the year of our Lord one thousand eight hundred and sixty-two, a proclamation was issued by the President of the United States, containing, among other things, the following, to wit:[1]

"That on the first day of January, in the year of our Lord one thousand eight hundred and sixty-three, all persons held as slaves within any State or designated part of a State, the people whereof shall then be in rebellion against the United States, shall be then, thenceforward, and forever free; and the Executive Government of the United States, including the military and naval
10 authority thereof, will recognize and maintain the freedom of such persons, and will do no act or acts to repress such persons, or any of them, in any efforts they may make for their actual freedom.

---
[1] to wit: namely.

> *It affects states or parts of states in rebellion against the United States.*

57

---

1. READ AND CITE TEXT EVIDENCE

Ⓐ **ASK STUDENTS** to use their marked text as evidence to explain what happened on January 1, 1863. *Students should cite evidence from lines 1–2 that Lincoln issued a proclamation in September of 1862 to all states "in rebellion against the United States" (lines 7–8) freeing the slaves in those states as of "the first day of January, in the year of our Lord one thousand eight hundred and sixty-three" (lines 5–6).*

"That the Executive will, on the first day of January aforesaid,[2] by proclamation, designate the States and parts of States, if any, in which the people thereof, respectively, shall then be in rebellion against the United States; and the fact that any State, or the people thereof, shall on that day be, in good faith, represented in the Congress of the United States by members chosen thereto at elections wherein a majority of the qualified voters of such State shall have participated, shall, in the absence of strong countervailing[3] testimony, be
20 deemed conclusive evidence that such State, and the people thereof, are not then in rebellion against the United States."

Now, therefore I, Abraham Lincoln, President of the United States, by virtue of the power in me vested as Commander-in-Chief, of the Army and Navy of the United States in time of actual armed rebellion against the authority and government of the United States, and as a fit and necessary war measure for **suppressing** said rebellion, do, on this first day of January, in the year of our Lord one thousand eight hundred and sixty-three, and in accordance with my purpose so to do publicly proclaimed for the full period of one hundred days, from the day first above mentioned, order and designate as
30 the States and parts of States wherein the people thereof respectively, are this day in rebellion against the United States, the following, to wit:

[2] **aforesaid:** stated before.
[3] **countervailing:** contradicting.

suppressing:
preventing;
restraining

Arkansas, Texas, Louisiana, (except the Parishes of St. Bernard, Plaquemines, Jefferson, St. John, St. Charles, St. James Ascension, Assumption, Terrebonne, Lafourche, St. Mary, St. Martin, and Orleans, including the City of New Orleans) Mississippi, Alabama, Florida, Georgia, South Carolina, North Carolina, and Virginia, (except the forty-eight counties designated as West Virginia, and also the counties of Berkley, Accomac, Northampton, Elizabeth City, York, Princess Ann, and Norfolk, including the cities of Norfolk and Portsmouth), and which excepted parts, are for the present, left precisely as if
40 this proclamation were not issued.

And by virtue of the power, and for the purpose aforesaid, I do order and declare that all persons held as slaves within said designated States, and parts of States, are, and henceforward shall be free; and that the Executive government of the United States, including the military and naval authorities thereof, will recognize and maintain the freedom of said persons.

And I hereby enjoin upon[4] the people so declared to be free to abstain from all violence, unless in necessary self-defence; and I recommend to them that, in all cases when allowed, they labor faithfully for reasonable wages.

And I further declare and make known, that such persons of suitable
50 condition, will be received into the armed service of the United States to **garrison** forts, positions, stations, and other places, and to man vessels of all sorts in said service.

[4] **enjoin upon:** direct.

Louisiana and Virginia have exceptions— counties that aren't considered in rebellion.

Slaves in rebel states are now free.

garrison:
to occupy as troops

2. **REREAD** Reread lines 13–21. What is Lincoln's purpose in this paragraph and how does he achieve it? Cite text evidence in your response.

His purpose is to define "in rebellion." He does so by defining who is "not then in rebellion" as "any State, or the people thereof . . . represented in the Congress . . . by members chosen thereto at elections...."

3. **READ** As you read lines 22–40, continue to cite text evidence.
• Circle the authority by which Lincoln makes the January 1, 1863, proclamation.
• Underline the reason Lincoln gives for making the proclamation.
• In the margin of lines 32–40, explain the reason for the exceptions.

4. **REREAD** Reread lines 22–31. Interpret the meaning of "the full period of one hundred days." Cite text evidence in your answer.

One hundred days is the period of time between Lincoln's September 22, 1861 proclamation and the date the proclamation goes into effect: "the first day of January, in the year of our Lord one thousand eight hundred and sixty-three."

5. **READ** As you read lines 41–60, continue to cite text evidence.
• In the margin, explain Lincoln's order and declaration (lines 41–45).
• Underline parts of Lincoln's message that are directed to newly freed people.
• Circle reasons Lincoln offers to support his argument that this proclamation is justified.

---

2. **REREAD AND CITE TEXT EVIDENCE**

B **ASK STUDENTS** to discuss their answer with a partner. *Students should state that Lincoln's purpose in these lines is to define "in rebellion" (line 15). He does so by defining who is "not then in rebellion" (line 21) as "any State, or the people thereof . . . represented in the Congress . . . by members chosen thereto at elections . . ." (lines 16–21).*

3. **READ AND CITE TEXT EVIDENCE**

C **ASK STUDENTS** to cite text evidence to support their explanation of the reasons there were exceptions to the states listed as "in rebellion." *Students should cite the exceptions listed in lines 32–39 to show that certain parts of Louisiana and Virginia were exempted from the proclamation.*

Critical Vocabulary: suppressing (line 26) Ask students to explain Lincoln's use of *suppressing*.

4. **REREAD AND CITE TEXT EVIDENCE**

D **ASK STUDENTS** to cite text evidence to support their interpretation. *Students should cite evidence in lines 1–2 and lines 26–27 to show that the "full period of one hundred days" (lines 28–29) is the period between the date the proclamation was issued and the date it went into effect.*

5. **READ AND CITE TEXT EVIDENCE**

E **ASK STUDENTS** to use their marked text as evidence to explain how Lincoln justified issuing and enforcing the proclamation. *Students should cite lines 53–54 as evidence that Lincoln justified the proclamation by stating that it was a just act necessitated by the war.*

Critical Vocabulary: garrison (line 51) Have students explain Lincoln's use of *garrison*. Whom is Lincoln addressing, and what does he suggest through this word?

invoke:

cite as an authority

E   And upon this act, sincerely believed to be an act of justice, warranted by the Constitution, upon military necessity, I **invoke** the considerate judgment of mankind, and the gracious favor of Almighty God.

In witness whereof, I have hereunto set my hand and caused the seal of the United States to be affixed.

Done at the City of Washington, this first day of January, in the year of our Lord one thousand eight hundred and sixty three, and of the Independence of
60   the United States of America the eighty-seventh.

By the President: ABRAHAM LINCOLN
WILLIAM H. SEWARD, Secretary of State.

6.   **◀ REREAD AND DISCUSS**   Reread lines 41–60. With a small group, discuss the purpose of these lines. What do you think Lincoln envisioned would happen as a result of this proclamation?

SHORT RESPONSE

Cite Text Evidence   Analyze Lincoln's argument that he is taking action that is of "military necessity." Refer to your reading notes, and **cite text evidence** in your response.

Lincoln's argument of military necessity depends on his claim that there are states and parts of states that are "in rebellion against the United States." He offers as evidence that these states are not represented in Congress and that they are in "actual armed rebellion against the authority and government of the United States." For these reasons, Lincoln asserts that the Emancipation Proclamation is a "necessary war measure for suppressing said rebellion."

60

6.   **REREAD AND DISCUSS USING TEXT EVIDENCE**

F   **ASK STUDENTS** to be prepared to share the results of their group discussions in a class discussion. *Students should cite evidence from lines 43–48.*

Critical Vocabulary: invoke (line 54) Have students compare definitions of *invoke*.

FOR ELL STUDENTS Explain the meaning of the archaic terms *whereof* ("of what") and *hereunto* ("to this document").

SHORT RESPONSE

Cite Text Evidence   Students should:

- determine a claim Lincoln makes.
- analyze Lincoln's argument.
- cite text evidence that delineates Lincoln's reasoning.

TO CHALLENGE STUDENTS . . .

For more information on Lincoln, students can view the video "The Story of Us: Abraham Lincoln" in their eBooks.

ASK STUDENTS to explain how Lincoln's position on slavery changed over time. *Students should note that initially Lincoln did not want slavery to be the central issue of the Civil War, but by the time of his death he not only thought all slaves should be freed but also that all African Americans should have equal rights.*

DIG DEEPER

With the class, return to Question 6, Reread and Discuss. Have students share the results of their discussions.

ASK STUDENTS whether they were satisfied with the outcome of their small-group discussions. Have each group share their findings about Lincoln's expectations of what would happen as a result of the Emancipation Proclamation. What textual evidence did students find to support their conclusions?

- Guide each group to share whether they came to a unanimous conclusion about Lincoln's expectations. How did they resolve any disagreement?
- Ask groups to explain how they determined which details in the text were relevant.
- After groups have shared the results of their discussions, ask students whether another group's contributions to the class discussion helped them understand Lincoln's expectations.

ASK STUDENTS to return to their Short Response answer and revise it based on the class discussion.

from **The Iroquois Constitution**

Public Document by Dekanawida

Why This Text

Students sometimes have difficulty understanding an author's purpose for writing a text. The Iroquois Constitution is a document with literary and historical significance. With the help of the close-reading questions, students will analyze the symbols and language in the document. This close reading will lead students to understand Dekanawida's purpose for writing the constitution and its central ideas.

Background Have students read the background and the information about the Iroquois. Explain to students that at the time the Iroquois Constitution was framed, the Iroquois did not have a written language. After a written language was developed, the constitution was written from oral sources. Thanks to the constitution they created, the Iroquois Confederacy became a formidable power. By 1750, it numbered about fifteen thousand people, and Iroquois hunters and warriors ranged over one million square miles.

AS YOU READ Ask students to pay attention to Dekanawida's purpose. How soon into the text can you identify his goals for the Iroquois Confederacy?

Common Core Support

- cite strong and thorough textual evidence
- determine two or more central ideas of a text
- determine an author's purpose in a text in which the rhetoric is particularly effective

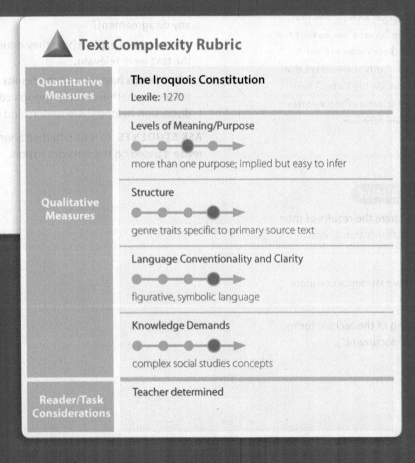

Text Complexity Rubric

Quantitative Measures

The Iroquois Constitution
Lexile: 1270

Qualitative Measures

Levels of Meaning/Purpose
more than one purpose; implied but easy to infer

Structure
genre traits specific to primary source text

Language Conventionality and Clarity
figurative, symbolic language

Knowledge Demands
complex social studies concepts

Reader/Task Considerations
Teacher determined

Analyze Author's Purpose

Students should read this document carefully all the way through. Close-reading questions at the bottom of the page will help them focus on a thorough analysis of the text. As they read, students should jot down comments or questions about the document in the side margins.

WHEN STUDENTS STRUGGLE . . .

To help students analyze Dekanawida's purpose, have them work in a small group to fill out a chart, such as the one shown below.

CITE TEXT EVIDENCE For practice in analyzing an author's purpose, ask students to identify Dekanawida's purpose, and how he proposes to achieve it.

detail: leaders will yearn "for the welfare of the people"

detail: weapons are buried in "the depths of the earth"

purpose: establish peace among the five nations

detail: five arrows symbolize the nations being stronger together

detail: women, not warriors, will "own the land"

Background *The Iroquois Confederacy, also known as the League of Five Nations, was a union of five American Indian tribes across upper New York State. Around 1570, so the legend goes, a visionary named* **Dekanawida** *convinced the nations to unite in order to establish peace. The Iroquois Constitution is regarded as the world's oldest living constitution. In 1988, to mark the bicentennial of the U.S. Constitution, Congress passed a resolution stating that "the confederation of the original Thirteen Colonies into one republic was influenced by the political system developed by the Iroquois Confederacy, as were many of the democratic principles which were incorporated into the Constitution itself."*

from The Iroquois Constitution

Public Document by Dekanawida

CLOSE READ
Notes

1. **READ ▶** As you read lines 1–24, begin to collect and cite text evidence.
   - Circle the author's name and his purpose in the first sentence.
   - In the margin, explain what Dekanawida does first.
   - Read the footnotes. In the margin, hypothesize the reason Dekanawida first addresses Adodarhoh.

Tree of Great Peace

I am Dekanawida[1] and with the Five Nations' Confederate Lords I plant the Tree of the Great Peace. I plant it in your territory, Adodarhoh,[2] and the Onondaga Nation, in the territory of you who are Firekeepers.

I name the tree the Tree of the Great Long Leaves. Under the shade of this Tree of the Great Peace we spread the soft white feathery down of the globe thistle as seats for you, Adodarhoh, and your cousin Lords.

We place you upon those seats, spread soft with the feathery down of the globe thistle, there beneath the shade of the spreading branches of the Tree of Peace. There shall you sit and watch the Council Fire of the Confederacy of the Five Nations, and all the affairs of the Five Nations shall be transacted at this place before you, Adodarhoh, and your cousin Lords, by the Confederate Lords of the Five Nations.

[1] **Dekanawida:** the legendary Great Peacemaker.
[2] **Adodarhoh:** the Onondaga Chief who was the last to join the peace pact.

He plants the Tree of the Great Peace.

Dekanawida wanted to be sure to have Adodarhoh's cooperation.

61

---

1. **READ AND CITE TEXT EVIDENCE**

A ASK STUDENTS to cite text evidence to support their hypothesis. *Students may cite evidence from lines 5–6 to show that Adodarhoh received special attention from Dekanawida, and 9–12 to show that Adodarhoh would hold a place of leadership, and that the Council Fire would be in his territory.*

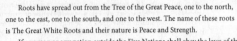

Roots have spread out from the Tree of the Great Peace, one to the north, one to the east, one to the south, and one to the west. The name of these roots **B** is The Great White Roots and their nature is Peace and Strength.

If any man or any nation outside the Five Nations shall obey the laws of the Great Peace and make known their **disposition** to the Lords of the Confederacy, they may trace the Roots to the Tree and if their minds are clean and they are obedient and promise to obey the wishes of the Confederate
20 Council, they shall be welcomed to take shelter beneath the Tree of the Long Leaves.

We place at the top of the Tree of the Long Leaves an Eagle who is able to see afar. If he sees in the distance any evil approaching or any danger threatening he will at once warn the people of the Confederacy.

disposition:
nature, character

Leaders

The Lords of the Confederacy of the Five Nations shall be mentors of the people for all time. The thickness of their skin shall be seven spans—which is to say that they shall be proof against anger, offensive actions, and criticism. Their hearts shall be full of peace and goodwill and their minds filled with a yearning for the welfare of the people of the Confederacy. With endless
30 patience they shall carry out their duty and their firmness shall be tempered with a tenderness for their people. Neither anger nor fury shall find lodgment in their minds and all their words and actions shall be marked by calm deliberation.

2. **◀ REREAD** Reread lines 1–24. What do you think was the author's purpose in using tree roots as the symbol for the Iroquois Confederacy? Cite text evidence to support your answer.

Tree roots go deep into the earth, stabilizing tall trees. In the same way, the roots of a peaceful confederacy must be deep, keeping stability in the Five Nations, "and their nature is Peace and Strength." Also, just as tree roots nourish a tree, peace and cooperation nourish the Confederacy.

3. **READ ▶** As you read lines 25–48, continue to cite text evidence.

• Underline language describing the leaders of the Confederacy of the Five Nations.
• In the margin, explain the special role given to women (lines 34–36).
• Circle text explaining the symbolism of the five arrows.

62

Clans
C The lineal descent[3] of the people of the Five Nations shall run in the female line. Women shall be considered the **progenitors** of the Nation. They shall own the land and the soil. Men and women shall follow the status of the mother.

progenitors:
ancestors

Symbols

Five arrows shall be bound together very strong and each arrow shall represent one nation. As the five arrows are strongly bound this shall
40 symbolize the complete union of the nations. Thus are the Five Nations united completely and enfolded together, united into one head, one body, and one mind. Therefore they shall labor, legislate, and council together for the interest of future generations.

Women define family relationships and also own the land.

War and Peace
D I, Dekanawida, and the Union Lords, now uproot the tallest pine tree and into the cavity thereby made we cast all weapons of war. Into the depths of the earth, down into the deep underearth currents of water flowing to unknown regions we cast all the weapons of strife. We bury them from sight and we plant again the tree. Thus shall the Great Peace be established and hostilities shall no longer be known between the Five Nations but peace to the United People.

---
[3] **lineal descent:** line of ancestors.

63

---

2. **REREAD AND CITE TEXT EVIDENCE**

B **ASK STUDENTS** to discuss their answer with a partner, and to include text evidence in their answer. *Students may suggest that the roots symbolize nourishing the Confederacy with "Peace and Strength" (line 15).*

3. **READ AND CITE TEXT EVIDENCE**

C **ASK STUDENTS** to cite text evidence to support their explanation of the special role given to women. *Students should cite evidence from lines 34–36, "They shall own the land and the soil."*

Critical Vocabulary: disposition (line 17) Ask students to explain Dekanawida's use of *disposition*.

Critical Vocabulary: progenitors (line 35) Tell students that the Iroquois are a matrilineal society. Ask them to explain this using the word *progenitors* in the same way it is used here.

FOR ELL STUDENTS Some students may be familiar with the term *cast*, referring to the people who act in a movie or a play. Explain that in this context the verb *to cast* means "to throw in a forceful way."

4. ◀ REREAD   Reread lines 43–48. What is the symbolic meaning of burying the weapons of war deep in the earth? How do the pine tree and the currents of water add to this symbol? Cite text evidence in your response.

The symbolic meaning of burying the weapons of war in the "depths of the earth" is that war is an unnatural way of relating, and is to be abandoned for all time. The water will carry the weapons to "unknown regions," so the weapons will be physically gone and absent from thought—"no longer be known." The warring way of life is symbolically replaced with peace when the tree that stands for "peace to the United People" is placed over the hole.

SHORT RESPONSE

Cite Text Evidence   What is Dekanawida's primary purpose for writing this constitution? What steps does he take to make sure the Confederacy is successful? Refer to your reading notes, and be sure to **cite text evidence** in your response.

Dekanawida wants peace among the Five Nations. He establishes new leaders who will be people with characters that are peaceful, "yearning for the welfare of the people." Women, not warriors, will "own the land and the soil." Symbols are established, such as the "five arrows," that remind them they are "bound together." Finally, Dekanawida supports his purpose of establishing peace by casting "all weapons of war" into "the depths of the earth."

64

TO CHALLENGE STUDENTS . . .

To learn more about the Iroquois and the meanings of their symbols, students can research the Five Nations online and in print resources.

ASK STUDENTS to research the symbols Dekanawida used in the Iroquois Constitution, and to learn more about what the symbols mean to the Iroquois people. Students should work in groups to find out about at least one symbol. Have groups share the results of their research with the class and discuss how their research helped them understand the symbolism.

DIG DEEPER

With the class, return to Question 2, Reread. Have students share their responses.

ASK STUDENTS to cite the text evidence that led to their interpretation of Dekanawida's use of tree roots as a symbol for the Iroquois Confederacy.

- Point out that lines 13–14 describe the roots spreading out in four directions. Ask students what the four directions symbolize. *Four directions symbolize everywhere on Earth.*
- Have students cite text that shows that the roots symbolize peace. *Dekanawida says that the nature of the roots is "Peace and Strength."*
- Read aloud lines 16–21. Ask students to comment on Dekanawida's use of the phrase "they may trace the Roots to the Tree" (line 18). *Students may see this as an invitation to any tribe or person to live according to this constitution.*

ASK STUDENTS to return to their Short Response answer and revise it based on the class discussion.

---

4. **REREAD AND CITE TEXT EVIDENCE**

D   **ASK STUDENTS** to cite text evidence to support their interpretation. *Students may say that burying weapons in the "depths of the earth" (lines 44–45) symbolizes the abandonment of war. They may say that water carrying the weapons to "unknown regions" (lines 45–46) symbolizes letting go of thoughts of war. They may say that the tree represents "peace to the United People" (line 48).*

SHORT RESPONSE

Cite Text Evidence   Student responses will vary, but they should cite evidence from the text to support their analysis of Dekanawida's purpose. Students should:

- determine Dekanawida's purpose.
- explain the steps he took to ensure the Confederacy was successful.
- support the central idea with details from the text.

Bonding Over a Mascot

Newspaper Article by Joe Lapointe

Why This Text

Students may have difficulty understanding an author's purpose for writing. In "Bonding Over a Mascot," Joe Lapointe investigates the NCAA ban of American Indian mascots and its effect on sports teams at Florida State University. With the help of the close-reading questions, students will analyze the positions of the people Lapointe interviews who are affected by this ban. This close reading will lead students to analyze Lapointe's purpose for writing "Bonding Over a Mascot."

Background Have students read the background. Introduce the selection by telling students that the debate over using Native American mascots and sports imagery intensified after 2006. In February of 2013, ESPN reporter Paul Lukas covered a symposium about Native American imagery in sports that took place at the National Museum of the American Indian, where Native Americans unanimously condemned insulting imagery.

AS YOU READ Ask students to pay attention to Lapointe's point of view. How soon into the text can you infer a reason for Lapointe to write about the mascot situation at Florida State University?

Common Core Support

- cite strong and thorough textual evidence
- analyze a complex set of ideas and explain how specific individuals or ideas develop over the course of a text
- determine an author's purpose

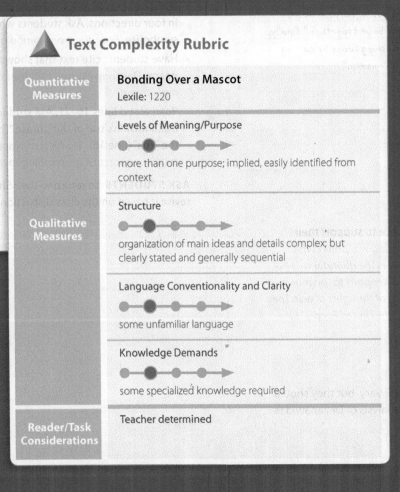

Text Complexity Rubric

Bonding Over a Mascot

Quantitative Measures	Lexile: 1220

Levels of Meaning/Purpose

more than one purpose; implied, easily identified from context

Structure

organization of main ideas and details complex; but clearly stated and generally sequential

Language Conventionality and Clarity

some unfamiliar language

Knowledge Demands

some specialized knowledge required

Reader/Task Considerations

Teacher determined

Strategies for CLOSE READING

Author's Purpose

Students should read this article carefully all the way through. Close-reading questions at the bottom of the page will help them focus on a thorough analysis of the text. As they read, students should jot down comments or questions about the article in the side margins.

WHEN STUDENTS STRUGGLE . . .

To help students analyze Lapointe's purpose, have them work in small groups to fill out a chart, such as the one shown below.

CITE TEXT EVIDENCE For practice in analyzing an author's purpose, ask students to identify choices Lapointe makes about what to focus on in his article.

detail: Lapointe focuses on Florida State's "harmonious relationship" with the Seminoles.

detail: Lapointe quotes Toni Sanchez: "the N.C.A.A. edict is 'beyond idiotic' and offensive."

detail: N.C.A.A. president Myles Brand said the edict raised "the level of awareness nationally about how we treat Native Americans."

topic: the N.C.A.A. ban of Native American sports imagery

detail: President of Florida State T. K. Wetherell said the edict was merely "politically correct," but the university still might use Native American imagery less in the future.

detail: Chairman of FSU history department, Neil Jumonville, says the N.C.A.A. ban accelerated the offering of a Seminole history course at the university.

detail: Seminole councilman Osceola describes the offensive Sammy Seminole mascot.

Background *In 2005, the National Collegiate Athletic Association (N.C.A.A.) banned the use of American Indian mascots by sports teams during their postseason tournaments. At least eighteen schools had mascots that the N.C.A.A. deemed "hostile or abusive." Almost immediately, protests arose, especially from Florida State University, home of the Florida Seminoles. Read the article below to find out what stirred the controversy and the result of the N.C.A.A. decision.*

Bonding Over a Mascot

Newspaper Article by Joe Lapointe

CLOSE READ Notes

1. **READD** As you read lines 1–25, begin to collect and cite evidence.

- Circle text that describes the relationship between the Seminoles and Florida State University.
- Underline how Toni Sanchez feels about the university's American Indian statue and the N.C.A.A. policy.
- In the margin, explain the N.C.A.A "crackdown."

December 29, 2006

A few new statues of a Seminole family in 19th-century clothing stand outside the football stadium at Florida State University. The father holds a long gun, the son a bow and arrow, and the mother an infant in her arms as she looks warily to her right.

The statues represent the era when the Seminoles and the United States were at war. The public art is part of a complex relationship between Seminole culture and sports at Florida State. This bond has strengthened since a crackdown by the National Collegiate Athletic Association last year against American Indian mascots, nicknames and imagery among sports teams.

Not every university enjoys a harmonious relationship with Indians. But a sense of cooperation seems to **permeate** the Florida State campus in Tallahassee, Fla., where Toni Sanchez was among 21 students to complete a new course this month called History of the Seminoles and Southeastern Tribes.

The "crackdown" bans the use of American Indian mascots for sports teams.

permeate: *pervade, soak through*

65

---

1. **READ AND CITE TEXT EVIDENCE**

A **ASK STUDENTS** to cite textual evidence that supports their explanation of the N.C.A.A. crackdown, and to explain how the crackdown affected the relationship between the Seminoles and FSU, where a sports team is called the Seminoles. *Students should cite lines 8–9 in explanation of the N.C.A.A. crackdown and cite line 7, which states that the bond between the Seminoles and the school "has strengthened."*

Critical Vocabulary: permeate (line 11) Have students explain why Lapointe uses the word *permeate* to describe the "sense of cooperation" at the FSU campus. *The cooperation is present in all areas of campus life.*

edict:
decree,
proclamation

Sanchez, a senior majoring in English, called the N.C.A.A. **edict** "beyond idiotic" and offensive. She described the new statues as beautiful.

"I know what a real Seminole is," she said. "This Anglo guilt and regret don't affect me."

Sanchez is from a family with Seminole and Hispanic ancestry. Her father, once a farm worker, is now a casino operator. Her mother is a teacher. Sanchez also plays trumpet at football games in a marching band that wears arrowheads on the back of its uniforms.

Of the tribal flag near the new statues, another recent addition, she said, "Every time I look at it, I get really giddy inside." Of the use of the Seminole imagery for the university's sports, she said, "I'm so proud of it."

Florida State was one of 18 institutions cited by the N.C.A.A. in August 2005 for "mascots, nicknames or images deemed hostile or abusive in terms of race, ethnicity or national origin." The institutions were forbidden to use the symbols in postseason events controlled by the N.C.A.A., like the national championship basketball tournament that begins in March.

Five programs have since received permission to continue using their imagery because they received approval from specific Indian groups, in Florida State's case the 3,200-member Seminole Tribe of Florida. Five others have changed or are in the process of changing, said Bob Williams, an N.C.A.A. spokesman. The other eight, he said, remain on the list and are subject to the policy, including the Illinois Fighting Illini and the North Dakota Fighting Sioux.

Myles Brand, the president of the N.C.A.A., said in a telephone interview last week that his organization made the right decision but witnessed more negative reaction to the ruling than expected.

"What we've accomplished in part is to raise the level of awareness nationally about how we treat Native Americans," Brand said. "If we don't stand by our values, we lose our integrity."

caricature:
cartoon,
parody

At times, Indians are reduced to casual **caricature** that would not be tolerated by other groups, he said, adding that the N.C.A.A. had been honored for its stance by Indian groups in Oklahoma and Indiana.

2. REREAD Reread lines 15–18. What does Sanchez imply is the real reason behind the N.C.A.A ban? Cite textual evidence.

Sanchez blames the N.C.A.A. ban on "guilt and regret."

3. READ As you read lines 26–51, circle text from the N.C.A.A.'s statement. Then, underline the opinions of Brand and Wetherell.

Less complimentary is T. K. Wetherell, the president of Florida State, who said the N.C.A.A. was "more interested in being politically correct" and did not consult the Seminole tribe before making its decision.

"The way they weaseled out was to say, 'O.K., as long as the tribe continues to support it,'" he said.

Wetherell, a former Florida State football player who also teaches history, wore a hunting outfit when interviewed recently in his office. He pointed to a team logo of an Indian's face that he said had elements of caricature. "That's not really a Seminole-looking deal," Wetherell said. "This is a marketing tool." He said the university might "gradually let certain things fade."

He said he told the Seminole Tribe of Florida's council, "If you don't want Florida State to be the Seminoles, we ain't Seminoles anymore." Wetherell said the tribe approved the use partly because the campus is in the capital and tribal leaders "are not only good businessmen, they are great politicians."

He said the new history course was proposed before the N.C.A.A. edict.

But Neil Jumonville, the chairman of the history department, said the N.C.A.A. resolution accelerated the creation of the class and that his staff received advice from local Seminole leaders.

Wetherell doesn't approve of the likeness of the Seminole and thinks the logo might change.

4. REREAD Reread lines 38–51. Explain the conflict between Brand and Wetherell.

Brand represents the N.C.A.A. and stands by their policy. This policy is meant to be enforced everywhere, regardless of whether or not a problem exists. Wetherell represents Florida State and disagrees with the policy because he understands the unique relationship between the university and the Seminole tribe.

5. READ As you read lines 52–81, continue to cite text evidence.

- Write in the margin what you can infer about Wetherell's comments about the team logo.
- Underline text explaining why the university keeps the mascot and why the Seminole tribe didn't fight to have it changed.
- Circle what Versen hopes the students will explore in the class.

---

2. **REREAD AND CITE TEXT EVIDENCE**

ASK STUDENTS to cite text evidence to support their analysis of Sanchez's position on the N.C.A.A. ban. *Students should recognize that Sanchez rejects the "Anglo" establishment's intervention: "I know what a real Seminole is…" (line 17).*

3. **READ AND CITE TEXT EVIDENCE**

ASK STUDENTS why Florida State was cited by the N.C.A.A. in August 2005. *Students should cite evidence that FSU used "mascots, nicknames or images deemed hostile or abusive in terms of race, ethnicity or national origin" (lines 27–28).*

Critical Vocabulary: edict (line 15) What tone is conveyed by Lapointe's choice of the word *edict*?

Critical Vocabulary: caricature (line 44) Why does Brand suggest it is offensive to be reduced to caricature?

4. **REREAD AND CITE TEXT EVIDENCE**

ASK STUDENTS to cite text evidence of Brand's and Wetherell's opinions of the N.C.A.A. ban. *Students will find evidence that Brand stands by the N.C.A.A.'s position in lines 38–43. Wetherell is critical of the N.C.A.A. and dismisses their efforts in line 48 by stating that they are merely "interested in being politically correct."*

5. **READ AND CITE TEXT EVIDENCE** Clarify for students that Wetherell's explanation of why the Seminoles approved the use of their name is an opinion, not a fact.

ASK STUDENTS to cite text evidence to support the inference they draw from Wetherell's comments about the team logo. *Students should cite evidence from lines 53–56.*

"These are people who are savvy about their place in the American myth," Jumonville said. "And they are smart enough to manipulate the myth for their own good."

The first class was taught by Christopher R. Versen, who recently earned his doctorate in American history.

70 "I wanted to challenge students to think about identity," Versen said. "What is it inside us that makes us identify ourselves one way or another? What external factors play into identity?"

(F) The Seminoles are an **amalgam** of several tribes, predominantly Creek, that included escaped slaves. They migrated south to the Everglades in retreat from the United States Army. Some were driven out during the Trail of Tears[1] period under President Andrew Jackson.

Those descendants live as the Seminole Nation of Oklahoma. The Seminoles in Florida once had a commercial hunting economy. Since 1979, their economic status has improved because of casino gambling.

80 Earlier this month, the Seminoles acquired Hard Rock International—the music-themed chain of restaurants, hotels and casinos—for $965 million.

Versen said he did not discuss sports identity with his students because he was afraid it would become a distraction. But a guest speaker who raised the mascot issue was Max Osceola, one of three councilmen for the Seminole Tribe of Florida.

amalgam:
mix, blend,
combination

[1] **Trail of Tears:** In 1838 and 1839, Jackson's policy forced the Cherokee nation to leave their home east of the Mississippi River and relocate to present-day Oklahoma. Over 4,000 people lost their lives to hunger, disease, and exhaustion during the march.

6. **◀ REREAD** Reread lines 52–81. Why does Lapointe include information about the Seminoles' history and their situation today?

He shows the struggles of the Seminole people to explain why the mascot issue is a sensitive one. They had to endure unfair treatment in the past and their descendants in Florida remember their ancestors' difficulties.

7. **READ ▶** As you read lines 82–118, continue to cite evidence.
- Circle the description of Max Osceola in lines 82–90. Circle his description of the old Sammy Seminole.
- Underline the description of the new mascot.
- In the margin, explain Max Osceola's point of view.

68

Toni Sanchez, a student who is from a family with Seminole and Hispanic ancestry, is proud of the use of Seminole imagery at Florida State.

"If I had a child and named it after you, would you consider it an honor?" Osceola said he asked the students. He also reflected on a former mascot, Sammy Seminole, who was retired in 1972.

(G) "He had a big nose and he lived in a teepee," Osceola said. "He looked like a buffoon."

90 The current mascot is named, coincidentally, Osceola, after a 19th-century warrior. A student dressed as Osceola rides a horse named Renegade onto the football field and throws a flaming spear. This mascot's clothing was designed by the tribe.

Tina Osceola, who is the executive director of the tribe's historical resources department and is a cousin of Max Osceola's, said, "We've given them license to be theatrical."

A statue of the warrior riding atop Renegade stands outside the stadium above the word "Unconquered," because the Seminoles never surrendered to

100 the United States.

When the Seminoles announced in New York the purchase of Hard Rock, Max Osceola joked that Indians once sold Manhattan for trinkets but were now "going to buy Manhattan back, one burger at a time."

Not everyone outside the tribe approves of all of the Indian trappings at sporting events, including the tomahawk chop hand gesture and a droning cheer that sounds like background music heard in old western movies.

Joe Quetone, the executive director of the nonprofit Florida Governor's Council on Indian Affairs Inc., said, "Things fans do are outrageous and ridiculous."

Osceola points out that having someone named after you is an honor, but it becomes an insult if it is a joke or a stereotype.

69

---

6. **REREAD AND CITE TEXT EVIDENCE**

(F) ASK STUDENTS to share their responses with a partner and revise their answers if necessary. *Answers should include inferences about Lapointe's inclusion of both Seminole history and their situation today. Students should cite text evidence from lines 73–81 in their responses. They should make a connection between Lapointe's purpose and this part of the text.*

7. **READ AND CITE TEXT EVIDENCE**

(G) ASK STUDENTS to summarize the changes in the FSU mascot. *Students should include evidence that Sammy Seminole was a degrading image (lines 89–90) and that the Seminoles participated in the design of the later mascot (lines 93–94).*

Critical Vocabulary: amalgam (line 73) Have students compare their definitions of *amalgam*. Ask them the difference between a mixture and an alloy.

FOR ELL STUDENTS Explain that the word *trappings* in this context has nothing to do with trapping an animal. It means "characteristic signs" or "articles associated with a particular group."

110   Bobby Bowden, the head football coach, did not respond to four recent requests for comment on the issue placed with the university's sports information department.

From a student's perspective, Sanchez said that people who were genuinely concerned with the circumstances of Indians should concentrate less on sports iconography and more on alcoholism, suicide, teen pregnancy and high school dropout rates.

"After all those years of diseases, occupation and war, we're still here," she said. "I refuse to believe that a silly mascot will take us down."

8. ◄ REREAD   Reread lines 82–118. What does Sanchez mean when she says that a mascot won't "take us down"?

> She means that the N.C.A.A. policy cannot undermine the
> Seminole. American Indians made it through worse trials, so they
> can make it through a collegiate policy.

SHORT RESPONSE

Cite Text Evidence   What is the author's purpose in writing this newspaper article? **Cite text evidence** to show how he supports his ideas in your response.

> The author wants to show differing opinions about the N.C.A.A.'s
> policy on American Indian mascots in colleges. The quotes from
> people at the university, including coaches, professors, and a student,
> show that not everyone agrees with the N.C.A.A.'s policy. Those
> who disagree provide qualifying evidence. Quotes from N.C.A.A.
> supporters are few and flimsy, but the underlying concern of respect
> for American Indians is still obvious. Including information about
> the Trail of Tears shows that Seminole Indians have a long history
> and that the memory of the past should be honored.

70

TO CHALLENGE STUDENTS . . .

The Saginaw Chippewa are another tribe that has granted permission for a sports team to use its name since the 2005 N.C.A.A. ban of Native American mascots.

ASK STUDENTS to research this decision by the Saginaw Chippewa and to compare their concerns and remedies with the solutions agreed to by FSU and the Seminole people. As a class, discuss the efforts of the Seminoles and Chippewa to convey accurate information about their cultures, such as the use of the word *unconquered* on the FSU statue, which informs people of the truth that the Seminoles never surrendered to the United States. What do the Saginaw Chippewa want "in return" for school sports teams using American Indian imagery? *The tribe suggests that those schools offer classes to teach their students about American Indian culture and create a relationship with the people whose name they are using.*

---

8.   REREAD AND CITE TEXT EVIDENCE

H   **ASK STUDENTS** to add text evidence to their answers to support their analysis of Sanchez's statement that a mascot won't "take us down." *Answers will vary. Students should cite evidence from lines 113–118.*

SHORT RESPONSE

Cite Text Evidence   Student responses will vary, but they should cite evidence from the essay to support their analysis of Lapointe's purpose. Students should:

- explain Lapointe's purpose.
- identify central ideas that support his purpose.
- cite text evidence that shows how Lapointe supports his central ideas.

DIG DEEPER

With the class, return to Question 2, Reread, and the analysis of Toni Sanchez's position on the N.C.A.A.'s ban on "mascots, nicknames or images deemed hostile or abusive in terms of race, ethnicity or national origin." Have students share their responses.

ASK STUDENTS to share their evidence, and to review the context provided in the article for Sanchez's position.

- How does Lapointe first identify Sanchez? *Students should cite evidence from lines 12–13, "Toni Sanchez was among 21 students to complete a new course this month called History of the Seminoles and Southeastern Tribes."*

- Have students find evidence in the article of Sanchez's ancestry and infer why Lapointe included this information. *Students will find evidence in lines 19–20 that Sanchez has "Seminole and Hispanic ancestry." They should recognize that Lapointe specifically chose a Seminole student because the topic of the article is the relationship between the Seminole tribe and FSU.*

- Ask students to cite text evidence that Sanchez is proud of her Seminole ancestry. *Students should cite her participation in the new history class (lines 12–14), her description of the statues as "beautiful" (line 16), and her statement in lines 17–18, in which she asserts that she is unaffected by decisions made by the N.C.A.A.*

ASK STUDENTS to return to their Short Response answer and to revise it based on the class discussion.

CLOSE READING NOTES

An Age of Realism

An Age of Realism

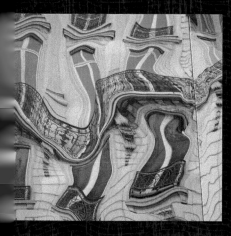

"Reality is that which, when you stop believing in it, doesn't go away."

—Phillip K. Dick

SHORT STORY

The Men in the Storm   **Stephen Crane**

SCIENCE WRITING

The Yuckiest Food in the Amazon   **Mary Roach**

SHORT STORY

A Journey   **Edith Wharton**

POEM

Ode to a Large Tuna in the Market   **Pablo Neruda**

The Men in the Storm

Short Story by Stephen Crane

Reality is that which, when you stop believing in it, doesn't go away.

Why This Text

Students may be unfamiliar with stories in which no single character stands out; in "The Men in the Storm," Crane aspires to represent the collective voice of the masses struggling to survive. As a realist, Crane included many specific details about daily life and sets his story among ordinary people. With the help of the close-reading questions, students will get a sense of the real lives of ordinary people facing difficult conditions on the city streets more than a hundred years ago.

Background Have students read the background information about the author. Point out that Crane's adventurous nature brought him into contact with a wide variety of experiences and provided him with countless opportunities for writing. Although his stories are set in very different places—from a Civil War battlefield to a shipwrecked dinghy en route to Cuba, to the mean streets of New York City—his unflinching commitment to exposing the plight of the common person never wavered.

AS YOU READ Ask students to pay attention to the way the author uses setting, tone, dialect, and style to add meaning and to underscore important themes.

Common Core Support

- cite strong and thorough textual evidence
- determine two or more themes or central ideas of a text
- analyze how a text's structure contributes to its aesthetic impact

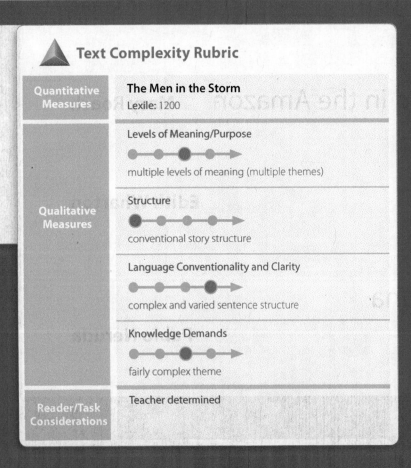

Text Complexity Rubric

The Men in the Storm
Lexile: 1200

Quantitative Measures

Qualitative Measures

Levels of Meaning/Purpose
multiple levels of meaning (multiple themes)

Structure
conventional story structure

Language Conventionality and Clarity
complex and varied sentence structure

Knowledge Demands
fairly complex theme

Reader/Task Considerations
Teacher determined

Strategies for CLOSE READING

Analyze Structure: Realism and Naturalism

Students should read this story carefully all the way through. Close-reading questions at the bottom of the page will help them analyze the techniques the author uses to paint a realistic portrait of downtrodden Americans at the turn of the century. As they read, students should jot down comments or questions about the text in the margins.

WHEN STUDENTS STRUGGLE . . .

To help students identify examples of realistic details used to establish tone and add meaning, have them work in small groups to fill out a chart like the one shown below.

CITE TEXT EVIDENCE For practice in recognizing how the author's word choice and tone reveal the story's central ideas, have them analyze each of the following details from the text.

Example from the Text	What It Reveals
"Those on the walks huddled their necks closely in the collars of their coats and went along stooping like a race of aged people." (lines 4–6)	The people are beaten down, tired, spent. The word "race" identifies people as a group rather than as individuals.
". . . scores of pedestrians and drivers . . . speeding for scores of unknown doors and entrances, scattering to an infinite variety of shelters. . ." (lines 24–26)	The image of a swarm of people mindlessly rushing toward a destination suggests the primitive forces that control our animal behavior.
"There was an absolute expression of hot dinners in the pace of the people." (line 28)	The people walking with an "expression of hot dinners" shows the single-minded focus of the crowd.
"During the afternoon of the storm, the whirling snows acted as drivers, as men with whips . . ." (lines 39–40)	Comparing the snow to a driver with a whip creates the sense that the snow is punishing.

Background Stephen Crane (1871–1900)—American novelist, poet, and short story writer—was one of the most innovative writers of his generation, known for his gritty realism and willingness to take on difficult themes such as fear, social isolation, and spiritual crisis. He is perhaps best known for his Civil War novel The Red Badge of Courage (1895), which depicts the psychological complexities of the battlefield. Crane, who dropped out of college and moved to New York to be a writer, had an adventurous life that was tragically cut short when he died of tuberculosis at the age of 28. Crane's work was nearly forgotten until two decades later when it was "rediscovered" by critics.

The Men in the Storm

Short Story by Stephen Crane

CLOSE READ
Notes

1. **READ** ▶ As you read lines 1–27, begin to collect and cite text evidence.
   - Underline images that help you visualize the weather.
   - Circle images of street life.
   - In the margin, describe the setting (lines 1–13).

A At about three o'clock of the February afternoon, the blizzard began to swirl great clouds of snow along the streets, sweeping it down from the roofs and up from the pavements until the faces of pedestrians tingled and burned as from a thousand needle-prickings. Those on the walks huddled their necks closely in the collars of their coats and went along stooping like a race of aged people. The drivers of vehicles hurried their horses furiously on their way. They were made more cruel by the exposure of their positions, aloft on high seats. The street cars, bound up-town, went slowly, the horses slipping and straining in the spongy brown mass that lay between the rails. The drivers,
10 muffled to the eyes, stood erect and facing the wind, models of grim philosophy. Overhead the trains rumbled and roared, and the dark structure of the elevated railroad, stretching over the avenue, dripped little streams and drops of water upon the mud and snow beneath it.

The story takes place in a winter blizzard in a big city.

73

1. **READ AND CITE TEXT EVIDENCE** In this section of text, the author uses sensory details to describe the setting.

   A **ASK STUDENTS** to cite details that appeal to sound, sight, and touch. *Students may identify the sense of sound: "overhead the trains rumbled and roared" (line 11); sight: "went along stooping like a race of aged people" (lines 5–6); and touch: "the faces of the pedestrians tingled and burned as from a thousand needle-prickings" (lines 3–4).*

All the clatter of the street was softened by the masses that lay upon the cobbles until, even to one who looked from a window, it became important music, a melody of life made necessary to the ear by the dreariness of the pitiless beat and sweep of the storm. Occasionally one could see black figures of men busily shovelling the white drifts from the walks. The sounds from their labor created new recollections of rural experiences which every man manages

20 to have in a measure. Later, the immense windows of the shops became aglow with light, throwing great beams of orange and yellow upon the pavement. They were infinitely cheerful, yet in a way they accented the force and discomfort of the storm, and gave a meaning to the pace of the people and the

B vehicles, scores of pedestrians and drivers, wretched with cold faces, necks and feet, speeding for scores of unknown doors and entrances, scattering to an infinite variety of shelters, to places which the imagination made warm with the familiar colors of home.

The thought of hot food is on everyone's mind.

C There was an absolute expression of hot dinners in the pace of the people. If one dared to speculate upon the destination of those who came trooping, he

30 lost himself in a maze of social calculations; he might fling a handful of sand and attempt to follow the flight of each particular grain. But as to the suggestion of hot dinners, he was in firm lines of thought, for it was upon every hurrying face. It is a matter of tradition; it is from the tales of childhood. It comes forth with every storm.

2. **◄ REREAD** Reread lines 1–27. Describe the contrast between the storm outside and the people who remain inside. Cite evidence from the text.

The storm consists of "great clouds of snow" that cause the "faces of pedestrians" to tingle and burn. On the other hand, the people viewing the storm from inside hear "a melody of life." The light from the shops is described as "infinitely cheerful," which contrasts with the "force and discomfort of the storm."

3. **READ ►** As you read lines 28–61, continue to cite textual evidence.

- In the margin, explain what is on everyone's mind.
- Underline examples of people moving toward their destination.
- Circle descriptions of men waiting near the "charitable house."

74

However, in a certain part of a dark West-side street, there was a collection of men to whom these things were as if they were not. In this street was located a charitable house where for five cents the homeless of the city could get a bed at night and, in the morning, coffee and bread.

D During the afternoon of the storm, the whirling snows acted as drivers, as

40 men with whips, and at half-past three, the walk before the closed doors of the house was covered with wanderers of the street, waiting. For some distance on either side of the place they could be seen lurking in doorways and behind projecting parts of buildings, gathering in close bunches in an effort to get warm. A covered wagon drawn up near the curb sheltered a dozen of them. Under the stairs that led to the elevated railway station, there were six or eight, their hands stuffed deep in their pockets, their shoulders stooped, jiggling their feet. Others always could be seen coming, a strange procession, some slouching along with the characteristic hopeless gait of professional strays, some coming with hesitating steps wearing the air of men to whom this sort of thing was

50 new.

4. **◄ REREAD** Reread lines 39–55. How is the situation getting worse for the men? Cite textual evidence in your response.

More and more men congregate on the street in front of the charitable house; the walk is "covered with wanderers of the street" who are "lurking in doorways and behind projecting parts of buildings" and "crowded together, muttering . . . their red, inflamed wrists covered by the cloth." The house shows no signs of opening.

75

---

2. **REREAD AND CITE TEXT EVIDENCE**

B **ASK STUDENTS** to review lines 24–26. Have them cite text evidence showing what the pedestrians are doing and thinking about. *They are "speeding . . . to an infinite variety of shelters"; they are thinking of "the familiar colors of home."*

3. **READ AND CITE TEXT EVIDENCE** Have students visualize the men moving toward their destination. Explain that no individual characters stand out. Point out the references to "the men" and "people."

C **ASK STUDENTS** what point the author is trying to make about the men. *They are undifferentiated; they are heading the same way, thinking the same thing.*

FOR ELL STUDENTS Challenge students to guess the meaning of the noun *clatter* (line 14) by looking for context clues.

4. **REREAD AND CITE TEXT EVIDENCE** Explain that in lines 39–55, the author uses specific language to describe the severity of the scene.

D **ASK STUDENTS** to find examples of words and phrases that reveal the condition of the men. *Students may cite "lurking in doorways" (line 42), "gathering in close bunches" (line 43), "sheltered a dozen of them" (line 44), "six or eight, their hands stuffed deep in their pockets, their shoulders stooped, jiggling their feet" (lines 45–47). What conclusions can be drawn from these details? The men represent the oppressed masses. How can the men be described? The men are without resources, anxious, living on the edges of society, clandestine.*

CLOSE READ Notes

It was an afternoon of incredible length. The snow, blowing in twisting clouds, sought out the men in their meagre hiding-places and skilfully beat in among them, drenching their persons with showers of fine, stinging flakes. They crowded together, muttering, and fumbling in their pockets to get their red, inflamed wrists covered by the cloth.

Newcomers usually halted at one of the groups and addressed a question, perhaps much as a matter of form, "Is it open yet?"

Those who had been waiting inclined to take the questioner seriously and become contemptuous. "No; do yeh think we'd be standin' here?"

60 The gathering swelled in numbers steadily and persistently. One could always see them coming, trudging slowly through the storm.

Finally, the little snow plains in the street began to assume a leaden hue from the shadows of evening. The buildings upreared gloomily save where various windows became brilliant figures of light that made shimmers and splashes of yellow on the snow. A street lamp on the curb struggled to illuminate, but it was reduced to impotent blindness by the swift gusts of sleet crusting its panes.

In this half-darkness, the men began to come from their shelter places and mass in front of the doors of charity. They were of all types, but the 70 nationalities were mostly American, German and Irish. Many were strong, healthy, clear-skinned fellows with that stamp of countenance which is not frequently seen upon seekers after charity. There were men of undoubted patience, industry and temperance, who in time of ill-fortune, do not habitually turn to rail at the state of society, snarling at the arrogance of the rich and bemoaning the cowardice of the poor, but who at these times are apt to wear a sudden and singular meekness, as if they saw the world's progress marching from them and were trying to perceive where they had failed, what they had lacked, to be thus vanquished in the race. Then there were others of

The "men of industry" were still healthy, not yet ground down by their poverty; the long-term poor lived in boarding houses and were angry at the world.

5. READID As you read lines 62–125, continue to cite textual evidence.
- Underline the descriptions of the "men of industry."
- In the margin, summarize the essential difference between the "men of industry" and the "Bowery lodging-house element."
- Circle the lines that describe the problem the men face, and explain the problem in the margin (lines 107–115).

the shifting, Bowery lodging-house element who were used to paying ten cents 80 for a place to sleep, but who now came here because it was cheaper.

But they were all mixed in one mass so thoroughly that one could not have discerned the different elements but for the fact that the laboring men, for the most part, remained silent and impassive in the blizzard, their eyes fixed on the windows of the house, statues of patience.

The sidewalk soon became completely blocked by the bodies of the men. They pressed close to one another like sheep in a winter's gale, keeping one another warm by the heat of their bodies. The snow came down upon this compressed group of men until, directly from above, it might have appeared like a heap of snow-covered merchandise, if it were not for the fact that the 90 crowd swayed gently with a unanimous, rhythmical motion. It was wonderful to see how the snow lay upon the heads and shoulders of these men, in little ridges an inch thick perhaps in places, the flakes steadily adding drop and drop, precisely as they fall upon the unresisting grass of the fields. The feet of the men were all wet and cold and the wish to warm them accounted for the slow, gentle, rhythmical motion. Occasionally some man whose ears or nose tingled acutely from the cold winds would wriggle down until his head was protected by the shoulders of his companions.

There was a continuous murmuring discussion as to the probability of the doors being speedily opened. They persistently lifted their eyes toward the 100 windows. One could hear little combats of opinion.

"There's a light in th' winder!"

"Naw; it's a reflection f'm across th' way."

"Well, didn't I see 'em lite it?"

"You did?"

"I did!"

"Well, then, that settles it!"

As the time approached when they expected to be allowed to enter, the men crowded to the doors in an unspeakable crush, jamming and wedging in a way that it seemed would crack bones. They surged heavily against the building 110 in a powerful wave of pushing shoulders. Once a rumor flitted among all the tossing heads.

"They can't open th' doors! Th' fellers er smack up ag'in 'em."

Then a dull roar of rage came from the men on the outskirts; but all the time they strained and pushed until it appeared to be impossible for those that they cried out against to do anything but be crushed to pulp.

"Ah, git away f'm th' door!"

The men are pushed so tightly against the door that it cannot be opened, and the surge of men crushes those at the door even more.

---

5. READ AND CITE TEXT EVIDENCE Have students read lines 68–84 and notice the descriptions of two types of men.

E ASK STUDENTS to cite evidence detailing the two types of men in the mass. *Students should cite lines 70–77 explaining that some of the men were "strong, healthy, clear-skinned fellows . . . who in time of ill-fortune, do not habitually turn to rail at the state of society." The other men were used to sleeping in lodging houses, but were trying to find someplace cheaper (79–80).*

FOR ELL STUDENTS Clarify the meaning of *swelled* (line 60). Explain that in this context it means "grew, expanded in size and number."

FOR ELL STUDENTS Dialect speech may be difficult for ELL students. Go over the dialogue section. Have a volunteer read it aloud (or read it aloud yourself) and ask students what familiar words sound like *naw, winder, f'm, th', 'em,* (lines 101–103), *fellers* (line 112), *and git* (line 116). *no, window, from, the, them, fellows, get*

"Git outa that!"

"Throw 'em out!"

"Kill 'em!"

120 "Say, fellers, now, what th' 'ell? Give 'em a chanct t' open th' door!"

"Yeh damned pigs, give 'em a chanct t' open th' door!"

Men in the outskirts of the crowd occasionally yelled when a boot-heel of one of frantic trampling feet crushed on their freezing extremities.

"Git off me feet, yeh clumsy tarrier!"

"Say, don't stand on me feet! Walk on th' ground!"

A man near the doors suddenly shouted: "O-o-oh! Le' me out—le' me out!" And another, a man of infinite valor, once twisted his head so as to half face those who were pushing behind him. "Quit yer shovin', yeh"—and he delivered a volley of the most powerful and singular **invective** straight into the faces of

130 the men behind him. It was as if he was hammering the noses of them with curses of triple brass. His face, red with rage, could be seen; upon it, an expression of sublime disregard of consequences. But nobody cared to reply to his imprecations; it was too cold. Many of them snickered and all continued to push.

invective:
an abusive expression; language used to attack somebody

---

6. **◀ REREAD** Reread lines 101–125. How does the author's use of dialect affect the story?

The dialect reflects the natural, everyday speech of the men. No speakers are identified; we only hear snippets of what might be a conversation. The language accentuates the chaos of the mass, the desperation of the men, and the tension of the scene.

---

7. **READ ▶** As you read lines 126–174, continue to cite textual evidence.

• Underline details that describe the conditions outside.

• Circle details that describe the man in the window across the street.

• In the margin, explain the reactions of the men to the man in the dry goods store.

78

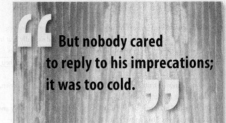

But nobody cared to reply to his imprecations; it was too cold.

In occasional pauses of the crowd's movement the men had opportunity to make jokes; usually grim things, and no doubt very uncouth. Nevertheless, they are notable—one does not expect to find the quality of humor in a heap of old clothes under a snowdrift.

The winds seemed to grow fiercer as time wore on. Some of the gusts of

140 snow that came down on the close collection of heads cut like knives and needles, and the men huddled, and swore, not like dark assassins, but in a sort of an American fashion, grimly and desperately, it is true, but yet with a wondrous under-effect, indefinable and **mystic**, as if there was some kind of humor in this catastrophe, in this situation in a night of snow-laden winds.

Once, the window of the huge dry-goods shop across the street furnished material for a few moments of forgetfulness. In the brilliantly-lighted space appeared the figure of a man. He was rather stout and very well clothed. His whiskers were fashioned charmingly after those of the Prince of Wales. He stood in an attitude of magnificent reflection. He slowly stroked his moustache

150 with a certain grandeur of manner, and looked down at the snow-encrusted mob. From below, there was denoted a supreme complacence in him. It seemed that the sight operated inversely, and enabled him to more clearly regard his own environment, delightful relatively.

One of the mob chanced to turn his head and perceive the figure in the window. "Hello, lookit 'is whiskers," he said genially.

Many of the men turned then, and a shout went up. They called to him in all strange keys. They addressed him in every manner, from familiar and cordial greetings to carefully-worded advice concerning changes in his personal appearance. The man presently fled, and the mob chuckled

160 ferociously like ogres who had just devoured something.

mystic:
spiritual, with a meaning beyond human understanding

The men mock the man in the store because he seems unconcerned about their situation.

---

8. **◀ REREAD AND DISCUSS** Reread lines 154–160. In a small group, discuss how the men show solidarity with one another.

79

---

6. **REREAD AND CITE TEXT EVIDENCE**

F ASK STUDENTS to draw conclusions about the men from the way they speak. What does their speech say about them? *They are rough, confrontational, and demonstrative; they understand each other; they are unified by language.*

7. **READ AND CITE TEXT EVIDENCE**

G ASK STUDENTS to think about the description of the man in the window in lines 146–153. Which words suggest royalty? *Students may note "Prince of Wales," (line 148), "magnificent reflection," (line 149), "grandeur of manner," (line 150), "supreme complacence" (line 151).* In contrast, how are the people on the street described? *They are a "snow-encrusted mob."*

Critical Vocabulary: invective (line 129) Have students share definitions. What can happen when people start hurling invectives at one another? *People may get into a fight.*

8. **REREAD AND DISCUSS USING TEXT EVIDENCE** Have students discuss how seeing the man in the window affects the men (lines 154–160).

H ASK STUDENTS to describe how the men's behavior toward each other contrasts with their earlier behavior in the story (lines 101–125). *They are suddenly unified in their ridicule of the man; they are able to see their commonalities rather than their differences.*

Critical Vocabulary: mystic (line 143) Have students share definitions of *mystic*. Why does the author describe the catastrophe as having an underlying "mystic" effect? *The author is saying that some catastrophes are so horrendous they are beyond human understanding.*

They turned then to serious business. Often they addressed the stolid front of the house.

"Oh, let us in fer Gawd's sake!"

"Let us in or we'll all drop dead!"

"Say, what's th' use o' keepin' all us poor Indians out in th' cold?"

And always some one was saying, "Keep off me feet."

The crushing of the crowd grew terrific toward the last. The men, in keen pain from the blasts, began almost to fight. With the pitiless whirl of snow upon them, the battle for shelter was going to the strong. It became known that the basement door at the foot of a little steep flight of stairs was the one to be opened, and they jostled and heaved in this direction like laboring fiends. One could hear them panting and groaning in their fierce exertion.

Usually some one in the front ranks was protesting to those in the rear: "O—o—ow! Oh, say, now, fellers, let up, will yeh? Do yeh wanta kill somebody?"

A policeman arrived and went into the midst of them, scolding and berating, occasionally threatening, but using no force but that of his hands and shoulders against these men who were only struggling to get in out of the storm. His decisive tones rang out sharply: "Stop that pushin' back there! Come, boys, don't push! Stop that! Here, you, quit yer shovin'! Cheese that!"

When the door below was opened, a thick stream of men forced a way down the stairs, which were of an extraordinary narrowness and seemed only wide enough for one at a time. Yet they somehow went down almost three abreast. It was a difficult and painful operation. The crowd was like a turbulent water forcing itself through one tiny outlet. The men in the rear, excited by the success of the others, made frantic exertions, for it seemed that this large band would more than fill the quarters and that many would be left upon the pavements. It would be disastrous to be of the last, and accordingly men with the snow biting their faces, writhed and twisted with their might. One expected that from the tremendous pressure, the narrow passage to the basement door

would be so choked and clogged with human limbs and bodies that movement would be impossible. Once indeed the crowd was forced to stop, and a cry went along that a man had been injured at the foot of the stairs. But presently the slow movement began again, and the policeman fought at the top of the flight to ease the pressure on those who were going down.

A reddish light from a window fell upon the faces of the men when they, in turn, arrived at the last three steps and were about to enter. One could then note a change of expression that had come over their features. As they thus stood upon the threshold of their hopes, they looked suddenly content and complacent. The fire had passed from their eyes and the snarl had vanished from their lips. The very force of the crowd in the rear, which had previously vexed them, was regarded from another point of view, for it now made it inevitable that they should go through the little doors into the place that was cheery and warm with light.

The tossing crowd on the sidewalk grew smaller and smaller. The snow beat with merciless persistence upon the bowed heads of those who waited. The wind drove it up from the pavements in frantic forms of winding white, and it seethed in circles about the huddled forms, passing in, one by one, three by three, out of the storm.

There may not be room for all the men, so those in the back struggle to improve their position and chances of getting in.

9. **READ ▶** As you read lines 175–208, continue to cite evidence.

- Underline the lines that depict the men as a force of nature.
- Circle text describing how the men change when they enter the doorway.
- In the margin, explain why those at the back of the crowd become frantic.
- Underline words that convey hopelessness in lines 204–208.

9. **READ AND CITE TEXT EVIDENCE** Have students visualize the crowd forcing its way into the narrow doorway (lines 175–208).

ASK STUDENTS to cite evidence showing the change in the men as they enter the doorway. *Students should cite lines 197–200 describing the men as "suddenly content and complacent" and "the snarl had vanished from their lips."*

FOR ELL STUDENTS *Content* (line 198) is a false cognate for the Spanish adjective *contento/a* ("happy"). Point out to your Spanish-speaking students that in English *content* has a different meaning, "satisfied."

10. **REREAD** As you reread lines 204–208, explain what happens at the end of the story.

As the men enter the doorway, the crowd on the street thins out but the snow continues to fall outside.

SHORT RESPONSE

Cite Text Evidence Identify the theme of the story and explain how its central ideas develop, interact, and build on one another throughout the course of the text. Be sure to support your ideas by **citing text evidence**.

The central theme of the story is that people feel desperate when confronted with the harshness of nature. The story begins with a cruel storm that mirrors the cruel fate of the men who are out of work. "The winds seemed to grow fiercer as time wore on," and the men get rowdier. The storm is a destructive force but also a unifying one, causing the men to forget their differences and live in the moment, achieving a kind of spirituality born of their misery: the author describes a man who acts in pure rage as "sublime" and the joking of the men as having a "wondrous under-effect, indefinable and mystic." Poverty, like the storm, is inevitable, persistent, and debilitating. Even as some manage to escape its clutches in a temporary shelter for the night, others line up to take their place.

82

---

10. **REREAD AND CITE TEXT EVIDENCE** Review what the men have been through up to this point in the text.

J ASK STUDENTS how what happens in lines 204–208 affects the men. *As the men get closer to the threshold, they calm down— relief will come soon.*

SHORT RESPONSE

Cite Text Evidence Students' responses should include text evidence that supports their positions. They should:

- cite strong and thorough textual evidence.
- determine two or more themes or central ideas of a text and how they develop, interact, and build on one another.
- analyze how the author's choices concerning how to structure a text contribute to its aesthetic impact.

TO CHALLENGE STUDENTS . . .

Tell students that Stephen Crane is known for his use of distinctive dialects to convey the voices of ordinary people. In "The Men in the Storm," the men speak in a regional English endemic to the time and place the story is set: New York City's Bowery district, circa 1900.

ASK STUDENTS to work with a partner or small group to translate the dialect in lines 101–125 of "The Men in the Storm."

- Explain that there are several ways to do a translation: either by focusing on the literal meanings of the words themselves, or by trying to re-create the sound and feel of realistic speech.
- Students can first put the dialogue into standard English (focusing on the literal meanings) and then do a second, more interpretative translation, in which they put the words into contemporary English—the English we speak today. Here's an example:

  Line of text: "Git off me feet, yeh clumsy tarrier!"
  Translation #1: "Get off my feet, you clumsy oaf!"
  Translation #2: "Move it, doofus."

- Point out that context is a strong factor in the way dialogue is interpreted. Students should consider the immediate effects of the storm on the men's physical and mental states, as well as long-term effects of grinding poverty: unemployment, hunger, and homelessness. Have them also consider the "mob mentality" aspect: the fact that people as individuals may not speak the same way as people in a large crowd.
- After they have written their dialogues, students can perform them aloud for the class.

DIG DEEPER

1. With the class, return to Question 8, Reread and Discuss. Have students share their responses.

   ASK STUDENTS to think about the men's response to the man in the window (lines 154–160). Have them:

   - paraphrase the episode in their own words.
   - describe the behavior of the men prior to, during, and after the event takes place.
   - make an inference about why seeing the man in the window changes the mood so abruptly. What does he represent to the men?
   - draw conclusions about the feeling of solidarity between the men. What makes them stop fighting one another?
   - make an inference about what causes the man in the window to flee. Have them cite text evidence depicting the men's sense of victory following his departure.

2. With the class, return to Question 10, Reread. Have students share their responses.

   ASK STUDENTS to think about the way the story ends. Have them:

   - describe what has happened to the men that makes them take on "another point of view." How does this point of view contrast with their earlier attitude?
   - cite text evidence describing the physical change in the men as they approach the threshold.
   - describe what the men see through the little doors. What words does the author use to describe what they see? What else in the story has been described this way?
   - draw conclusions, based on the story, about what happens to people when their basic needs are not met. What is the effect on society as a whole?

   ASK STUDENTS to return to their Short Response answer and revise it based on the class discussion.

CLOSE READING NOTES

The Yuckiest Food in the Amazon

Science Writing by Mary Roach

Why This Text

Students are likely to encounter unfamiliar, complex ideas in science writing, which may make it difficult for them to determine the author's purpose. With the help of the close-reading questions, students will analyze how a set of ideas is developed in the article. This close reading will lead students to understand the author's purpose.

Background Have students read the background and information about the author and the article. Introduce the article by explaining that Mary Roach is known for writing about unusual science topics—such as cadavers, the alimentary canal, packing for Mars—in a lively and humorous style. Her style does not detract from the seriousness of her work, which has won numerous accolades from within and outside of the scientific establishment.

AS YOU READ Ask students to pay attention to the tone of the article. How does the tone help illuminate the author's purpose?

Common Core Support

- cite strong and thorough textual evidence
- determine central ideas of a text
- determine the meaning of words and phrases as they are used in a text
- determine an author's point of view and purpose, analyzing how style and content contribute to the text

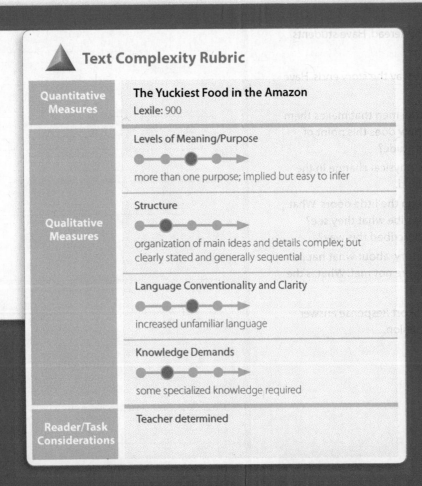

Text Complexity Rubric

The Yuckiest Food in the Amazon
Lexile: 900

Quantitative Measures

Qualitative Measures

Levels of Meaning/Purpose
more than one purpose; implied but easy to infer

Structure
organization of main ideas and details complex; but clearly stated and generally sequential

Language Conventionality and Clarity
increased unfamiliar language

Knowledge Demands
some specialized knowledge required

Reader/Task Considerations
Teacher determined

Strategies for CLOSE READING

Determine Author's Purpose

Students should read this essay carefully all the way through. Close-reading questions at the bottom of the page will help them focus on a thorough analysis of the author's purpose. As they read, students should jot down comments or questions about the text in the margins.

WHEN STUDENTS STRUGGLE . . .

To help students determine the author's purpose in "The Yuckiest Food in the Amazon," have them work in small groups to fill out a chart like the one shown below.

CITE TEXT EVIDENCE For practice analyzing an author's purpose, ask students to cite evidence of the author's rhetorical choices that advanced that purpose.

Title	"The Yuckiest Food in the Amazon"
Tone	"I have frequently . . . felt the need to put . . . my mouth . . . where it would rather not go." (lines 11–12) "Now I am getting my come-uppance." (line 18) "My problem . . . is a knee. . . . quietly genuflecting in a bowl of oily broth." (lines 33–34)
Rhetoric	"a raw fish eye and its accompanying musculature" (line 14) "You eat what they hunt." (lines 25–26) "The knee is one of nature's marvels, a busy intersection of tendon, bone and cartilage." (lines 39–40)
Language	"I come from a tribe that eats Vienna sausages." (lines 150–151) "Every few seconds, he looks back at me, his face changing channels from disgust to bewilderment and back" (lines 164–165)
Author's Purpose:	to show that the concept of "disgust" varies across cultures.

Background *What tastes worse than rodent knee and saliva-flavored manioc mash? It depends on where you come from, as writer Mary Roach learned in a remote Amazon village. In 1998, Roach accompanied anthropologist John Patton to the village of Conambo in Ecuador, where he was studying the Achuar people. Although usually up for any adventure, Roach had some hesitation when faced with the local food, as described in the following article.*

The Yuckiest Food in the Amazon

Science Writing by Mary Roach

CLOSE READ
Notes

1. **READ** ▶ As you read lines 1–38, begin to collect and cite evidence.
   - Underline conclusions that Rozin learns from his research.
   - Circle examples of things Roach has eaten in her travels.
   - In the margin, explain the "huge difference" Roach describes in lines 27–32.

In 1986, a psychologist named Paul Rozin took a group of toddlers and did a peculiar thing. One by one, he sat them down at a table and presented them with a plate of what he said was dog-doo and asked them if they'd like to eat it. (In fact, it was peanut butter, scented with bleu cheese.) Then he did the same with a sterilized grasshopper. Sixty-two percent of the children under 2 happily dispatched the **ersatz** turd; 31 percent the insect. Older children invariably rejected both plates. His point: Disgust is learned. Culture is our instructor. We are taught that horse meat is disgusting but chicken embryos are not; that Slim Jims are tasty and crickets are gross.

10   **Espousing**, as I have, a belief that nothing is inherently disgusting, that it's all a case of mind over culture, I have frequently, in my travels, felt the need to put my money where my mouth is and my mouth where it would rather not go. I have eaten walrus meat left buried on an Arctic beach to "ferment" for a month, a raw fish eye and its accompanying musculature, duck tongue, caribou marrow, brain, flipper, ant. I am, yes, one of those annoying travelers who

ersatz:
fake, pretend

espouse:
promote,
support

83

---

1. **READ AND CITE TEXT EVIDENCE**   Explain to students that the author begins her essay by recounting a psychological study that frames the topic she will explore.

Ⓐ ASK STUDENTS how they identified Rozin's conclusions. *Students should distinguish between Rozin's results—62% of the children ate the fake turd, etc.—and his conclusions. The results lead to his conclusions, which are introduced with the phrase, "His point."*

Critical Vocabulary: ersatz (line 6) Have students share their definitions of *ersatz*, and ask volunteers to use the adjective in sentences about food. *Example: Our vegetarian friends prepared a magnificent meal of ersatz turkey.*

Critical Vocabulary: espouse (line 10) Have students suggest synonyms for *espouse* that could be used in this context. *advocate, champion, embrace, uphold*

boast about the disgusting food they've lived to tell about (and tell about and tell about).

Now I am getting my come-uppance. I am getting it big-time, in a small
20 village in the Ecuadorian Amazon. I have come here to do a story on an
anthropologist named John Patton. Patton studies a tribe called the Achuar,
notable for their skill in blowgun-making and their long-ago rivalry with the
head-shrinking Chuar. (If you've seen an authentic South American shrunken
head, you've probably seen an Achuar tribesman.) Patton's base is Conambo, a
scatter of houses along a fast, muddy river, reachable every now and again by a
four-seater missionary plane. There is no hotel, no restaurant, no store. You eat
what they hunt.

I am fast coming to understand that there is a huge difference, a vast
yawning canyon of difference, between tasting something deeply unappealing
and living on it. Anyone, if he tries, can suppress his disgust long enough to
30 swallow a single fish eye or a mouthful of decaying walrus. Eating enough of
this sort of thing to live on is altogether a different matter. I am here for five
days. I'm not doing very well.

My problem at the moment is a knee. It's a rodent knee, quietly
genuflecting in a bowl of oily broth. Earlier today, the knee was attached to a
happy, hairy, spaniel-sized rodent, **gamboling** and cavorting in the wee hours
of the rain forest morning until our host happened along and plugged it full of
buckshot. (Blowguns are used only on birds and pack animals like monkeys,
which would be scared off by gunshot.)

The knee is one of nature's marvels, a busy intersection of tendon, bone
40 and cartilage. Be that as it may, "marvel" does not exactly describe my state of

She learns the
difference
between
eating
something just
once and
eating it for
days at a time.

gambol:
skip, hop

2. **REREAD** Reread lines 10–38. Describe the tone Roach uses as she
writes about "yucky" foods. Cite examples from the text.

Roach has a light-hearted tone, and she also doesn't steer clear of
making fun of herself. She repeats words to emphasize these points,
as in, "to tell about (and tell about and tell about)."

3. **READ** As you read lines 39–80, continue to cite evidence.

• Underline examples of Roach's humorous tone.
• In the margin, make an inference about why Roach must "clean my plate."
• Circle text that describes how Patton feels about his soup.

mind at the moment. Extreme psychic discomfort comes closer. The hunter
and the chef are sitting directly across from me. Their generosity is
heartbreaking. I have to clean my plate. I must force apart the gristly
abomination with my teeth, work my tongue into its fissures and slimy orifices,
extract anything vaguely chewable, and swallow it. I lean over to scout the
contents of Patton's bowl.

He got the ankle. The thing about ankle bones, as schoolchildren
everywhere know, is that they're attached to foot bones. And foot bones are
attached to toe bones and toenails and those filthy little rubbery pads on the
50 bottom of the foot. No matter how good a meat may taste, the experience is
indelibly marred by the act of spitting ghastly unchewables out into your
fingers.

Patton is undaunted. He has the entire thing in his mouth. He stops
sucking and gumming long enough to say: "The foot pads are a good source of
fat." He is enjoying his rodent soup in the way that only a man who has been
served steamed tapir[1] fetus and live palm beetles can. A hail of tiny foot bones
accumulates on the ground beside him.

The knee awaits. I've finished my broth. To stall any longer would betray
my revulsion. I manage to locate a couple of pockets of reasonably normal-
60 looking flesh. My inclination is to chew these slowly, forever if need be, until
my hosts tire of sitting here and go off to tend the manioc[2] garden. The
problem with this tactic is that boiled rodent flesh isn't the sort of thing you
want to have hanging around your tongue for any longer than is strictly
necessary for purposes of not choking to death. It's not really that bad, it's just
strong. As in overpowering, as in taste buds passing out and waving white
flags. It doesn't, in short, taste anything like chicken. I find myself chewing
with my mouth open, hoping my hosts will take this for an endearing cultural
peculiarity, rather than an attempt to bypass the tasting portion of my meal.

[1] **tapir:** a mammal related to the horse and the rhinoceros, with a flexible snout.
[2] **manioc:** a shrubby tropical plant, also known as cassava.

These people
share what
they have. It
would be rude
to decline the
food.

indelibly:
forever,
permanently

4. **REREAD** Reread lines 53–57. Why does Patton seem "undaunted" about
eating his rodent soup?

Patton likes the soup because he's eaten it before, and because
he's eaten more disgusting foods such as "tapir fetus" and "live
palm beetles." As stated previously, taste is relative.

---

2. **REREAD AND CITE TEXT EVIDENCE**

B **ASK STUDENTS** to describe the tone the author takes
toward herself. *Students should recognize that Roach has a
self-deprecating tone: "I am, yes, one of those annoying travelers"
(line 15), "Now I am getting my come-uppance. I am getting it
big-time" (line 18).*

3. **READ AND CITE TEXT EVIDENCE**

C **ASK STUDENTS** how they made their inference. *Students
should note that the generosity of the hunter and chef "is
heartbreaking," which implies there isn't much food to share.*

Critical Vocabulary: gambol (line 35) Ask students how the
word *gambol* helps the author convey her purpose. *Gambol
creates a lighthearted and ironic image—a rodent skipping around
and playing in the morning is now served in a soup.*

4. **REREAD AND CITE TEXT EVIDENCE**

D **ASK STUDENTS** to compare Roach's reaction to the soup
with that of Patton's. *Roach is having a terrible time—her state of
mind is "extreme psychic discomfort." But Patton is calmly and
expertly dispatching his rodent ankle.* How do their reactions
underline one of the essay's themes, that "disgust is learned"?
*Both Patton and Roach are eating unfamiliar food, but Patton, who
studies and lives with the Achuar, has grown accustomed to their diet
and simply looks at the rodent ankle as a "good source of fat."*

Critical Vocabulary: indelibly (line 51) Have students suggest
synonyms for the adverb *indelibly.* enduringly, lastingly,
unforgettably

FOR ELL STUDENTS Point out to Spanish speakers that
the word *abomination* has a cognate, *abominación.* It means
"something that causes disgust."

I beg Patton to take my meat. (Our hosts speak no English.) Kind soul that
70 he is, he relieves me of the knee. The man of the house makes a comment,
which Patton translates: "She doesn't like to eat?" He has seen Westerners who
don't have any children, who don't know how to shoot a rifle. Perhaps there are
Westerners who don't like eating. "She had a big breakfast," fibs Patton.

It was in fact a big breakfast, but I didn't do very much having. Someone
shot an alligator, and I had some leg. (It's a leg sort of day.) I have eaten alligator
meat before, in Florida, but someone, bless him, had taken it upon himself to
remove the scales before cooking it. (See "ghastly unchewables," above.) I tried
to pretend that the leg was something else, something bland and comforting.
After several false starts—Melba toast? lettuce?—my brain, clearly shaken,
80 presented me with "orange roughy."[5]

Patton maintains that the bulk of an Achuar's daily calories do not come
from meat. They come from *chicha*, a mildly alcoholic, vaguely nutritious,
watered-down manioc mash. Achuar men drink up to four gallons a day. If you
like chicha, you can live well in Conambo. In about an hour, I will get to try it.
Patton's friend Isaac is hosting a *minga*, a work party for the villagers who
helped Isaac's family dig a new manioc plot. It's similar in concept to the
Amish barn-raising, with marathon chicha-drinking taking the place of
square-dancing.

I am of two minds about chicha. On the one hand, it's a beverage. In the
90 land of scary food, the beverage is your friend.

On the other hand. We are talking about a beverage fermented with
human saliva. <u>Achuar women chew boiled manioc into the desired mashed-
potato texture, and then spit-spray the contents of their bulging cheeks out into
the chicha urn.</u> While I know that, percentage-wise, we're talking a tiny
fraction of the mixture, I'm having difficulty embracing the idea. I have a little
agreement with myself: When spittle finds its way onto the ingredient list, I
find a way to say no.

*On the one
hand, drinking
something
"yucky" is
probably
easier than
eating it. But
this drink is
made with
human saliva.*

[5] **orange roughy:** a large, deep-sea fish native to New Zealand, also known as slimehead.

5. (**READ** ▶) As you read lines 81–135, continue to cite text evidence.
  • In the margin, explain why Roach is "of two minds about chicha" (lines 89–97).
  • Underline facts you learn about the etiquette of chicha making and consumption.
  • In the margin of lines 100–108, make an inference about why Roach includes the description of Isaac's living room.

86

Indians in Ecuador cook manioc to make chicha.

(**E**) "<u>You can't say no</u>," says Patton, tossing ankle carcass to a cringing,
harelipped dog. "It's just not done."
100 Patton and I are seated on a low log bench in the open-walled platform that
serves as Isaac's living room. The man of the house whittles blowgun darts as
he chats. A pair of black horn-rim glasses sits askew on his face. One lens is
violently cracked, as though someone stepped on it, though no one here has the
kind of shoes for that. The floor is dirty but uncluttered. Decor runs to parrot
feathers and jaguar skulls, a government poster urging vaccinations for
children. In the corner, a little girl has set up a chicha tea party with her dolls,
the tenderness of the scene marred only by the knowledge that the tiny chicha
bowls are made from howler monkey voice boxes.

Isaac's wife and mother are in constant motion, serving bowls of chicha to
110 the 10 or so guests. Chicha is the backbone of Achuar society. As with the ankle
bone and the knee bone, you feel an unalterable pressure to accept. Chicha is

*Roach draws
parallels
between
Isaac's home
and American
homes.
Therefore the
odd details she
includes seem
truly weird.*

87

---

5. (**READ AND CITE TEXT EVIDENCE**)

(**E**) **ASK STUDENTS** to paraphrase the unwritten rules for
drinking chicha. *A guest cannot refuse chicha without being
considered "irretrievably rude." Chicha is drunk at every meal,
celebration, and visit. If a visitor tries to refuse chicha, the host will
insist.* Have students discuss why Roach might have included this
section on chicha etiquette. *Students should understand that
Roach is setting up the essay's climax. By explaining the importance
of chicha consumption—and the rules surrounding it—Roach
describes a seemingly intractable predicament. She cannot bear to
drink the bowl of chicha, but she must.*

FOR ELL STUDENTS Explain that the word *whittle* means "to
cut or shave small bits from a piece of wood." It can be used
figuratively, as in the sentence *My car payments have whittled
away my savings.*

the holy communion, the Manischewitz,[4] the kava-kava[5] of Achuar life. It's present at every ceremony, every visit, every meal. An Achuar woman's desirability rests in no small part on her skill at chicha brewing and serving.

F   Isaac's mother dips a clay bowl into an urn of eggnog-hued liquid. Something slimy dangles off the bottom of the bowl, waving howdy-doo as she crosses the floor to our bench. Her hand is coated with a mucilaginous[6] yellow fluid with flecks of manioc fiber. The sidewalk outside a frat house on a Sunday morning comes, unbidden and unwelcome, to mind.

120   "It's Miller time," says Patton as he takes the bowl. After 10 minutes, he warns, she'll return to take the bowl away and give it to someone else, most likely me. It is considered irretrievably rude to refuse a bowl of chicha, or even to set it down. (In a maddening instance of form following etiquette, the ceramic bowls in which chicha is served are rounded on the bottom, so that the drinker cannot set one down without spilling the contents.)

A refusal is interpreted as a bluff and triggers a ritualized pas de deux:[7] "No, really, I shouldn't." "Yes, yes, I insist." Woe unto the visitor: The host never backs down.

Which means I have 10 minutes to talk myself out of the revulsion that's
130 building in my gut, jostling for space among the pinworms and protozoa. My mouth is full of saliva anyway, I tell myself. What's a little more? Myself isn't buying it. Myself is noting the vast and unsettling difference between oral hygiene practices around the Amazon basin and around the basin in our bathroom at home. This isn't a matter of disgust, I tell Patton. It's a matter of gum disease.

Patton wipes manioc slime from his beard. Intelligent chicha drinkers, he holds, don't fret about the saliva it's made with. They fret about the giardia[8] and

---

[4] **Manischewitz:** a popular brand of kosher products.
[5] **kava-kava:** a ceremonial drink used in the Pacific Islands, made up of chewed or ground pulp and cold water.
[6] **mucilaginous:** moist and sticky.
[7] **pas de deux:** a dance for two people.
[8] **giardia:** a protozoán parasite that lives inside the intestines of infected humans and animals. It is contracted through consuming contaminated food or liquids.

---

6. ◄ **REREAD AND DISCUSS** Reread lines 115–135. With a small group, discuss Roach's tone in these lines. Why does she refer to herself as "myself" in lines 129–135?

7. **READ ▶** As you read lines 136–169, continue to cite text evidence.
   • In the margin, explain Roach's reaction to chicha in lines 141–149.
   • Underline text describing the Achuar's reaction to the energy bar.

> **I come from a tribe that eats Vienna sausages. I should be able to cope.**

amoebas in the unfiltered river water it's made with. It is at this moment that Isaac's mother gets up to retrieve the chicha bowl from Patton, fill it to near
140 overflow and present it to me.

The first thing that hits you is the smell. Fruity and fetid, a whiff of drinker's breath on a late-night bus. I put my lips to the rim of the bowl, bumpy-slimy with manioc pulp. I hold my breath and drink.

G   The taste is not awful. It's chalky, rummy, indifferent. But this was never about taste. It's about distaste. Did you ever drop something into a toilet and have to roll up your sleeve and retrieve it? That's how I'm feeling right now. Only I've got to keep going. I've got to lift the lid, step right in, and hunker down in the toilet bowl. As soon as the level of chicha lowers visibly, Isaac's mother will step up to refill the bowl.

150   I disappoint and surprise myself. I come from a tribe that eats Vienna sausages. I should be able to cope. But I can't. I cannot drink this bowl of chicha.

An idea alights. I ask Patton to hold my bowl and rummage in my backpack for the crinkle of airtight cellophane: a raspberry-chocolate Trader Joe's energy bar. The room falls abruptly quiet. Foreigner's backpacks are known to hold all manner of otherworldly wonders: sugar packets, earplugs, contact lenses.

H   The energy bar makes the rounds. A few of the men sniff at it. Only Isaac takes a bite. He chews vigorously at first, then stops, suddenly and with alarm,
160 as though someone had snuck up behind him and put a gun to his head. His eyebrows bunch together like drawn drapes. His lips go all abstract and jumpy. He stands, grabs hold of a roof post, and spits forcefully. He coughs, arrghs, hawks, spits again.

The chicha does not taste bad, but her mind won't let her get past the sense of distaste and she cannot drink it.

---

6. **REREAD AND DISCUSS USING TEXT EVIDENCE**

F **ASK STUDENTS** in each group to give examples of word choices that help convey Roach's tone. *Students could cite "eggnog-hued liquid" (line 115), "waving howdy-doo" (line 116), "The sidewalk outside a frat house on a Sunday morning" (lines 118–119), "jostling for space among the pinworms and protozoa" (line 130).* Have students characterize Roach's conversation with herself. *Students should realize that the conversation is funny and a little desperate. By using "myself" ungrammatically as the subject of sentences, she pokes fun at herself and draws attention to her plight.*

7. **READ AND CITE TEXT EVIDENCE**

G **ASK STUDENTS** why the author talks about dropping something into a toilet (line 145). *Students should realize that Roach is trying to connect with her readers, who surely have never drunk a bowl of chicha. So, she creates an analogy from everyday life—a comparison that any reader will be able to relate to.*

CLOSE READ
Notes

Every few seconds, he looks back at me, his face changing channels from disgust to bewilderment and back. After a good minute of this, he hands back the energy bar, grinning now that the taste is gone, shaking his head at the foreigner's unfathomable tastes.

The way I see it, permission has been granted to back out of the next bowl of chicha.

8. **◄ REREAD** Reread lines 153–169 to cite evidence. Why does Roach give the men the energy bar?

She wants the men to have the same experience of trying a new food. She predicts that they will think it's gross, and will then use their reaction as an excuse to decline the next bowl of chicha.

SHORT RESPONSE

Cite Text Evidence What is Roach's purpose in writing this article? How does her tone convey this purpose? Review your reading notes, and be sure to **cite text evidence** in your response.

Roach's purpose is to show that the concept of "disgust" varies across cultures. She is experienced in eating many foods that most Americans would not want to eat, but chicha is the yuckiest food she has come across. The term "yucky" is relative: Roach includes Rozin's study to enforce this idea. Patton likes the rodent and chicha because his taste buds have become accustomed to eating them. Roach's humorous tone makes the cultural differences seem funny, instead of awkward or uncomfortable. Rather than seeing the Achuar as weird, we see them as people like us who just have different eating habits.

90

---

8. **REREAD AND CITE TEXT EVIDENCE**

H **ASK STUDENTS** to discuss Roach's decision to give the Achuar an energy bar. How does this scene reinforce the central idea of the essay? *Just as she dislikes the chicha, the Achuar men will probably be similarly revolted by something completely foreign to them, an energy bar. Their reaction proves her correct and supports the idea that disgust is learned. Only Isaac dares to take a bite of the energy bar, and he reacts with disgust.*

SHORT RESPONSE

Cite Text Evidence Students' responses should include text evidence that supports their positions. They should:

- state Roach's purpose in the article.
- give examples that illustrate or support the author's purpose.
- describe the author's tone and explain how it helps her convey her purpose.

TO CHALLENGE STUDENTS . . .

For greater context and understanding, students can research the Achuar online.

ASK STUDENTS to describe the main sources of food for the Achuar. *As mentioned in Roach's essay, the men hunt game from the rain forest. This game constitutes an important part of their diet. Also, Achuar women and girls tend gardens in forest clearings. These gardens are the source of manioc, from which they make chicha. A third important part of the Achuar diet is fish. Families generally live near lakes or rivers, which provide fish for a good part of the year.* What socioeconomic forces are threatening the Achuar's livelihood? *Oil was discovered in the Achuar's territory in the 1970s. The oil companies damage the forest and pollute the rivers, making it hard for the Achuar to continue their hunting-and-gathering life. Also, oil workers bring in a lot of new foods, so the Achuar may gradually learn not to be disgusted by western food.*

DIG DEEPER

With the class, return to Question 3, Read. Have students share their examples of Roach's humorous tone.

ASK STUDENTS to analyze the techniques that Roach uses to convey her tone.

- What words and phrases help the author convey humor? *Students should realize that Roach uses words and phrases that vividly evoke her dismay at the rodent knee. The vividness of her language—and the imagery it calls up in the reader's mind—is funny. She calls the knee "a busy intersection of tendon, bone and cartilage" (lines 39–40); she explains that she must "work [her] tongue into its fissures and slimy orifices" (line 44), and she describes the flavor as strong, "[as] in overpowering, as in taste buds passing out and waving white flags" (lines 65–66).*

- How does Roach get humor out of the cultural divide between her and her hosts? *Roach sees humor in how unfathomable her actions must appear to her hosts. She vainly hopes that when she chews with her mouth open, her hosts "will take this for an endearing cultural peculiarity" (lines 67–68), and when Patton finally takes the knee from her, she imagines her hosts thinking that perhaps "there are Westerners who don't like eating" (lines 72–73).*

ASK STUDENTS to return to their Short Response answer and revise it based on the class discussion.

A Journey

Short Story by Edith Wharton

Why This Text

Students may have difficulty analyzing the point of view in which a story is told. In addition, stories such as this one by Edith Wharton may be difficult for students to comprehend because of its subtle use of irony. Students will need to deconstruct the text by distinguishing between what is directly stated in the text and what is really meant. With the help of the close-reading questions, students will be able to understand the use of irony in the story.

Background Have students read the background and the information about the author. Introduce the selection by telling students that Edith Wharton's long and distinguished career as an American author spanned forty years and included the publication of more than forty books. Although she did not publish her first work of fiction until the age of thirty-six, Wharton had been writing since adolescence, composing poems and stories, and completing her first short novel, *Fast and Loose,* at the age of fifteen!

AS YOU READ Ask students to pay close attention to the irony in the story. How soon into the story do they begin to detect its ironic tone?

Common Core Support

- cite multiple pieces of textual evidence
- determine the theme and analyze its development over the course of the text
- analyze a text in which grasping point of view requires analyzing irony

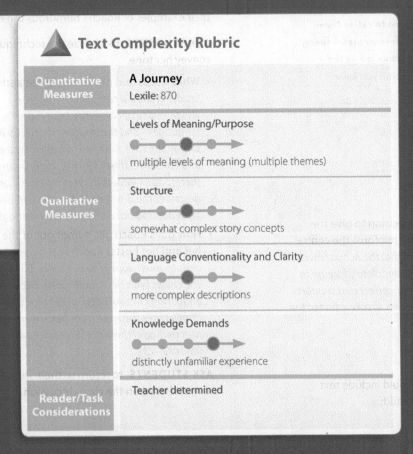

Text Complexity Rubric

Quantitative Measures

A Journey
Lexile: 870

Qualitative Measures

Levels of Meaning/Purpose
multiple levels of meaning (multiple themes)

Structure
somewhat complex story concepts

Language Conventionality and Clarity
more complex descriptions

Knowledge Demands
distinctly unfamiliar experience

Reader/Task Considerations
Teacher determined

Strategies for CLOSE READING

Analyze Author's Point of View: Irony

Students should read this short story carefully all the way through. Close-reading questions at the bottom of the page will help them focus on a thorough analysis of irony in the text. As they read, students should record comments or questions about the text in the side margins.

WHEN STUDENTS STRUGGLE . . .

To help them understand the use of irony in the text, have students work in small groups to fill out a chart such as the one shown as they analyze the story.

CITE TEXT EVIDENCE For practice in tracing the three basic types of irony in the text—verbal irony, situational irony, and dramatic irony—have students cite textual evidence from the story to complete the chart.

Verbal Irony	Situational Irony	Dramatic Irony
When the wife calls her husband's irritability in the sickroom "helpless tyrannies" (line 18), her statement is a contradiction and can be interpreted as verbal irony.	The journey home is an example of situational irony since the couple is returning there because the husband is expected to die. At the end, when the wife thinks that "the worst terror was past" (line 345), she has an unexpected, tragic accident—the opposite of what was expected to happen.	The reader and the wife know that the husband is dead, but the passengers and train crew do not know this.

Background Edith Wharton (1862–1937) was born into a wealthy family in New York City. From her earliest days, Wharton displayed an exceptional visual memory. Before she was eight, she was composing stories in her head, later committing them to paper. By the time she was thirteen, she was writing sonnets. The novel that brought Wharton her first great success was The House of Mirth (1905), the story of a young woman crushed by the ranks of old New York when she tries to live by her own moral standards. The most celebrated American female writer of her time, she had a skeptical view of personal fulfillment. "If only we'd stop trying to be happy," she once said, "we could have a pretty good time."

A Journey

Short Story by Edith Wharton

CLOSE READ
Notes

1. **READ ▶** As you read lines 1–23, begin to collect and cite text evidence.

- Underline the images that the wife sees from her berth in lines 1–6, and in the margin, note what mood they suggest.
- Circle text describing changes in the husband in lines 7–23.
- In the margin of the next page, explain the simile Wharton uses in lines 11–15.

As she lay in her berth, staring at the shadows overhead, the rush of the wheels was in her brain, driving her deeper and deeper into circles of wakeful lucidity. The sleeping-car had sunk into its night-silence. Through the wet window-pane she watched the sudden lights, the long stretches of hurrying blackness. Now and then she turned her head and looked through the opening in the hangings at her husband's curtains across the aisle. . . .

She wondered restlessly if he wanted anything and if she could hear him if he called. His voice had grown very weak within the last months and it irritated him when she did not hear. This irritability, this increasing childish
10 **petulance** seemed to give expression to their imperceptible estrangement.

They suggest a dark, lonely mood.

petulance:
irritation over a small annoyance

91

---

1. **READ AND CITE TEXT EVIDENCE**

Ⓐ **ASK STUDENTS** to cite evidence for their explanation of the simile Wharton uses in lines 11–15. *The comparison Wharton makes by stating that the couple is now "like two faces looking at one another through a sheet of glass . . . close together, almost touching, but . . . not hear[ing] or feel[ing] each other: the conductivity between them . . . broken" (lines 11–13) suggests that although physically close, they have lost their emotional connection. The connotative meaning of conductivity (line 13) highlights the loss of the spark between them, supported by this image: "Now their energies no longer kept step" (line 21).*

Critical Vocabulary: petulance (line 10) Have students share their definitions of the word and use it in a sentence.

CLOSE READ
Notes

A Like two faces looking at one another through a sheet of glass they were close together, almost touching, but they could not hear or feel each other: the conductivity between them was broken. She, at least, had this sense of separation, and she fancied sometimes that she saw it reflected in the look with which he supplemented his failing words. Doubtless the fault was hers. She was too impenetrably healthy to be touched by the irrelevancies of disease. Her

B self-reproachful tenderness was tinged with the sense of his irrationality: she had a vague feeling that there was a purpose in his helpless tyrannies. The suddenness of the change had found her so unprepared. A year ago their pulses had beat to one robust measure; both had the same **prodigal** confidence in an exhaustless future. Now their energies no longer kept step: hers still bounded ahead of life, preempting unclaimed regions of hope and activity, while his lagged behind, vainly struggling to overtake her.

When they married, she had such arrears of living to make up: her days had been as bare as the whitewashed school-room where she forced innutritious facts upon reluctant children. His coming had broken in on the slumber of circumstance, widening the present till it became the encloser of remotest chances. But imperceptibly the horizon narrowed. Life had a grudge against her: she was never to be allowed to spread her wings.

At first the doctors had said that six weeks of mild air would set him right; but when he came back this assurance was explained as having of course included a winter in a dry climate. They gave up their pretty house, storing the

Margin left:
Although physically close, they have lost their emotional connection.

prodigal: generous; abundant

2. ◀ REREAD Reread lines 7–23. What do the contrasting descriptions of health and sickness suggest about the wife's relationship with her husband? How does she describe her own reactions to her husband's health? Support your answer with explicit textual evidence.

The contrasting descriptions of health and sickness reflect the growing estrangement between the narrator and her husband. The husband is "irritated" when she doesn't hear him; she describes herself as at fault and having a "self-reproachful tenderness." She is critical of her own response to his failing health.

3. READ ▶ As you read lines 24–63, continue to cite textual evidence.
- Underline text that shows the wife's negative feelings in lines 24–45.
- In the margin, describe in your own words how the husband used to be (lines 30–45).
- Underline text that describes the wife's fear in lines 46–63.

> ❝ It frightened her to feel that this was the man she loved . . . ❞

wedding presents and new furniture, and went to Colorado. She had hated it there from the first. Nobody knew her or cared about her; there was no one to wonder at the good match she had made, or to envy her the new dresses and the visiting-cards which were still a surprise to her. And he kept growing

C worse. She felt herself beset with difficulties too evasive to be fought by so direct a temperament. She still loved him, of course; but he was gradually, undefinably ceasing to be himself. The man she had married had been strong, active, gently masterful: the male whose pleasure it is to clear a way through the material obstructions of life; but now it was she who was the protector, he who must be shielded from importunities and given his drops or his beef-juice though the skies were falling. The routine of the sick-room bewildered her; this punctual administering of medicine seemed as idle as some uncomprehended religious mummery.[1]

D There were moments, indeed, when warm gushes of pity swept away her instinctive resentment of his condition, when she still found his old self in his eyes as they groped for each other through the dense medium of his weakness. But these moments had grown rare. Sometimes he frightened her: his sunken expressionless face seemed that of a stranger; his voice was weak and hoarse; his thin-lipped smile a mere muscular contraction. Her hand avoided his damp soft skin, which had lost the familiar roughness of health: she caught herself furtively watching him as she might have watched a strange animal. It frightened her to feel that this was the man she loved; there were hours when to tell him what she suffered seemed the one escape from her fears. But in general she judged herself more leniently, reflecting that she had perhaps been too long alone with him, and that she would feel differently when they were at home again, surrounded by her robust and buoyant family. How she had rejoiced when the doctors at last gave their consent to his going home! She knew, of course, what the decision meant; they both knew. It meant that he was to die; but they dressed the truth in hopeful euphemisms, and at times, in the joy of preparation, she really forgot the purpose of their journey, and slipped into an eager allusion to next year's plans.

Margin right:
He used to be strong, active, and protective.

furtively: secretly

---

[1] **mummery:** a ridiculous performance or ceremony.

CLOSE READ
Notes

---

2. REREAD AND CITE TEXT EVIDENCE

B **ASK STUDENTS** to find phrases in the text that show that the wife is of two minds about her feelings for her husband. *"increasing childish petulance" (lines 9–10), "self-reproachful tenderness" (line 17), "helpless tyrannies" (line 18), "vainly struggling" (line 23)*

3. READ AND CITE TEXT EVIDENCE

C **ASK STUDENTS** to cite evidence for their description of how the husband had been before his illness. *Students should note that he had been "strong, active" (lines 39–40), and protective (line 41).*

Critical Vocabulary: prodigal (line 20) Have students explain *prodigal* as Wharton uses it here.

Critical Vocabulary: furtively (line 53) Have students share their definitions of *furtively*. Ask how *furtively* fits into Wharton's discussion of the growing sense of separation that the wife feels toward her husband. *Students should point out that as the wife watches her husband grow progressively worse, and as the "estrangement" between them deepens, she secretly watches him "as she might have watched a strange animal" (line 53).*

FOR ELL STUDENTS Clarify that the word *contraction* (line 51) is a multiple-meaning word, and that in this context, it does not refer to the grammatical construction, but instead means "a shortening or tensing of a muscle."

ASK STUDENTS to look for other multiple-meaning words in the text and cite them in the margin.

CLOSE READ
Notes

E **F** At last the day of leaving came. She had a <u>dreadful fear</u> that they would never get away; that somehow at the last moment he would fail her; that the doctors held one of their <u>accustomed treacheries</u> in reserve; but nothing happened. They drove to the station, he was installed in a seat with a rug over his knees and a cushion at his back, and she hung out of the window waving <u>unregretful farewells</u> to the acquaintances she had really never liked till then.

70 The first twenty-four hours had passed off well. He revived a little and it amused him to look out of the window and to observe the humours of the car. The second day he began to grow weary and to chafe under the **dispassionate** stare of the freckled child with the lump of chewing-gum. She had to explain to the child's mother that her husband was too ill to be disturbed: a statement received by that lady with a resentment visibly supported by the maternal sentiment of the whole car. . . .

That night he slept badly and the next morning his temperature frightened her: she was sure he was growing worse. The day passed slowly, punctuated by the <u>small irritations</u> of travel. Watching his tired face, she traced in its

80 contractions every rattle and jolt of the tram, till her own body vibrated with sympathetic fatigue. She felt the others observing him too, and hovered restlessly between him and the line of <u>interrogative eyes</u>. The freckled child hung about him like a fly; offers of candy and picture-books failed to dislodge her: she twisted one leg around the other and watched him **imperturbably**. The porter, as he passed, lingered with vague proffers of help, probably inspired by philanthropic passengers swelling with the sense that "something ought to

dispassionate:
free from personal feeling or bias

imperturbably:
calmly; without being upset

---

4. **◀ REREAD** Reread lines 46–63. From what point of view is the story being told? How do you know?

The story is told from the third-person limited point of view, because the reader's view of the characters, events, and situation is limited to the views of the wife.

5. **READ ▶** As you read lines 64–105, continue to cite textual evidence.
   - Underline phrases that help set the tone of the story.
   - In the margin, explain why the return home is an example of situational irony (lines 95–105).

94

CLOSE READ
Notes

> "She had a dreadful fear . . . that the doctors held one of their accustomed treacheries in reserve . . ."

be done;" and one nervous man in a skull-cap was audibly concerned as to the possible effect on his wife's health.

The hours dragged on in a <u>dreary inoccupation</u>. Towards dusk she sat

90 down beside him and he laid his hand on hers. The touch startled her. He seemed to be calling her from far off. She looked at him helplessly and his smile went through her like a physical pang.

"Are you very tired?" she asked.

"No, not very."

"We'll be there soon now."

"Yes, very soon."

"This time to-morrow—"

He nodded and they sat silent. When she had put him to bed and crawled into her own berth she tried to cheer herself with the thought that in less than

100 twenty-four hours they would be in New York. Her people would all be at the station to meet her—she pictured their round unanxious faces pressing through the crowd. She only hoped they would not tell him too loudly that he was looking splendidly and would be all right in no time: the subtler sympathies developed by long contact with suffering were making her aware of a certain coarseness of texture in the family **sensibilities**.

Suddenly she thought she heard him call. <u>She parted the curtains and listened.</u> No, it was only a man snoring at the other end of the car. His snores had a greasy sound, as though they passed through tallow. <u>She lay down and tried to sleep</u> . . . Had she not heard him move? <u>She started up trembling</u> . . .

The situation is ironic because they are returning home only because the husband is expected to die.

sensibility:
the capacity to feel, react, or respond to emotion

6. **◀ REREAD AND DISCUSS** Reread lines 64–105. With a small group, discuss the wife's concern about the journey. Why is she worried about "her people"?

7. **READ ▶** As you read lines 106–150, continue to cite textual evidence.
   - Underline actions the wife takes in lines 106–121.
   - In the margin, explain what is ironic, or surprising, about her actions (lines 114–121).
   - Circle text that describes a change in the wife's outlook in lines 122–132.

95

---

4. **REREAD AND CITE TEXT EVIDENCE**

D **ASK STUDENTS** to explain how the point of view used in the description of the wife in lines 46–48 shows the point of view from which the story is being told. *Students should note that in these lines the narrator is not a character in the story but presents a point of view limited to one character—to what the wife thinks or feels.*

5. **READ AND CITE TEXT EVIDENCE**

E **ASK STUDENTS** to cite text evidence explaining why the return home is an example of situational irony. *Students should cite evidence from lines 58–63 that explains that the doctors "at last gave their consent to his going home. . . . It meant that he was to die."*

Critical Vocabulary: dispassionate (line 72) and **imperturbably** (line 84) Have students define these words.

6. **REREAD AND DISCUSS USING TEXT EVIDENCE**

F **ASK STUDENTS** to cite specific textual evidence to support the reasons for the wife's concern about the journey home. *Students should cite evidence in lines 100–105 to explain the wife's concerns about the unctuous comments her "people" might make to her husband.*

7. **READ AND CITE TEXT EVIDENCE**

G **ASK STUDENTS** to cite evidence that explains irony in the wife's actions. *Students should cite textual evidence from lines 114–117 and 119–121 to explain that her reaction is ironic because if she could not "endure her fears [about her husband] a moment longer" (lines 119–120), she would not be expected to turn over and go to sleep.*

Critical Vocabulary: sensibility (line 105) Have students explain *sensibility* and use it in a sentence.

Her reaction is
ironic because if
she could not
"endure her
fears a moment
longer," you
would not
expect her to go
to sleep.

110 The silence frightened her more than any sound. He might not be able to make her hear—he might be calling her now . . . What made her think of such things? It was merely the familiar tendency of an over-tired mind to fasten itself on the most intolerable chance within the range of its forebodings. . . .

G Putting her head out, she listened; but she could not distinguish his breathing from that of the other pairs of lungs about her. She longed to get up and look at him, but she knew the impulse was a mere vent for her restlessness, and the fear of disturbing him restrained her. . . . The regular movement of his curtain reassured her, she knew not why; she remembered that he had wished her a cheerful good-night; and the sheer inability to endure her fears a moment

120 longer made her put them from her with an effort of her whole sound tired body. She turned on her side and slept.

She sat up stiffly, staring out at the dawn. The train was rushing through a region of bare hillocks huddled against a lifeless sky. It looked like the first day of creation. The air of the car was close, and she pushed up her window to let in the keen wind. Then she looked at her watch: it was seven o'clock, and soon the people about her would be stirring. She slipped into her clothes, smoothed her

dishevelled:
untidy

dishevelled hair and crept to the dressing-room. When she had washed her face and adjusted her dress she felt more hopeful. It was always a struggle for her not to be cheerful in the morning. Her cheeks burned deliciously under the

130 coarse towel and the wet hair about her temples broke into strong upward tendrils. Every inch of her was full of life and elasticity. And in ten hours they would be at home!

She stepped to her husband's berth: it was time for him to take his early glass of milk. The window-shade was down, and in the dusk of the curtained enclosure she could just see that he lay sideways, with his face away from her. She leaned over him and drew up the shade. As she did so she touched one of his hands. It felt cold. . . .

H She bent closer, laying her hand on his arm and calling him by name. He did not move. She spoke again more loudly; she grasped his shoulder and

140 gently shook it. He lay motionless. She caught hold of his hand again: it slipped from her limply, like a dead thing. A dead thing? . . . Her breath caught. She must see his face. She leaned forward, and hurriedly, shrinkingly, with a sickening reluctance of the flesh, laid her hands on his shoulders and turned him over. His head fell back; his face looked small and smooth; he gazed at her with steady eyes.

She remained motionless for a long time, holding him thus; and they looked at each other. Suddenly she shrank back: the longing to scream, to call out, to fly from him, had almost overpowered her. But a strong hand arrested her. Good God! If it were known that he was dead they would be put off the

150 train at the next station—

I In a terrifying flash of remembrance there arose before her a scene she had once witnessed in travelling, when a husband and wife, whose child had died in the train, had been thrust out at some chance station. She saw them standing on the platform with the child's body between them; she had never forgotten the dazed look with which they followed the receding train. And this was what would happen to her. Within the next hour she might find herself on the platform of some strange station, alone with her husband's body. . . . Anything but that! It was too horrible—She quivered like a creature at bay.

As she cowered there, she felt the train moving more slowly. It was coming

160 then—they were approaching a station! She saw again the husband and wife standing on the lonely platform; and with a violent gesture she drew down the shade to hide her husband's face.

Feeling dizzy, she sank down on the edge of the berth, keeping away from his outstretched body, and pulling the curtains close, so that he and she were

J shut into a kind of **sepulchral** twilight. She tried to think. At all costs she must conceal the fact that he was dead. But how? Her mind refused to act: she could not plan, combine. She could think of no way but to sit there, clutching the curtains, all day long. . . .

She heard the porter making up her bed; people were beginning to move

170 about the car; the dressing-room door was being opened and shut. She tried to rouse herself. At length with a supreme effort she rose to her feet, stepping into

She is afraid
that if her
husband's
death is
discovered,
they will be
left at the
next station.

sepulchral:
of a tomb,
vault, or grave

---

8. **◄ REREAD** Reread lines 138–150. Why is the wife's reaction to her husband's death ironic?

Her reaction is ironic because she's more concerned about being put off the train than she is upset that her husband has just died.

---

9. **READ ►** As you read lines 151–188, continue to cite textual evidence.
- Underline text describing what the wife remembers.
- In the margin, explain why the wife conceals her husband's death (lines 151–162).

WHEN STUDENTS STRUGGLE . . . To help students understand Wharton's subtle use of irony and how irony can help them grasp the narrator's point of view, ask them to reread lines 122–132. Invite groups to discuss how this paragraph uses irony to reinforce the contrast between the wife's health and the husband's illness ("Every inch of her was full of life" [line 131]), while highlighting the situational irony expressed in the fact that the husband is lying dead just a few feet away.

Critical Vocabulary: dishevelled (line 127) Have students share their definitions of *dishevelled*. What is "dishevelled" in the text? *the wife's hair* What else can be dishevelled? *Students might cite a person's clothing or appearance.*

8. **REREAD AND CITE TEXT EVIDENCE**

H **ASK STUDENTS** to assess whether the wife's reaction to her husband's death is an effective use of irony. How does it help students grasp the narrator's point of view of the wife? *Students should cite evidence from lines 138–144 and 146–150 showing that her response is ironic—it's not the way one would expect the wife to feel. The narrator sees her as a selfish person more concerned about being put off the train than grieving for her husband.*

9. **READ AND CITE TEXT EVIDENCE**

I **ASK STUDENTS** to cite evidence supporting their response as to why the wife keeps her husband's death hidden from the people on the train. *She had once seen "a husband and wife, whose child had died in the train . . . thrust out at some chance station. . . . And this was what would happen to her. . . . Anything but that! It was too horrible . . ." (lines 152–158).*

Critical Vocabulary: sepulchral (line 165) Have students explain the meaning of *sepulchral* and the image it creates.

the aisle of the car and drawing the curtains tight behind her. She noticed that they still parted slightly with the motion of the car, and finding a pin in her dress she fastened them together. Now she was safe. She looked round and saw the porter. She fancied he was watching her.

"Ain't he awake yet?" he enquired.

"No," she faltered.

"I got his milk all ready when he wants it. You know you told me to have it for him by seven."

180 She nodded silently and crept into her seat.

At half-past eight the train reached Buffalo. By this time the other passengers were dressed and the berths had been folded back for the day. The porter, moving to and fro under his burden of sheets and pillows, glanced at her as he passed. At length he said: "Ain't he going to get up? You know we're ordered to make up the berths as early as we can."

She turned cold with fear. They were just entering the station.

"Oh, not yet," she stammered. "Not till he's had his milk. Won't you get it, please?"

"All right. Soon as we start again."

190 When the train moved on he reappeared with the milk. She took it from him and sat vaguely looking at it: her brain moved slowly from one idea to another, as though they were stepping-stones set far apart across a whirling flood. At length she became aware that the porter still hovered expectantly.

K

"Will I give it to him?" he suggested.

"Oh, no," she cried, rising. "He—he's asleep yet, I think—"

10. **◄ REREAD** Reread lines 151–188. Explain the dramatic irony implicit in the wife's attempts to hide her husband's death from the people on the train.

This episode is an example of dramatic irony because the reader knows something (in this case, that the husband is dead) that characters in the story do not know.

11. **READ ►** As you read lines 189–210, continue to cite textual evidence.
- Circle the simile Wharton uses to describe the wife's mental state.
- In the margin, explain why she decides to drink the milk (lines 194–202).

98

She waited till the porter had passed on; then she unpinned the curtains and slipped behind them. In the semi-obscurity her husband's face stared up at her like a marble mask with agate eyes. The eyes were dreadful. She put out her hand and drew down the lids. Then she remembered the glass of milk in her 200 other hand: what was she to do with it? She thought of raising the window and throwing it out; but to do so she would have to lean across his body and bring her face close to his. She decided to drink the milk.

L

She returned to her seat with the empty glass and after a while the porter came back to get it.

"When'll I fold up his bed?" he asked.

"Oh, not now—not yet; he's ill—he's very ill. Can't you let him stay as he is? The doctor wants him to lie down as much as possible."

He scratched his head. "Well, if he's *really* sick—"

He took the empty glass and walked away, explaining to the passengers 210 that the party behind the curtains was too sick to get up just yet.

She found herself the centre of sympathetic eyes. A motherly woman with an intimate smile sat down beside her.

M

"I'm real sorry to hear your husband's sick. I've had a remarkable amount of sickness in my family and maybe I could assist you. Can I take a look at him?"

"Oh, no—no, please! He mustn't be disturbed."

The lady accepted the **rebuff** indulgently.

"Well, it's just as you say, of course, but you don't look to me as if you'd had much experience in sickness and I'd have been glad to assist you. What do you 220 generally do when your husband's taken this way?"

She decides to drink the milk rather than having to lean across her husband to throw it out the window.

rebuff: *a blunt refusal of a friendly offer*

12. **◄ REREAD** Reread lines 203–210. Why are the porter's actions ironic? Cite evidence in your response.

The porter's actions are ironic because he doesn't know the husband is dead. He inadvertently does the wife a favor by explaining to the other passengers that "the party behind the curtains was too sick to get up just yet."

13. **READ ►** As you read lines 211–239, continue to cite textual evidence.
- Underline the questions that the "motherly woman" asks.
- Circle the wife's responses.

99

---

10. **REREAD AND CITE TEXT EVIDENCE**

J ASK STUDENTS in what way the wife's furtive actions are an example of dramatic irony. *Since the reader and the wife know that the husband is dead, but the characters do not know this fact, the wife's attempts at hiding his dead body from everyone on the train is an example of dramatic irony. Students should cite evidence from lines 165–168, 172–179, and 181–188.*

11. **READ AND CITE TEXT EVIDENCE**

K ASK STUDENTS to cite evidence explaining why the woman drinks the milk that the porter has brought for her husband. *Students should cite specific textual evidence in lines 194–195 and 199–202 to explain that she decides to drink the milk because she does not want the porter to suspect that her husband is dead. She also does not want to throw the milk from the window because she would have to lean across her husband's dead body.*

12. **REREAD AND CITE TEXT EVIDENCE**

L ASK STUDENTS to explain what the porter believes has happened to the milk. In what way is this ironic? *He thinks that the husband has drunk the milk but is really sick and should be left alone. However, the wife and the reader know he is dead.*

13. **READ AND CITE TEXT EVIDENCE**

M ASK STUDENTS to point out the disparity that exists between what the "motherly woman" seems to be and what she is. *Students should cite evidence from the questions she asks the wife and from her last statement (lines 229–230). When she says that the wife "don't look to me as if you'd had much experience in sickness," she seems more judgmental than caring.*

Critical Vocabulary: rebuff (line 217) Have students define the word.

"I—I let him sleep."

"Too much sleep ain't any too healthful either. Don't you give him any medicine?"

"Y—yes."

"Don't you wake him to take it?"

"Yes."

"When does he take the next dose?"

"Not for—two hours—"

The lady looked disappointed. "Well, if I was you I'd try giving it oftener. That's what I do with my folks."

230   After that many faces seemed to press upon her. The passengers were on their way to the dining-car, and she was conscious that as they passed down the aisle they glanced curiously at the closed curtains. One lantern-jawed man with prominent eyes stood still and tried to shoot his projecting glance through the division between the folds. The freckled child, returning from breakfast, waylaid the passers with a buttery clutch, saying in a loud whisper, "He's sick;" and once the conductor came by, asking for tickets. She shrank into her corner and looked out of the window at the flying trees and houses, meaningless hieroglyphs of an endlessly unrolled papyrus.

240   Now and then the train stopped, and the newcomers on entering the car stared in turn at the closed curtains. More and more people seemed to pass—their faces began to blend fantastically with the images surging in her brain. . . .

Later in the day a fat man detached himself from the mist of faces. He had a creased stomach and soft pale lips. As he pressed himself into the seat facing her she noticed that he was dressed in black broadcloth, with a soiled white tie.

14. ◀ REREAD   Reread lines 231–239. What is the result of the conversation between the wife and the "motherly woman"? How is the wife affected? Support your answer with text evidence.

The conversation has made the wife more nervous, even though the "motherly woman" was just trying to help. The wife now thinks "that many faces seemed to press upon her," as if she is going to be found out.

15. READ ▶   As you read lines 240–290, continue to cite text evidence.

• Underline text used to describe the fat man in lines 243–249.

• In the margin, explain who he might be.

• Underline text describing the confusion the wife feels in lines 255–272.

"Husband's pretty bad this morning, is he?"

"Yes."

"Dear, dear! Now that's terribly distressing, ain't it?" An apostolic smile revealed his gold-filled teeth.

250   "Of course you know there's no sech thing as sickness. Ain't that a lovely thought? Death itself is but a deloosion of our grosser senses. On'y lay yourself open to the influx of the sperrit, submit yourself passively to the action of the divine force, and disease and **dissolution** will cease to exist for you. If you could indooce your husband to read this little pamphlet—"

The faces about her again grew indistinct. She had a vague recollection of hearing the motherly lady and the parent of the freckled child ardently disputing the relative advantages of trying several medicines at once, or of taking each in turn; the motherly lady maintaining that the competitive system saved time; the other objecting that you couldn't tell which remedy had effected 260 the cure; their voices went on and on, like bell-buoys droning through a fog. . . . The porter came up now and then with questions that she did not understand, but that somehow she must have answered since he went away again without repeating them; every two hours the motherly lady reminded her that her husband ought to have his drops; people left the car and others replaced them . . .

Her head was spinning and she tried to steady herself by clutching at her thoughts as they swept by, but they slipped away from her like bushes on the side of a sheer **precipice** down which she seemed to be falling. Suddenly her mind grew clear again and she found herself vividly picturing what would 270 happen when the train reached New York. She shuddered as it occurred to her that he would be quite cold and that some one might perceive he had been dead since morning.

She thought hurriedly:—"If they see I am not surprised they will suspect something. They will ask questions, and if I tell them the truth they won't believe me—no one would believe me! It will be terrible"—and she kept repeating to herself:—"I must pretend I don't know. I must pretend I don't

Margin notes:

He may be a clergyman or someone religious.

dissolution: *death*

precipice: *the edge of a steep cliff*

16. ◀ REREAD   Reread lines 273–279. What new concerns occur to the narrator in these lines? How is this an example of situational irony?

She is worried that she won't look sufficiently surprised when they find her husband dead. She is afraid they will notice he has been dead since the morning. The situation is ironic because she is more worried about her behavior than her husband's death.

---

14. REREAD AND CITE TEXT EVIDENCE

N   ASK STUDENTS to explain the irony in the wife's perception of the passengers after she has spoken with the "motherly woman." How does her perception of them contrast with what is probably true? *Students should cite evidence from lines 231–235 to emphasize that the conversation has made the wife even more nervous, causing her to believe that "many faces seemed to press upon her" (line 231) and that one man's "prominent eyes" (line 234) were trying to peer through her husband's curtain (line 235). Her paranoia increases, causing a disjunction between appearance and reality and heightening the irony.*

15. READ AND CITE TEXT EVIDENCE

O   ASK STUDENTS to cite specific textual evidence of the wife's confused mental state. *Students should cite examples in lines 255, 260–264, and 266–268 to indicate the vagueness she feels, the droning voices she hears, and the dizziness she experiences.*

16. REREAD AND CITE TEXT EVIDENCE

P   ASK STUDENTS to explain the wife's thoughts about what will happen when the train crew discovers that her husband is dead. How will she really be feeling? *Students should cite evidence from lines 273–279 to explain the wife's new concern that she will not look sufficiently surprised when the crew finds that her husband is dead. To deflect suspicion from herself, she must pretend that his death is a shock to her—and even scream to make the pretense more convincing.*

Critical Vocabulary: dissolution (line 253) Have students explain *dissolution* as Wharton uses it here. Then have them give the scientific (or technical) meaning of the word.

Critical Vocabulary: precipice (line 268) Have students share their definitions of the word and use it in sentences.

know. When they open the curtains I must go up to him quite naturally—and then I must scream." . . . She had an idea that the scream would be very hard to do.

280   Gradually new thoughts crowded upon her, vivid and urgent: she tried to separate and restrain them, but they beset her clamorously, like her schoolchildren at the end of a hot day, when she was too tired to silence them. Her head grew confused, and she felt a sick fear of forgetting her part, of betraying herself by some unguarded word or look.

    "I must pretend I don't know," she went on murmuring. The words had lost their significance, but she repeated them mechanically, as though they had been a magic formula, until suddenly she heard herself saying: "I can't remember, I can't remember!"

    Her voice sounded very loud, and she looked about her in terror; but no 290 one seemed to notice that she had spoken.

(Q)   As she glanced down the car her eye caught the curtains of her husband's berth, and she began to examine the monotonous **arabesques** woven through their heavy folds. The pattern was intricate and difficult to trace; she gazed fixedly at the curtains and as she did so the thick stuff grew transparent and through it she saw her husband's face—his dead face. She struggled to avert her look, but her eyes refused to move and her head seemed to be held in a vice. At last, with an effort that left her weak and shaking, she turned away; but it was of no use; close in front of her, small and smooth, was her husband's face. It seemed to be suspended in the air between her and the false braids of the 300 woman who sat in front of her. With an uncontrollable gesture she stretched out her hand to push the face away, and suddenly she felt the touch of his smooth skin. She **repressed** a cry and half started from her seat. The woman with the false braids looked around, and feeling that she must justify her movement in some way she rose and lifted her travelling-bag from the opposite seat. She unlocked the bag and looked into it; but the first object her hand met was a small flask of her husband's, thrust there at the last moment, in the haste of departure. She locked the bag and closed her eyes . . . his face was there again, hanging between her eye-balls and lids like a waxen mask against a red curtain. . . .

310   She roused herself with a shiver. Had she fainted or slept? Hours seemed to have elapsed; but it was still broad day, and the people about her were sitting in the same attitudes as before.

17. **(READ ▶)** Read lines 291–332, and continue to cite textual evidence.

- Underline text describing the wife's confusion in lines 291–322.
- In the margin, explain what is happening in these lines.
- Underline images of death in the wife's dream (lines 323–332).

arabesque:
a design of intertwined flowing lines

repress:
to hold back or stifle

    A sudden sense of hunger made her aware that she had eaten nothing since morning. The thought of food filled her with disgust, but she dreaded a return of faintness, and remembering that she had some biscuits in her bag she took one out and ate it. The dry crumbs choked her, and she hastily swallowed a little brandy from her husband's flask. The burning sensation in her throat acted as a counter-irritant, momentarily relieving the dull ache of her nerves. Then she felt a gently-stealing warmth, as though a soft air fanned her, and the 320 swarming fears relaxed their clutch, receding through the stillness that enclosed her, a stillness soothing as the spacious quietude of a summer day. She slept.

(R)   Through her sleep she felt the impetuous rush of the train. It seemed to be life itself that was sweeping her on with headlong **inexorable** force—sweeping her into darkness and terror, and the awe of unknown days.—Now all at once everything was still—not a sound, not a pulsation . . . She was dead in her turn, and lay beside him with smooth upstaring face. How quiet it was!—and yet she heard feet coming, the feet of the men who were to carry them away . . . She could feel too—she felt a sudden prolonged vibration, a series of hard shocks, 330 and then another plunge into darkness: the darkness of death this time—a black whirlwind on which they were both spinning like leaves, in wild uncoiling spirals, with millions and millions of the dead. . . .

(S)   She sprang up in terror. Her sleep must have lasted a long time, for the winter day had paled and the lights had been lit. The car was in confusion, and as she regained her self-possession she saw that the passengers were gathering up their wraps and bags. The woman with the false braids had brought from the dressing-room a sickly ivy-plant in a bottle, and the Christian Scientist was reversing his cuffs. The porter passed down the aisle with his impartial brush. 340 An impersonal figure with a gold-banded cap asked for her husband's ticket. A voice shouted "Baig-gage express!" and she heard the clicking of metal as the passengers handed over their checks.

The wife's mental state is disintegrating. She is having hallucinations and is confused.

inexorable:
unyielding

18. **(◀ REREAD)** Reread lines 323–332. Why do you think Wharton uses these deathly images in these lines?

Wharton might be emphasizing the severity of the wife's confusion. The wife feels as if she has died.

19. **(READ ▶)** As you read lines 333–352, continue to cite textual evidence.

- Underline text describing the porter's actions.
- In the margin, explain what happens to the wife (lines 350–352).

---

17. **READ AND CITE TEXT EVIDENCE**

Q **ASK STUDENTS** to explain the wife's deteriorating mental state in lines 291–332. *Students should emphasize that she is experiencing disordered thinking and hallucinations as she thinks she sees her husband's dead face (line 295), sometimes suspended in mid-air (lines 298–302 and 307–309). She is also experiencing a sense of timelessness (lines 310–312) and "terror" (line 325), as well as dreams (nightmares) of her own death (lines 330–332).*

Critical Vocabulary: arabesque (line 292) and **repress** (line 302) Have students share their definitions.

FOR ELL STUDENTS Explain that homographs are words that are spelled alike but have different meanings. Point out that *object* (line 305) is a homograph. Ask what part of speech it is here *noun* and what it means. *It means "thing."* Ask students to pronounce and define the verb *object*. What does it mean? *to protest.* Have them use both words in sentences.

18. **REREAD AND CITE TEXT EVIDENCE**

R **ASK STUDENTS** to cite the deathly images in lines 323–332. *"sweeping her into darkness" (lines 324–325), "She was dead in her turn" (line 326), "the darkness of death" (line 330), "with millions and millions of the dead" (line 332)*

19. **READ AND CITE TEXT EVIDENCE**

S **ASK STUDENTS** to cite evidence for their explanation for what happens to the wife at the end of the story. *Students should cite evidence from lines 350–352 to explain that she has an accident. Upon the porter's approach, she panics, faints, and hits her head against her dead husband's berth, perhaps signifying her death.*

Critical Vocabulary: inexorable (line 324) Have students share their definitions of the word and use it in a sentence.

The wife panics, faints, and hits her head.

T   Presently her window was blocked by an expanse of sooty wall, and the train passed into the Harlem tunnel. The journey was over; in a few minutes she would see her family pushing their joyous way through the throng at the station. Her heart dilated. The worst terror was past. . . .

"We'd better get him up now, hadn't we?" asked the porter, touching her arm.

He had her husband's hat in his hand and was meditatively revolving it under his brush.

350   She looked at the hat and tried to speak; but suddenly the car grew dark. She flung up her arms, struggling to catch at something, and fell face downward, striking her head against the dead man's berth.

20. **◀ REREAD** Reread lines 342–345. Explain the irony of the text "The journey was over" in line 343.

At first, the reader feels relief that the "journey" is over, but then the wife herself has an unfortunate accident.

SHORT RESPONSE

Cite Text Evidence What do you think is the theme of "A Journey"? How does Wharton's use of irony hint at a deeper message about life that the author wants to convey? Support your response with **explicit textual evidence.**

The theme of "A Journey" is that life itself is a journey. The wife herself makes the comparison: "It seemed to be life itself that was sweeping her on with headlong inexorable force—sweeping her into darkness and terror . . ." Wharton points out that a journey, just like life is unpredictable. The wife is so preoccupied with concealing her husband's death that at the moment "the journey is over" she hits her head "against the dead man's berth." Just as "the worst terror" has passed, the wife has an accident and the story ends abruptly.

104

TO CHALLENGE STUDENTS . . .

For more context about the life and legacy of the great American author Edith Wharton, students can conduct print or online research to write a report.

ASK STUDENTS to do some research to find a topic about Wharton that interests them. You may suggest the following:

- Wharton's travels and their influence on her work
- women in Wharton's fiction
- Wharton's use of irony

Discuss these features of a research report:

- Plan your research
  - —Write questions about your topic.
  - —Research your topic, take notes, and organize them.
  - —Write an outline based on your notes.
- Write your report
  - —Keep your purpose and audience in mind.
  - —Write a draft, revise your report, and proofread it.
  - —Check that your bibliography is accurate.
- Publish and share

ASK STUDENTS what they hope to discover about Wharton as they research their report.

---

20. **REREAD AND CITE TEXT EVIDENCE**

T **ASK STUDENTS** what the word *journey* can mean as a metaphor. *Students may suggest that it can mean any process: the journey from innocence to worldliness; the journey through high school; the journey from apprentice to master craftsman; the journey of life.*

SHORT RESPONSE

Cite Text Evidence Student responses will vary, but students should cite specific evidence from the text to support their statement of the theme. Students should:

- explain the theme of the text.
- give reasons to support how the theme of the text conveys a deeper message about life.
- cite specific evidence from the text to support their reasons.

DIG DEEPER

With the class, return to Question 6, Reread and Discuss. Have students share the results of their discussion.

ASK STUDENTS whether they were satisfied with the outcome of their small-group discussions. Have each group share the details they discussed about the wife's concern regarding the journey home. What fears does she have about the trip? How does the journey home suggest an ironic situation in the text?

- Have each group share what the wife's overriding concern is about the journey home. What specific textual evidence did the groups cite to support this opinion? Did anyone in the group disagree? If so, how did the group resolve this disagreement or difference of opinion?

- Lead each group to share its discussion about why the wife is concerned about meeting her "people." What is the cause of her concern? How does her ironic treatment in the text cast doubt on her belief that she has developed "subtler sympathies" due to her "long contact with suffering"?

ASK STUDENTS to return to their Short Response answer about the theme and revise it based on the class discussion.

CLOSE READING NOTES

Ode to a Large Tuna in the Market

Poem by Pablo Neruda

Why This Text

Students sometimes have difficulty analyzing what a symbol in a poem represents—the meaning it has beyond its literal meaning. With the help of the close-reading questions, students will identify details in the text that describe the fish—the subject of the poem. The results of their close reading and analysis will help students develop an understanding of how poets use symbols to represent abstract ideas and qualities.

Background Have students read the background information about the poet Pablo Neruda. Introduce the selection by pointing out to students that though the poet claims not to believe in symbols, many of his poems, including the one they are about to read, have as their subject a single object. Explain that by contemplating the object and describing it very carefully and unusually, the poet turns the object, which is real to him, into a symbol of ideas and universal qualities.

AS YOU READ Tell students to pay close attention to the details the poet uses to describe the fish as well as the impact these word choices have on the meaning of the poem.

 Common Core Support

- cite strong and thorough textual evidence
- determine the meanings of words and phrases in the text, including figurative meanings
- analyze how an author's choices contribute to structure and meaning, as well as aesthetic impact

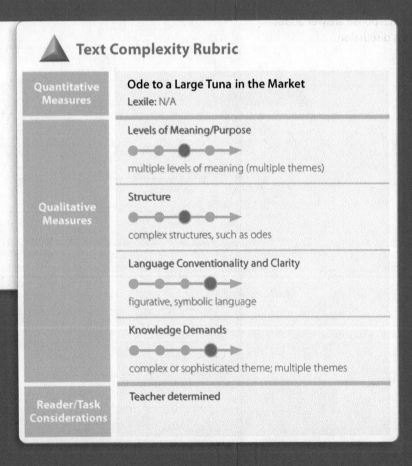

Text Complexity Rubric

Quantitative Measures	**Ode to a Large Tuna in the Market** **Lexile:** N/A
Qualitative Measures	**Levels of Meaning/Purpose** multiple levels of meaning (multiple themes)
	Structure complex structures, such as odes
	Language Conventionality and Clarity figurative, symbolic language
	Knowledge Demands complex or sophisticated theme; multiple themes
Reader/Task Considerations	Teacher determined

Strategies for CLOSE READING

Analyze Structure: Symbol

Students should read the poem closely, paying special attention to words the poet uses to describe the fish. Close-reading questions will help students cite text evidence in order to determine the figurative meanings of words and phrases, including symbols. As they read, students should note in the margin words the poet uses to describe the tuna and the ocean.

WHEN STUDENTS STRUGGLE . . .

To help students analyze how the author uses figurative language and symbols to create meaning in the poem, have them work in small groups to fill out a chart like the one shown below.

CITE TEXT EVIDENCE For practice analyzing figurative language and symbolism, ask students to explain the effects that these words from the poem create for the reader.

Lines from the Poem	Symbolic Meaning of the Lines
"this torpedo from the ocean depths" (lines 3–5)	These words make the tuna seem to be a powerful force from a mysterious place.
"the unknown, the unfathomable darkness, the depths of the sea" (lines 18–21)	These words make the ocean seem like a dark, mysterious place that people cannot understand.

Background Pablo Neruda *(1904–1973) was a Chilean poet who won the Nobel Prize for Literature in 1971. His book Odas Elementals (Elementary Odes) consists of poems that delve into everyday things, often things that do not readily seem to be inspirations for poetry. Neruda has written odes to his socks, salt, and the atom, as well as the large tuna you will read about here. The odes are written for everyday people, with a form and language that are simple and clear. In a 1970 interview with The Paris Review, Neruda said, "I don't believe in symbols. They are simply material things. The sea, fish, birds exist for me in a material way."*

Ode to a Large Tuna in the Market

Poem by Pablo Neruda

CLOSE READ
Notes

1. **READ ▷** As you read lines 1–14, begin to collect and cite text evidence.

- Underline the first word of the poem.
- Circle figurative language that describes the tuna and the market vegetables.
- In the margin, explain the impact of the descriptions in lines 1–10.

A Here,
among the market vegetables,
this (torpedo)
from the ocean
5 depths,
a (missile)
that swam,
now
lying in front of me
10 dead.

Describing the fish as a "torpedo" and a "missile" makes it seem powerful and deadly.

105

---

1. **READ AND CITE TEXT EVIDENCE**

A ASK STUDENTS to identify the words used to describe the tuna as it was alive and as it is now in the market. *Possible response: Students should identify "torpedo from the ocean depths" (lines 3–5) and "a missile that swam" (lines 6–7) as descriptions of the tuna alive. "Lying in front of me dead" (lines 9–10) describes the fish now.*

FOR ELL STUDENTS Spanish-speaking students will recognize the word *torpedo* because it has a Spanish cognate—*torpedo*—with the same meaning, "an underwater missile."

Only the tuna
has experience
of the deep
sea. **C**

Surrounded
by (the earth's green froth) **B**
—these lettuces,
bunches of carrots—
15 only you
lived through
the sea's truth, survived
the unknown, the
unfathomable
20 darkness, the depths
of the sea,
the great
abyss,
le grand abime,[1]
25 only you:
varnished
black-pitched
witness
to that deepest night.

varnish:
gloss

[1] **le grand abime:** French for "the large abyss."

30 Only you: **D**
dark bullet
barreled
from the depths,
carrying
35 only
your
one wound,
but resurgent,
always renewed,
40 locked into the current,
fins fletched[2]
like wings
in the torrent,
in the coursing
45 of
the
underwater
dark,
like a grieving arrow,
50 sea-javelin, a nerveless
oiled harpoon.

[2] **fletched:** feathered.

Dead
in front of me,
catafalqued[3] king
55 of my own ocean;
once **E**
sappy as a sprung fir
in (the green turmoil,)
once seed
60 to (sea-quake,)
(tidal wave,) now
simply
dead remains;
in the whole market
65 yours
was the only shape left
with purpose or direction
in this
jumbled ruin
70 of nature;

[3] **catafalque:** a platform used to support a coffin.

you are
a solitary man of war
among these frail vegetables,
your flanks and prow
75 black
and slippery
as if you were still
a well-oiled ship of the wind,
the only
80 true
machine
of the sea: unflawed,
undefiled,
navigating now
85 the waters of death. **F**

chaotic,
powerful,
dangerous

2. ◄ REREAD Reread lines 1–14. Analyze the contrast Neruda makes between the fish and the vegetables. Cite text evidence in your answer.

Describing the market vegetables as "earth's green froth" evokes water or sea foam, and reinforces the idea that the tuna is no longer a "missile" or a "torpedo" but is in a surreal new place.

3. READ ► As you read lines 15–51, continue to cite text evidence.
- Underline repeated phrases.
- In the margin, explain what makes the tuna unique.

4. ◄ REREAD Reread lines 15–51. How does Neruda continue to compare the tuna to a missile? Cite text evidence in your answer.

Neruda continues the comparison by evoking images of the tuna when it was alive as a "dark bullet . . . in the coursing of the underwater dark."

5. READ ► As you read lines 52–85, continue to cite text evidence.
- Circle text that describes the ocean.
- Underline text that describes the tuna.
- In the margin, write three adjectives describing Neruda's ocean.

2. REREAD AND CITE TEXT EVIDENCE

B ASK STUDENTS to identify words and phrases that describe and help them visualize the vegetables. *earth's green froth (line 12), lettuces (line 13), bunches of carrots (line 14)* Then have students identify the one word used to describe the vegetables that is similar to a word used to describe the ocean. *froth (line 12)*

3. READ AND CITE TEXT EVIDENCE

C ASK STUDENTS to explain what effect the repetition of the words *only you* has. *Possible response: The words set the tuna apart from everything else, including the speaker. They help create the sense of the tuna as mysterious and unique.*

Critical Vocabulary: varnish (line 26) Ask students to share their definitions of *varnish*. In the poem, *varnish* ends with *-ed* and acts as an adjective describing the fish. Ask students what the word helps them see about the fish. *The fish's skin is shiny.*

4. REREAD AND CITE TEXT EVIDENCE Have students identify words and phrases the speaker uses to describe the tuna when it was alive in the ocean. *dark bullet (line 31), grieving arrow (line 49), sea-javelin (line 50), nerveless oiled harpoon (lines 50–51)*

D ASK STUDENTS to describe how these words affect their understanding of what the tuna represents in the poem. *Possible response: The tuna is a sad, almost tragic, yet powerful force in nature.*

5. READ AND CITE TEXT EVIDENCE Encourage students to compare and contrast the words and phrases used to describe the living tuna with those used to describe it dead in the market.

E ASK STUDENTS to explain the effect that the repetition of the word *once* has in the poem. *Possible response: The word once reminds the reader that the tuna had once been a live, powerful force that is not dead and motionless.*

CLOSE READ
Notes

6. ◀ REREAD What are "the waters of death" that Neruda mentions in the last line of the poem? In what way is this description ironic? Cite text evidence in your explanation.

The "waters of death" are the "frail vegetables," the "jumbled ruin of nature" around the dead tuna. This description is ironic because the tuna was once alive in the water.

SHORT RESPONSE

Cite Text Evidence In the Background section, you read that Neruda does not "believe in symbols." What do you think the tuna means to him? Review your reading notes, and remember to **cite text evidence** in your response.

The images Neruda chooses to describe or characterize the tuna are carefully selected. There are objects that are related to the military and to hunting: torpedo, missile, man of war, arrow, javelin, harpoon. There are images of virility: "sappy as a sprung fir," "seed to sea-quake," and "solitary man of war." Through his choices, Neruda creates a symbol of virility, power, and life in the tuna and ties it to himself with the phrase "my own ocean." The tuna is a symbol of life.

108

TO CHALLENGE STUDENTS . . .

Through translations, Pablo Neruda's poems became very popular in this country in the 1960s and 1970s. Neruda was, however, a political activist in his native Chile, as well as a poet.

ASK STUDENTS to research the political causes that Neruda supported in his native country of Chile. Point out to students that though Neruda once said in a radio interview, "I insist on telling you that I am not a political poet," he may not have been entirely forthcoming. In fact, controversy about the cause of his death exists to this day. Some people claim that he was murdered by the Chilean government in power at the time. Have students work in small groups to explore Neruda's political beliefs, the Chilean government during the 1970s, and the circumstances of his death. Groups can present their findings and compare their interpretations of Neruda's beliefs and politics.

DIG DEEPER

With the class, return to Question 6, Reread. Have students share and discuss their answers.

ASK STUDENTS to note whether they think the ending is ironic or not ironic. Have students cite evidence from the text to support their thinking.

- Have students discuss the language the poet uses to describe the tuna throughout the poem.

- Have students compare and contrast the descriptions of the tuna in the first part of the poem with those at the end of the poem. How are the descriptions similar? How are they different?

- Have students compare and contrast the descriptions of the ocean in the first part of the poem with the image of the ocean in the last lines.

ASK STUDENTS to return to their response to the Short Response question and revise it based on the class discussion.

---

6. REREAD AND CITE TEXT EVIDENCE Emphasize that there is no strictly right or wrong interpretation of the final lines of the poem.

🅕 **ASK STUDENTS** to cite text evidence that expresses the tuna's place in "the waters of death." *"a solitary man of war" (line 72), "a well-oiled ship of the wind" (line 78), "the only true machine of the sea" (lines 79–82)*

SHORT RESPONSE

Cite Text Evidence Students' responses will vary, but they should cite evidence from the text to support their answers. Students should:

- include words and phrases from the text that describe the tuna.
- explain in their own words what they think the tuna symbolizes.
- cite other specific evidence from the text to support their ideas.

The Modern World

The Modern World

"Everybody gets so much information all
day long that they lose their common sense."

—Gertrude Stein

SHORT STORY

Ambush

Tim O'Brien

Selections from the Harlem Renaissance

ESSAY

How It Feels to Be Colored Me

Zora Neale Hurston

POEM

The Weary Blues

Langston Hughes

DRAMA

from The Crucible

Arthur Miller

ESSAY

Science, Guided by Ethics

Freeman Dyson

Ambush

Short Story by Tim O'Brien

Why This Text

Students reading literature about war may have a hard time relating to characters who are immersed in a world that is starkly alien to them. They may have a hard time understanding the motivations that drive characters in the middle of war. With the help of the close-reading questions, students will analyze the story's elements, including the emotional struggles of the main character. This close reading will lead students to understand the character's motivation behind a story from his past.

Background Have students read the background and information about the author. Introduce the story by pointing out the ambiguity at its core: as with the rest of the stories in *The Things They Carried*, the main character is Tim O'Brien, who fought in Vietnam like the author did, and who, years later, writes about the war, as the author does. Although the story is fictional, it is driven by some of the author's own experiences.

AS YOU READ Ask students to pay attention to the narrator's statements, feelings, and reactions to events. How do they help the reader understand the narrator's motivation?

Common Core Support

- cite strong and thorough textual evidence
- analyze the impact of an author's choices on story elements, including character motivation
- determine the meaning of words

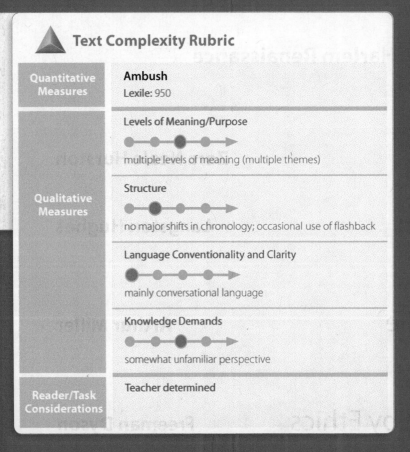

Text Complexity Rubric

	Ambush
Quantitative Measures	**Lexile:** 950

Qualitative Measures

Levels of Meaning/Purpose
multiple levels of meaning (multiple themes)

Structure
no major shifts in chronology; occasional use of flashback

Language Conventionality and Clarity
mainly conversational language

Knowledge Demands
somewhat unfamiliar perspective

Reader/Task Considerations
Teacher determined

Strategies for CLOSE READING

Analyze Story Elements: Motivation

Students should read this story carefully all the way through. Close-reading questions at the bottom of the page will help them focus on a thorough analysis of story elements, including the motivations of the main character. As they read, students should jot down comments or questions about the text in the margins.

WHEN STUDENTS STRUGGLE . . .

To help students analyze the narrator's motivation in "Ambush," have them work in small groups to fill out a chart like the one shown below.

CITE TEXT EVIDENCE For practice analyzing a character's motivation, ask students to cite text evidence and then interpret what it reveals about the character's motivation.

Text Evidence	What It Reveals About the Character's Motivation
"Someday, I hope, she'll ask again." (line 6)	The narrator wants a chance to tell the truth.
"This is why I keep writing war stories . . ." (line 9)	The narrator writes to try to resolve his feelings.
"I did not hate the young man; I did not see him as the enemy . . ." (lines 35–36)	The narrator felt he must kill the man but could not really justify it.
"The grenade was to make him go away . . ." (lines 39–40)	The narrator wanted the situation to disappear.
"I wanted to warn him." (line 50)	The narrator regrets what he has done; he wishes he could save the man.

Background Tim O'Brien's *military experience in Vietnam provides much of the material for his fiction and personal narratives. In 1990, O'Brien published* The Things They Carried, *a remarkable fictional memoir about the Vietnam War and its human effects. The book is made up of interconnected stories narrated by a character named Tim O'Brien, who, the author says, is not himself. "Ambush" comes from that collection.*

Ambush

Short Story by Tim O'Brien

CLOSE READ
Notes

1. **READD** ▶ As you read lines 1–13, begin to collect and cite text evidence.
 • Underline text that explains why the narrator is telling this story.
 • Circle text that explains why the narrator continues to write war stories.

A B When she was nine, my daughter Kathleen asked if I had ever killed anyone. She knew about the war; she knew I'd been a soldier. "You keep writing these war stories," she said, "so I guess you must've killed somebody." It was a difficult moment, but I did what seemed right, which was to say, "Of course not," and then to take her onto my lap and hold her for a while. Someday, I hope, she'll ask again. But here I want to pretend she's a grown-up. I want to tell her exactly what happened, or what I remember happening, and then I want to say to her that as a little girl she was absolutely right. This is why I keep writing war stories:

10 He was a short, slender young man of about twenty. I was afraid of him—afraid of something—and as he passed me on the trail I threw a grenade that exploded at his feet and killed him.

Or to go back:

Kathleen asks if he has killed anyone.

He says no.

He hopes she'll ask again.

2. **◀ REREAD** As you reread lines 1–9, make notes in the margin about Kathleen's question, the narrator's answer at the time, and the narrator's desire to explain more.

111

---

1. **READ AND CITE TEXT EVIDENCE**

A **ASK STUDENTS** to make an inference about the narrator based on his conversation with his daughter in lines 1–9. *Students may say that the narrator seems like he is thoughtful and loves his daughter. He wants to protect her by not telling the truth about his experiences because he thinks she's too young, but also hopes he will have a chance to tell her the truth when she's older.*

2. **REREAD AND CITE TEXT EVIDENCE**

B **ASK STUDENTS** to summarize the narrator's conversation with his daughter. *Students should note that Kathleen wants to know if he has killed anyone (lines 1–2), the narrator says "no" (line 5), and then he hopes that he can tell her the truth someday (lines 6–9).*

CLOSE READ
Notes

Shortly after midnight we moved into the ambush site outside My Khe. The whole platoon was there, spread out in the dense brush along the trail, and for five hours nothing at all happened. We were working in two-man teams—one man on guard while the other slept, switching off every two hours—and I remember it was still dark when Kiowa shook me awake for the final watch. The night was foggy and hot. For the first few moments I felt lost, not sure about directions, groping for my helmet and weapon. I reached out and found three grenades and lined them up in front of me; the pins had already been straightened for quick throwing. And then for maybe half an hour I kneeled there and waited. Very gradually, in tiny slivers, dawn began to break through the fog, and, from my position in the brush I could see ten or fifteen meters up the trail. The mosquitoes were fierce. I remember slapping at them, wondering if I should wake up Kiowa and ask for some repellent, then thinking it was a bad idea, then looking up and seeing the young man come out of the fog. He wore black clothing and rubber sandals and a gray ammunition belt. His shoulders were slightly stooped, his head **cocked** to the side as if listening for something. He seemed at ease. He carried his weapon in one hand, muzzle down, moving without any hurry up the center of the trail. There was no sound at all—none that I can remember. In a way, it seemed, he was part of the morning fog, or my own imagination, but there was also the reality of what was happening in my stomach. I had already pulled the pin on a grenade. I had come up to a crouch. It was entirely automatic. I did not hate the young man; **I did not see him as the enemy; I did not ponder issues of morality or politics or military duty. I crouched and kept my head low. I tried to swallow whatever was rising from my stomach, which tasted like lemonade, something fruity and sour. I was terrified.** There were no thoughts about killing. The grenade was to make him go away—just evaporate—and I leaned back and felt my head go empty and then felt it fill up again. I had already thrown the grenade before telling myself to throw it. The brush was thick and I had to lob it high, not aiming, and I remember the grenade seeming to freeze above me for an instant,

cocked:
tilted

3. **READ** ▶ As you read lines 14–71, continue to cite text evidence.

- Underline text describing the narrator's feelings.
- Circle text where the narrator says "I remember" in his story.
- In the margin, make an inference about how the narrator feels after he throws the grenade (lines 39–55).

CLOSE READ
Notes

> "For me, it was not a matter of live or die. I was in no real peril."

as if a camera had clicked, and I remember ducking down and holding my breath and seeing little wisps of fog rise from the earth. The grenade bounced once and rolled across the trail. I did not hear, it but there must have been a sound, because the young man dropped his weapon and began to run, just two or three quick steps, then he hesitated, swiveling to his right, and he glanced down at the grenade and tried to cover his head but never did. It occurred to me then that he was about to die. I wanted to warn him. The grenade made a popping noise—not soft but not loud either—not what I'd expected—and there was a puff of dust and smoke—a small white puff—and the young man seemed to jerk upward as if pulled by invisible wires. He fell on his back. His rubber sandals had been blown off. He lay at the center of the trail, his right leg beneath him, his one eye shut, his other eye a huge star-shaped hole.

For me, it was not a matter of live or die. I was in no real **peril**. Almost certainly the young man would have passed me by. And it will always be that way.

Later, I remember Kiowa tried to tell me that the man would've died anyway. He told me that it was a good kill, that I was a soldier and this was a war, that I should shape up and stop staring and ask myself what the dead man would've done if things were reversed.

None of it mattered. The words seemed far too complicated. All I could do was **gape** at the fact of the young man's body.

He is stunned and shocked.

peril:
danger

gape:
stare, with open mouth

---

3. **READ AND CITE TEXT EVIDENCE**

C **ASK STUDENTS** to find and cite text evidence for the narrator's feelings on the morning of the killing. *Students should mention the narrator's feeling "lost, not sure about directions" (lines 19–20); his "wondering" if he should wake Kiowa up to get some repellent (lines 25–27); the "reality" of what was happening in his stomach (lines 33–34); his terror (line 39); he felt his head "go empty" and then "fill up again" (lines 40–41); and his wanting to warn the young man before the grenade exploded (line 50).*

Critical Vocabulary: cocked (line 29) Have students share their definitions of *cocked*, and ask volunteers to use the word in a sentence.

Critical Vocabulary: peril (line 56) Have students suggest synonyms for the noun *peril* that would work in this context. risk, trouble, jeopardy

Critical Vocabulary: gape (line 64) Have students share their definitions of *gape*. How did the narrator look at the young man's body? *He could only gape—he stared with an open mouth.*

FOR ELL STUDENTS Tell students that the verb *duck* (line 44) has nothing to do with water birds. Ask students to infer the meaning from the context. Ducking down *must mean "lowering your head to avoid being seen or hit by something."*

D Even now I haven't finished sorting it out. Sometimes I forgive myself, other times I don't. In the ordinary hours of life I try not to dwell on it, but now and then, when I'm reading a newspaper or just sitting alone in a room, I'll look up and see the young man step out of the morning fog. I'll watch him walk toward me, his shoulders slightly stooped, his head cocked to the side,

70 and he'll pass within a few yards of me and suddenly smile at some secret thought and then continue up the trail to where it bends back into the fog.

4. **◄ REREAD** Reread lines 65–71. How does the vision the narrator imagines in these lines help resolve his conflict?

The narrator's vision at the end of the story allows him to imagine that he did not throw the grenade, and that the solider continued up the trail unharmed. It helps relieve the guilt he feels for killing the soldier.

SHORT RESPONSE

Cite Text Evidence What is the narrator's motivation for telling this story? Take into consideration that he doesn't tell his daughter the truth. What conclusions can you draw about the narrator? Review your reading notes, and be sure to **cite text evidence** in your response.

The narrator tells the story because he knows he must tell his daughter the truth someday. The beginning and ending of the story frame the narrator's actual experiences in Vietnam. We know he is still very much affected by his actions there. As he tells the story, he explains his actions more than his emotions. He writes war stories to try to resolve his conflicting feelings about the war.

114

---

4. **REREAD AND CITE TEXT EVIDENCE**

D ASK STUDENTS to infer how the narrator feels about the young man's death. *Students can infer that the narrator is deeply troubled and is still not sure whether he was justified in killing him. Sometimes he forgives himself, other times he doesn't (lines 65–66).*

SHORT RESPONSE

Cite Text Evidence Students' responses should include text evidence that supports their positions. They should:

- describe the narrator's motivation.
- cite evidence of the narrator's motivation.
- make inferences about the narrator's character.

TO CHALLENGE STUDENTS . . .

For more context on an American soldier's life in Vietnam during the war, students can view the video "On Patrol" in their eBooks.

ASK STUDENTS how the portrayals of the life of a soldier in Vietnam in the video and in the short story were similar and how they differed. *Both presentations showed a similar setting, though the story took place at night. The dangers and the conditions were similar in both media. In the story, the soldiers were spread out in groups of two, whereas in the video, the soldiers were generally in larger groups.*

DIG DEEPER

With the class, return to Question 4, Reread. Have students share their responses to the question.

ASK STUDENTS about the beginning and end of the story.

- Have students discuss the opening scene and its tone. *The narrator is with his nine-year-old daughter, who asks him if he killed someone in Vietnam. Despite the question, the tone is peaceful and loving—the narrator does "what seemed right," holds his daughter in his lap, and tells her a lie.*

- Have students compare and contrast the opening and closing scenes. *The story begins and ends in the present—far from Vietnam—and on a similar note. When the story begins, the narrator is talking to his young daughter, a conversation that spurs his memories. When the story ends, he is "reading a newspaper or just sitting alone," now imagining that the young man is still alive with a smile on his face.*

ASK STUDENTS to return to their Short Response answer and revise it based on the class discussion.

The Harlem Renaissance

How It Feels to Be Colored Me

Essay by Zora Neale Hurston

The Weary Blues

Poem by Langston Hughes

Why These Texts

Students may have difficulty appreciating foundational works without understanding the context in which they were written. With the help of the close-reading questions, students will identify details that help clarify the context and express the themes addressed by both writers. This close reading will lead students to develop an understanding of these two key works from the Harlem Renaissance.

Background Have students read the background about the Harlem Renaissance and the biographical information about the writers. Tell students that they are going to read an essay that describes Zora Neale Hurston's experience as an African American, first as a young girl in the South and later as a woman in New York City. Then they will read a poem by Langston Hughes about a jazz singer in Harlem in the 1920s.

AS YOU READ Ask students to pay attention to how both writers use figurative language to describe their subjects. What themes were especially relevant to African Americans early in the twentieth century?

Common Core Support

- cite strong and thorough textual evidence
- determine the meaning of words and phrases, including figurative and connotative meanings
- analyze how an author's choices concerning text structure contribute to a text's meaning and aesthetic impact
- demonstrate knowledge of early twentieth-century foundational texts

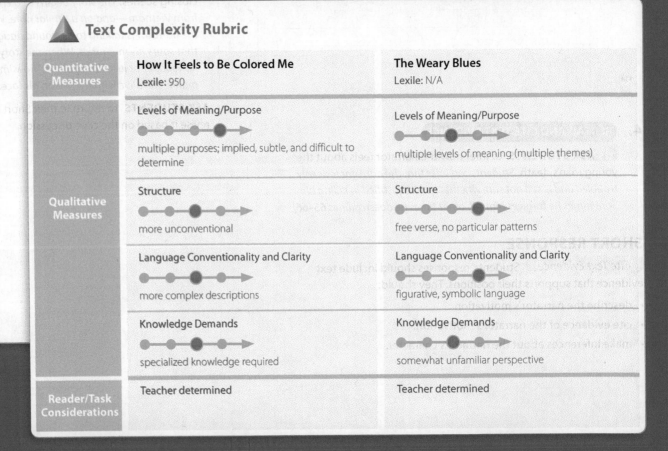

Text Complexity Rubric

	How It Feels to Be Colored Me	The Weary Blues
Quantitative Measures	Lexile: 950	Lexile: N/A
Qualitative Measures	**Levels of Meaning/Purpose** — multiple purposes; implied, subtle, and difficult to determine	**Levels of Meaning/Purpose** — multiple levels of meaning (multiple themes)
	Structure — more unconventional	**Structure** — free verse, no particular patterns
	Language Conventionality and Clarity — more complex descriptions	**Language Conventionality and Clarity** — figurative, symbolic language
	Knowledge Demands — specialized knowledge required	**Knowledge Demands** — somewhat unfamiliar perspective
Reader/Task Considerations	Teacher determined	Teacher determined

Strategies for CLOSE READING

Demonstrate Knowledge of Foundational Works

Students should read the essay and poem carefully all the way through. Close-reading questions at the bottom of the page will help them identify details, including figurative and connotative language, that express the themes of these texts. As they read, students should jot down comments or questions about the text in the margins.

WHEN STUDENTS STRUGGLE...

To help students demonstrate knowledge of foundational works, have them work in small groups to fill out a chart like the one shown below.

CITE TEXT EVIDENCE For practice analyzing foundational works, ask students to cite text evidence that provides details of life as an African American in the United States during the early twentieth century.

"How It Feels to Be Colored Me"

Topic	Theme	Text Evidence
childhood in a small southern town	A young girl was not defined by her race.	"I'd wave at them and when they returned my salute, I would say something like this: 'Howdy-do-well-I-thank-you-where-you-goin'?'" (lines 17–19)
being an adult in the outside world	People are often defined by race.	"In my heart as well as in the mirror, I became a fast brown . . ." (lines 38–39)

"The Weary Blues"

Topic	Theme	Text Evidence
musician playing blues in Harlem	Blues expresses both sadness and beauty.	"He played that sad raggy tune like a musical fool./Sweet Blues!" (lines 13–14)

Background In the early 1920s, African American artists, writers, musicians, and performers were part of a great cultural movement known as the Harlem Renaissance. The huge migration to the north after World War I brought African Americans of all ages and walks of life to the thriving New York City neighborhood called Harlem. Black men and women drew on their own cultural resources—their folk traditions as well as a new urban awareness—to produce unique forms of expression. These young black writers were the founders of a new era in literature. Looking inward, they expressed what it meant to be black in a white-dominated world.

Selections from

The Harlem Renaissance

How It Feels to Be Colored Me . . . . . . Essay by Zora Neale Hurston

The Weary Blues . . . . Poem by Langston Hughes

Zora Neale Hurston (1891–1960) grew up in the all-black town of Eatonville, Florida. Hurston was 13 when her family fell apart: her mother died, her father remarried, and by the age of 14, Hurston was on her own. In 1925, she moved to New York to study anthropology. Encouraged by her professors, she returned to the South to collect African American folklore, which she published in the collection Mules and Men. Sadly, her work fell out of favor in the 1940s, and Hurston died poor and nearly forgotten.

Langston Hughes (1902–1967) was one of the leading poets of the Harlem Renaissance. On a March night in 1922, Hughes sat in a small Harlem cabaret and wrote "The Weary Blues." In this poem, he incorporated the many elements of his life—the music of Southern black speech, the lyrics of the first blues he heard, and traditional poetic forms he learned in school. While the body of the poem took shape quickly, it took Hughes two years to get the ending right.

CLOSE READ
Notes

1. **READ** ▶ As you read lines 1–25, begin to collect and cite text evidence.

- Underline text that is comic or ironic.
- Circle the extended metaphor in lines 14–17.
- In the margin, explain her description of the Northerners in lines 4–13.

How It Feels to Be Colored Me
Essay by Zora Neale Hurston

extenuating:

lessening the severity of

The Northerners were a spectacle to be "peered at cautiously"

I am colored but I offer nothing in the way of **extenuating** circumstances except the fact that I am the only Negro in the United States whose grandfather on the mother's side was *not* an Indian chief.

I remember the very day that I became colored. Up to my thirteenth year I lived in the little Negro town of Eatonville, Florida. It is exclusively a colored town. The only white people I knew passed through the town going to or coming from Orlando. The native whites rode dusty horses, the Northern tourists chugged down the sandy village road in automobiles. The town knew the Southerners and never stopped cane chewing when they passed. But the Northerners were something else again. They were peered at cautiously from behind curtains by the timid. The more venturesome would come out on the porch to watch them go past and got just as much pleasure out of the tourists as the tourists got out of the village.

The front porch might seem a daring place for the rest of the town, but it was a gallery seat to me. My favorite place was atop the gate-post. Proscenium box for a born first-nighter.[1] Not only did I enjoy the show, but I didn't mind the actors knowing that I liked it. I actually spoke to them in passing. I'd wave at them and when they returned my salute, I would say something like this: "Howdy-do-well-I-thank-you-where-you-goin'?" Usually automobile or the horse paused at this, and after a queer exchange of compliments, I would probably "go a piece of the way" with them, as we say in farthest Florida. If one of my family happened to come to the front in time to see me, of course negotiations would be rudely broken off. But even so, it is clear that I was the first "welcome-to-our-state" Floridian, and I hope the Miami Chamber of Commerce will please take notice.

[1] **proscenium . . . first-nighter:** A proscenium box is a box near the stage. A first-nighter is a person who attends the opening night of a performance.

During this period, white people differed from colored to me only in that they rode through town and never lived there. They liked to hear me "speak pieces" and sing and wanted to see me dance the parse-me-la,[2] and gave me generously of their small silver for doing these things, which seemed strange to me for I wanted to do them so much that I needed bribing to stop. Only they didn't know it. The colored people gave no dimes. They **deplored** any joyful tendencies in me, but I was their Zora nevertheless. I belonged to them, to the nearby hotels, to the county—everybody's Zora.

But changes came in the family when I was thirteen, and I was sent to school in Jacksonville. I left Eatonville, the town of the oleanders,[3] as Zora. When I disembarked from the riverboat at Jacksonville, she was no more. It seemed that I had suffered a sea change.[4] I was not Zora of Orange County any more, I was now a little colored girl. I found it out in certain ways. In my heart as well as in the mirror, I became a fast brown—warranted not to rub nor run.

But I am not tragically colored. There is no great sorrow dammed up in my soul, nor lurking behind my eyes. I do not mind at all. I do not belong to the sobbing school of Negrohood who hold that nature somehow has given them a low-down dirty deal and whose feelings are all hurt about it. Even in the helter-skelter skirmish that is my life, I have seen that the world is to the strong regardless of a little pigmentation more or less. No, I do not weep at the world—I am too busy sharpening my oyster knife.[5]

deplore:

to strongly disapprove

Away from her home, she notices her own color for the first time.

[2] **parse-me-la:** a dance movement popular with Southern African Americans of the period.
[3] **oleanders:** evergreen shrubs with fragrant flowers.
[4] **sea change:** a complete transformation.
[5] **oyster knife:** a reference to the saying "The world is my oyster," implying that the world contains treasure waiting to be taken, like the pearl in an oyster.

2. **◀ REREAD** Reread lines 4–25. Explain the extended metaphor. What can you infer about Hurston's character in these lines?

The extended metaphor compares the front porch to a "gallery seat." Her interactions with the northern tourists were staged—funny and harmless. Although she pokes fun at her younger self, she also shows a girl who is curious, self-confident, and fearless.

3. **READ** ▶ As you read lines 26–46, continue to cite text evidence.

- Underline text describing the differences between whites and blacks.
- In the margin, summarize how Zora becomes "a little colored girl."

---

1. **READ AND CITE TEXT EVIDENCE** Remind students that a metaphor is a form of figurative language in which one thing is compared to another.

Ⓐ ASK STUDENTS to identify details in lines 14–17 that help them understand that the author is comparing her front porch to a theater. *gallery seat, proscenium box, first-nighter, actors*

Critical Vocabulary: extenuating (line 1) Have students share their definitions of *extenuating*. Ask students to define *extenuating circumstances.* *"special circumstances that account for an irregular or improper way of doing something"*

2. **REREAD AND CITE TEXT EVIDENCE** Remind students that they have identified details in lines 14–17 that they can use to describe the extended metaphor.

Ⓑ ASK STUDENTS to identify evidence in the text that tells what Hurston was like as a young girl. *". . . I didn't mind the actors knowing that I liked it. I actually spoke to them . . ." (lines 16–17); "Howdy-do-well-I-thank-you-where-you-going?" (line 19); ". . . I would probably 'go a piece of the way' with them . . ." (lines 20–21)*

3. **READ AND CITE TEXT EVIDENCE**

Ⓒ ASK STUDENTS to identify details in lines 34–39 that help them understand the change that occurred in Hurston on the trip from Eatonville to Jacksonville. *Students should cite evidence from lines 38–39.*

Critical Vocabulary: deplore (line 31) Ask students why the older people deplored Zora's joyful tendencies.

D Someone is always at my elbow reminding me that I am the grand-daughter of slaves. It fails to register depression with me. Slavery is sixty years in the past. The operation was successful and the patient is doing well, thank
50 you. The terrible struggle that made me an American out of a potential slave said "On the line!" The Reconstruction said "Get set!"; and the generation before said "Go!" I am off to a flying start and I must not halt in the stretch to look behind and weep. Slavery is the price I paid for civilization, and the choice was not with me. It is a bully adventure and worth all that I have paid through my ancestors for it. No one on earth ever had a greater chance for glory. The world to be won and nothing to be lost. It is thrilling to think—to know that for any act of mine, I shall get twice as much praise or twice as much blame. It is quite exciting to hold the center of the national stage, with the spectators not knowing whether to laugh or to weep.
60   The position of my white neighbor is much more difficult. No brown **specter** pulls up a chair beside me when I sit down to eat. No dark ghost thrusts its leg against mine in bed. The game of keeping what one has is never so exciting as the game of getting.
    I do not always feel colored. Even now I often achieve the unconscious Zora of Eatonville before the Hegira.[6] I feel most colored when I am thrown against a sharp white background.
    For instance at Barnard. "Beside the waters of the Hudson"[7] I feel my race. Among the thousand white persons, I am a dark rock surged upon, overswept by a creamy sea. I am surged upon and overswept, but through it all, I remain
70 myself. When covered by the waters, I am; and the ebb but reveals me again.
    Sometimes it is the other way around. A white person is set down in our midst, but the contrast is just as sharp for me. For instance, when I sit in the drafty basement that is The New World Cabaret with a white person, my color comes. We enter chatting about any little nothing that we have in common and are seated by the jazz waiters. In the abrupt way that jazz orchestras have, this

specter:
ghost

She says slavery is in the past. Now she has a chance for victory, "the world to be won."

---
[6] **Hegira:** journey (from the name given to Muhammad's journey from Mecca to Medina in 622).
[7] **Barnard . . . Hudson:** Barnard is the college in New York City from which Hurston graduated in 1928. "Beside the water . . ." is a reference to the first line of the college song. The college is located near the Hudson River.

---

4. **READ ▶** As you read lines 47–94, continue to cite text evidence.
   • Underline examples of repetition in lines 47–59.
   • Circle words and phrases that show the transformative power of the jazz music in lines 71–88.
   • In the margin, summarize what Hurston says about slavery.

E one plunges into a number. It loses no time in **circumlocutions**, but gets right down to business. It constricts the thorax and splits the heart with its tempo and narcotic harmonies. This orchestra grows rambunctious, rears on its hind legs and attacks the tonal veil with primitive fury, rending it, clawing it until it
80 breaks through to the jungle beyond. I follow those heathen—follow them exultingly. I dance wildly inside myself; I yell within, I whoop; I shake my assegai[8] above my head, I hurl it true to the mark *yeeeeoooww*! I am in the jungle and living in the jungle way. My face is painted red and yellow, and my body is painted blue. My pulse is throbbing like a war drum. I want to slaughter something—give pain, give death to what, I do not know. But the piece ends. The men of the orchestra wipe their lips and rest their fingers. I creep back slowly to the **veneer** we call civilization with the last tone and find the white friend sitting motionless in his seat, smoking calmly.
    "Good music they have here," he remarks, drumming the table with his
90 fingertips.
    Music! The great blobs of purple and red emotion have not touched him. He has only heard what I felt. He is far away and I see him but dimly across the ocean and the continent that have fallen between us. He is so pale with his whiteness then and I am *so* colored.
    At certain times I have no race, I am *me*. When I set my hat at a certain angle and saunter down Seventh Avenue, Harlem City, feeling as snooty as the lions in front of the Forty-Second Street Library, for instance. So far as my

circumlocutions:
roundabout expressions that serve to avoid the main point

veneer:
a deceptive outer covering; facade

---
[8] **assegai:** a type of light spear used in southern Africa.

---

5. **◀ REREAD** Reread lines 71–94. How is Hurston affected by the jazz performance? What does it reveal about her?

The music pulls her powerfully into a colorful, raw, primitive jungle, bringing out the "heathen" in her. She is made aware of how "colored" she is compared to her white friend who experienced the music in a completely different way.

6. **READ ▶** As you read lines 95–120, continue to cite text evidence.
   • Underline text that shows Hurston's pride and positive feelings about herself.
   • In the margin, summarize why people are like "bags of miscellany" (lines 108–120).

---

4. **READ AND CITE TEXT EVIDENCE**

D **ASK STUDENTS** to find details in lines 47–56 that help them understand Hurston's thoughts about slavery. *"Slavery is sixty years in the past." (lines 48–49); ". . . the patient is doing well . . ." (line 49); "The terrible struggle that made me an American out of a potential slave . . ." (line 50); "The world to be won and nothing to be lost." (lines 55–56)*

Critical Vocabulary: specter (line 61) Have students share their definitions of *specter* and identify the context clue that could help them figure out the meaning. ghost *in line 61* Ask students why Hurston thinks white people might feel haunted by the specter of a black person. *They feel guilty about how African Americans were treated in the past.*

FOR ELL STUDENTS Explain that the word *bully* (line 54) has more than one meaning. As a noun, it means "someone who is cruel to others, especially those smaller and weaker." Here, as an adjective, *bully* means "excellent, splendid."

5. **REREAD AND CITE TEXT EVIDENCE**

E **ASK STUDENTS** to share the details they underlined that describe Hurston's experience and that of her white friend at the jazz club. *Students should emphasize that Hurston's experience was more powerful and primal than that of her friend.*

6. **READ AND CITE TEXT EVIDENCE**

F **ASK STUDENTS** to work with a partner to identify details in lines 108–120 that can help them understand why people are like "bags of miscellany."

Critical Vocabulary: circumlocutions (line 76) Ask students to share their definitions.

Critical Vocabulary: veneer (line 87) Ask students how the word *veneer* fits in with Hurston's experience. *As she listened to the music, she broke through the veneer, or deceptive facade, of polite civilization.*

(Page 120)

raiment:
clothing

feelings are concerned, Peggy Hopkins Joyce on the Boule Mich[9] with her gorgeous **raiment**, stately carriage, knees knocking together in a most aristocratic manner, has nothing on me. The cosmic Zora emerges. I belong to no race nor time; I am the eternal feminine with its string of beads.

I have no separate feeling about being an American citizen and colored. I am merely a fragment of the Great Soul that surges within the boundaries. My country, right or wrong.

Sometimes, I feel discriminated against, but it does not make me angry. It merely astonishes me. How *can* any deny themselves the pleasure of my company! It's beyond me.

miscellany:
a collection of various items

People are all different, like bags filled with random treasure.

But in the main, I feel like a brown bag of **miscellany** propped against a wall. Against a wall in company with other bags, white, red, and yellow. Pour out the contents, and there is discovered a jumble of small things priceless and worthless. A first-water[10] diamond, an empty spool, bits of broken glass, lengths of string, a key to a door long since crumbled away, a rusty knife-blade, old shoes saved for a road that never was and never will be, a nail bent under the weight of things too heavy for any nail, a dried flower or two, still a little fragrant. In your hand is the brown bag. On the ground before you is the jumble it held—so much like the jumble in the bags, could they be emptied, that all might be dumped in a single heap and the bags refilled without altering the content of any greatly. A bit of colored glass more or less would not matter. Perhaps that is how the Great Stuffer of Bags filled them in the first place—who knows?

[9] **Peggy . . . Boule Mich:** a wealthy woman of Hurston's day, walking along the Boulevard Saint-Michel in Paris.
[10] **first-water:** of the highest quality or purity.

7. **REREAD** Reread lines 108–120. What does Hurston's statement about "bags" say about human character?

Hurston believes each person is a jumble of content. While people often say that people's characters distinguish them from each other, Hurston points out that the random and diverse nature of the content of our characters is something that makes us all alike.

(Page 121)

8. **READ** As you read "The Weary Blues," continue to cite text evidence.
- Underline pairs of words with alliteration within a line.
- Circle the words or phrases describing sadness or defeat.

The Weary Blues
Poem by Langston Hughes

croon:
a low, soft voice

pallor:
lack of color

Droning a drowsy syncopated[11] tune,
Rocking back and forth to a mellow **croon**,
   I heard a Negro play.
Down on Lenox Avenue[12] the other night
5 By the pale dull **pallor** of an old gas light
   He did a lazy sway. . . .
   He did a lazy sway. . . .
To the tune o' those Weary Blues
With his ebony hands on each ivory key
10 He made that poor piano moan with melody.
   O Blues!
Swaying to and fro on his rickety stool
He played that sad raggy tune like a musical fool.
   Sweet Blues!
15 Coming from a black man's soul.
   O Blues!
In a deep song voice with a melancholy tone
I heard that Negro sing, that old piano moan—
   "Ain't got nobody in all this world,
20   Ain't got nobody but ma self.
   I's gwine to quit ma frownin
   And put ma troubles on the shelf."
Thump, thump, thump, went his foot on the floor.
He played a few chords then he sang some more—
25   "I got the Weary Blues
   And I can't be satisfied.
   Got the Weary Blues
   And can't be satisfied—

[11] **syncopated:** characterized by a shifting of stresses from normally strong to normally weak beats.
[12] **Lenox Avenue:** a main north-south street in Harlem.

---

7. REREAD AND CITE TEXT EVIDENCE

G **ASK STUDENTS** to work with a partner to identify evidence in the text that helps them understand how Hurston believes that people are like bags of miscellany. *". . . I feel like a brown bag of miscellany . . ." (line 108); ". . . other bags, white, red, and yellow." (line 109); ". . . how the Great Stuffer of Bags filled them . . ." (line 119)*

Critical Vocabulary: raiment (line 99) Ask students to name some specific articles of clothing that might qualify as a "gorgeous raiment." *Students might suggest expensive gowns or dresses, silk blouses, or fur coats.*

Critical Vocabulary: miscellany (line 108) Have students identify the various items in the miscellany Hurston describes. *diamond, thread spool, broken glass, string, key, knife blade, old shoes, nail, dried flower*

8. READ AND CITE TEXT EVIDENCE

Remind students that alliteration is the repetition of usually initial consonant sounds in two or more words that appear close together in a text.

H **ASK STUDENTS** to cite examples of repetition in lines 1–24. *Examples include "He did a lazy sway. . . " (lines 6, 7), "Thump, thump, thump" (line 23), and "Blues!" (lines 11, 14, and 16).*

Critical Vocabulary: croon (line 2) Have students share their definitions of *croon*. Then ask them how the word *croon* helps establish the mood of the poem and what it says about Harlem in the 1920s. *The word is in keeping with the sad or mellow mood of the night scene.*

Critical Vocabulary: pallor (line 5) Ask students what color they see in their mind's eye when they read line 5. *Students may suggest very pale or washed-out yellow.*

CLOSE READ
Notes

> I ain't happy no mo'
> 30   And I wish that I had died.
> And far into the night he crooned that tune.
> The stars went out and so did the moon.
> The singer stopped playing and went to bed
> While the Weary Blues echoed through his head.
> 35   He slept like a rock or a man that's dead

9.   **◄ REREAD** Hughes was one of the first innovators of "jazz poetry"—poetry with a jazz-like rhythm and feeling of improvisation. Reread the poem and then describe the effect of its rhythm and repetitions on your experience as a reader.

The rhythm of the poem changes as it shifts from the listener to the singer. The rhyme scheme is loose and unpredictable, like jazz music.

SHORT RESPONSE

Cite Text Evidence Discuss how Hurston's essay and Hughes's poem—in their subject matter, style, form, and content—exemplify the themes of the Harlem Renaissance. Review your reading notes, and **cite text evidence** in your response.

Both Hurston and Hughes focus on the African American experience at a specific place and time. They use dialect; they improvise with word choice, rhythm, pace, and tone; they are moved and thrilled by the power of African American musical forms (jazz and blues). Hurston, however, places her own life and experience at the center of her writing. She is relentlessly positive about herself, and that positivity rubs off on her view of race relations. Hughes's poem is an observation, from the outside, of a black musician. Although he depicts the music as profoundly powerful, the poem expresses an undeniable and pervasive melancholy.

122

9.   **REREAD AND CITE TEXT EVIDENCE**   Have students work with a partner to identify the words that rhyme throughout the poem and words and phrases that are repeated.

ⓘ **ASK STUDENTS** to explain what characteristics of the poem give it a feeling of improvisation, or being made up on the spot. *Students should mention the repetition of words and the changing, irregular rhyme schemes.*

SHORT RESPONSE

Cite Text Evidence   Students' responses will vary but should include evidence from the text that supports their answers. Students should:

- identify details in both the essay and the poem that relate to the Harlem Renaissance of the 1920s.
- address the subject matter, style, form, and content of the texts.
- explain how the experiences described in the two texts are alike and different.

TO CHALLENGE STUDENTS . . .

For more context, students can research the Harlem Renaissance online.

ASK STUDENTS to work in small groups to answer the following questions.

- Have students identify the causes for the migration of African Americans from the South to the northern cities of Chicago, Detroit, and New York.
- Have students describe the nature of the Harlem Renaissance and discuss the different arts that flourished in New York during the 1920s.
- Have students identify some of the major artists of the period as well as some of their accomplishments. (The cover of Langston Hughes's poetry book *The Weary Blues* is featured in the video.)
- Finally, have students identify the causes for the decline of the Harlem Renaissance and discuss its lasting significance.

DIG DEEPER

With the class, return to Question 5, Reread. Have students share and discuss their responses.

ASK STUDENTS to identify specific text evidence in lines 86–94 that helps them more fully understand the response of the white man with whom Hurston is sitting.

- Encourage students to identify details that describe what the man is doing when the music stops. *". . . sitting motionless in his seat, smoking calmly"*
- Have students discuss what the words *motionless* and *calmly* imply about the white man. *He has not been excited by the music in the way that Hurston was.*
- Have students cite evidence to explain how Hurston describes the white man in lines 91–94 and the conclusion she draws about their differences. *"The great blobs of purple and red emotion have not touched him." (line 91) "He is far away." (line 92) "He is so pale with his whiteness then and I am so colored." (lines 93–94)*

ASK STUDENTS to revise their Short Response answers using details from the class discussion.

from The Crucible

Drama by Arthur Miller

 For more historical context, students can view the video "Salem Witch Trials" in their eBooks.

Why This Text

Students may have difficulty with this play for several reasons: its unusual form, in which the dialogue is sprinkled with stage directions and lengthy narrative "asides"; its archaic syntax, meant to simulate seventeenth-century speech; the tangled relationships between the characters; the unfamiliar historical setting; and, lastly, the parallels Miller draws between the play's events and events taking place at the time of its writing. With the help of the close-reading questions, students will examine how all those elements work together to produce a great piece of theater whose message is a call for sanity.

Background Have students read the background information. For more context, they can view the video "Salem Witch Trials" in their eBooks. Point out that the House Committee on Un-American Activities was set up to target Communists within the federal government, but its focus turned to Hollywood. In 1947 a group of writers, directors, and actors known as the Hollywood Ten were convicted of contempt of Congress for refusing to answer questions about their political beliefs. Over the next ten years, several hundred artists would be blacklisted by the film industry, including Arthur Miller, who was convicted of contempt of Congress in 1957 for refusing to name names.

AS YOU READ Ask students to pay attention to the way the author weaves together dramatic elements and exposition.

COMMON CORE: Common Core Support

- cite strong and thorough textual evidence
- analyze the impact of the author's choices of dramatic structure
- examine the use of direct and indirect characterization
- analyze the characters' motivations and their effect on each other, as well as how they develop and change during the play

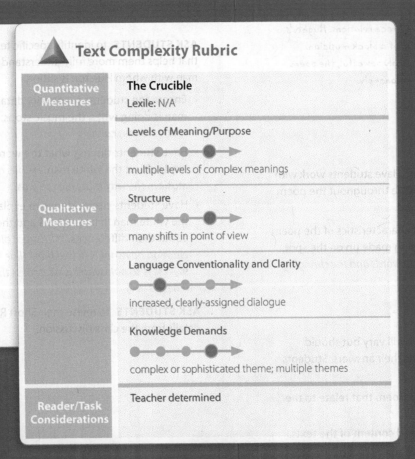

Text Complexity Rubric

The Crucible

Quantitative Measures	Lexile: N/A
Qualitative Measures	**Levels of Meaning/Purpose** — multiple levels of complex meanings
	Structure — many shifts in point of view
	Language Conventionality and Clarity — increased, clearly-assigned dialogue
	Knowledge Demands — complex or sophisticated theme; multiple themes
Reader/Task Considerations	Teacher determined

Strategies for CLOSE READING

Analyze Drama Elements

Students should read this drama excerpt carefully all the way through. Close-reading questions at the bottom of the page will help them follow the plot and keep track of the characters' interactions. As they read, students should jot down comments or questions about the text in the margins.

WHEN STUDENTS STRUGGLE . . .

To help students analyze drama elements in this excerpt from *The Crucible*, have them work in small groups to fill out a chart like the one shown below.

CITE TEXT EVIDENCE For practice recognizing how the author uses dialogue and exposition to reveal details about the characters, have students study this chart.

Example	What It Shows
". . . when . . . wonders are brought forth from below the social surface, it is too much to expect people to hold back very long from laying on the victims with all the force of their frustrations." (lines 102–105)	The people of Salem were so repressed that what happened was inevitable.
"Tituba . . . is also very frightened because her slave sense has warned her that, as always, trouble in this house eventually lands on her back." (lines 144–149)	This presents Tituba as a character with self-knowledge and a sense of her own vulnerability within the community.
"Parris: . . . I know that you— you least of all, Thomas, would ever wish so disastrous a charge laid upon me. . . . They will howl me out of Salem for such corruption in my house." (lines 290–293)	Parris is begging Putnam to keep things quiet in the hope that he will identify with his desperation.

Background Arthur Miller (1915–2005) is considered one of the major dramatists of 20th-century American theater. His politics and private life often put him in the public eye (he was once married to Marilyn Monroe). The Crucible, one of his most celebrated plays, is about an entire town caught up in a mad witch-hunt. It's set in 1692, but Miller wrote it during the "Communist scare," when a witch-hunt of a different sort was being conducted on the floor of the U.S. Congress.

from
The Crucible

Drama by Arthur Miller

CLOSE READ
Notes

CAST OF CHARACTERS
(IN ORDER OF APPEARANCE)

Reverend Samuel Parris

Betty Parris

Tituba

Abigail Williams

Susanna Walcott

Mrs. Ann Putnam

Thomas Putnam

Mercy Lewis

Mary Warren

John Proctor

Rebecca Nurse

Giles Corey

123

1. **READ** ▶ As you read lines 1–40, begin to collect and cite text evidence.
   - Underline details that describe Reverend Samuel Parris.
   - Circle details that describe the setting.
   - In the margin, explain the purpose of the exposition. For whose benefit does Miller include this text?

ACT ONE

An Overture

(A small upper bedroom in the home of Reverend Samuel Parris, *Salem, Massachusetts, in the spring of the year 1692.*

There is a narrow window at the left. Through its leaded panes the morning sunlight streams. A candle still burns near the bed, which is at the right. A chest, a chair, and a small table are the other furnishings. At the back a door opens on the landing of the stairway to the ground floor. The room gives off an air of clean spareness. The roof rafters are exposed, and the wood colors are raw and unmellowed.

Readers, directors, and actors would all benefit from Miller's exposition.

10 *As the curtain rises, Reverend Parris is discovered kneeling beside the bed, evidently in prayer. His daughter, Betty Parris, aged ten, is lying on the bed, inert.)*

A At the time of these events Parris was in his middle forties. In history he cut a villainous path, and there is very little good to be said for him. He believed he was being **persecuted** wherever he went, despite his best efforts to win people and God to his side. In meeting, he felt insulted if someone rose to shut the door without first asking his permission. He was a widower with no interest in children, or talent with them. He regarded them as young adults, and until this strange crisis he, like the rest of Salem, never conceived that the children were anything but thankful for being permitted to walk straight, eyes

20 slightly lowered, arms at the sides, and mouths shut until bidden to speak. His house stood in the "town"—but we today would hardly call it a village. The meeting house¹ was nearby, and from this point outward—toward the bay or inland—there were a few small-windowed, dark houses snuggling against the raw Massachusetts winter. Salem had been established hardly forty years before. To the European world the whole province was a

persecuted: wronged, mistreated

¹ **meeting house:** the most important building in the Puritan community, used both for worship and for meetings.

---

barbaric frontier inhabited by a sect of fanatics who, nevertheless, were shipping out products of slowly increasing quantity and value.

No one can really know what their lives were like. They had no novelists—and would not have permitted anyone to read a novel if one were
30 handy. Their creed forbade anything resembling a theater or "vain enjoyment." They did not celebrate Christmas, and a holiday from work meant only that they must concentrate even more upon prayer.

B Which is not to say that nothing broke into this strict and somber way of life. When a new farmhouse was built, friends assembled to "raise the roof," and there would be special foods cooked and probably some potent cider passed around. There was a good supply of ne'er-do-wells in Salem, who dallied at the shovelboard² in Bridget Bishop's tavern. Probably more than the creed, hard work kept the morals of the place from spoiling, for the people were forced to fight the land like heroes for every grain of corn, and
40 no man had very much time for fooling around.

C That there were some jokers, however, is indicated by the practice of appointing a two-man patrol whose duty was to "walk forth in the time of God's worship to take notice of such as either lye about the meeting house, without attending to the word and ordinances, or that lye at home or in the fields without giving good account thereof, and to take the names of such persons, and to present them to the magistrates, whereby they may be accordingly proceeded against." This **predilection** for minding other people's business was time-honored among the people of Salem, and it undoubtedly created many of the suspicions which were to feed the coming
50 madness. It was also, in my opinion, one of the things that a John Proctor would rebel against, for the time of the armed camp had almost passed, and since the country was reasonably—although not wholly—safe, the old disciplines were beginning to rankle. But, as in all such matters, the issue

² **shovelboard:** a game in which a coin or disc is shoved across a board by hand.

barbaric: uncivilized, primitive

predilection: liking, preference

2. **◀ REREAD** Reread lines 28–40. What commonalities kept the people of the Massachusetts colony together? Cite evidence from the text.

The people valued hard work and prayer; they did not favor creativity or "vain enjoyment"; "no man had very much time for fooling around."

3. **READ** ▶ As you read lines 41–77, continue to cite textual evidence.
   - Underline text describing things the people of Salem were suspicious of.
   - Circle text describing the realities of life in a new colony.
   - In the margin, describe the people of Salem in your own words (lines 56–77).

---

1. READ AND CITE TEXT EVIDENCE

A **ASK STUDENTS** to describe the effect of the exposition on readers (lines 12–40). What mood does it evoke? *Students may say the mood is somber, dark, intense, bleak, forbidding, joyless.*

Critical Vocabulary: persecuted (line 14) Have students explain the meaning of *persecuted*. What example in lines 12–20 describes Reverend Parris's feelings about his persecution? *Students may cite the example of someone shutting the door without his permission.*

2. REREAD AND CITE TEXT EVIDENCE

B **ASK STUDENTS** to cite evidence from lines 34–38 describing what the Massachusetts colonists did for fun. *They assembled to "raise the roof" on a new farmhouse; the event was accompanied by food and drink; they "dallied at the shovelboard."*

3. READ AND CITE TEXT EVIDENCE

C **ASK STUDENTS** to cite evidence explaining the purpose of the "two-man patrol" in the village. What was their job? *They spied on the villagers and presented names to the magistrate.*

Critical Vocabulary: barbaric (line 26) Have students explain the meaning of *barbaric*.

Critical Vocabulary: predilection (line 47) Have students explain the meaning of *predilection*. What predilections do students have when it comes to food? *Students should name a kind of food they like.*

They were
hardworking,
somber,
disciplined,
autocratic,
fearful, and
suspicious.

was not clear-cut, for danger was still a possibility, and in unity still lay the best promise of safety.

The edge of the wilderness was close by. The American continent stretched endlessly west, and it was full of mystery for them. It stood, dark and threatening, over their shoulders night and day, for out of it Indian tribes marauded from time to time, and Reverend Parris had parishioners who had lost relatives to these heathen.

D The parochial snobbery of these people was partly responsible for their failure to convert the Indians. Probably they also preferred to take land from heathens rather than from fellow Christians. At any rate, very few Indians were converted, and the Salem folk believed that the virgin forest was the Devil's last preserve, his home base and the citadel of his final stand. To the best of their knowledge the American forest was the last place on earth that was not paying homage to God.

For these reasons, among others, they carried about an air of innate resistance, even of persecution. Their fathers had, of course, been persecuted in England. So now they and their church found it necessary to deny any other sect its freedom, lest their New Jerusalem[3] be defiled and corrupted by wrong ways and deceitful ideas.

They believed, in short, that they held in their steady hands the candle that would light the world. We have inherited this belief, and it has helped and hurt us. It helped them with the discipline it gave them. They were a dedicated folk, by and large, and they had to be to survive the life they had chosen or been born into in this country.

The proof of their belief's value to them may be taken from the opposite character of the first Jamestown settlement, farther south, in Virginia. The **E** Englishmen who landed there were motivated mainly by a hunt for profit. They had thought to pick off the wealth of the new country and then return

---

[3] **New Jerusalem:** in Christianity, a heavenly city and the last resting place of the souls saved by Jesus. It was considered the ideal city, and Puritans modeled their communities after it.

---

4. **◀ REREAD** Reread lines 61–77. How did the wilderness setting and proximity to the Indians affect the beliefs of "the Salem folk"?

The wilderness was full of danger and dangerous "heathens." The
people of Salem felt that the forest was evil and was the "Devil's last
preserve."

---

rich to England. They were a band of individualists, and a much more **ingratiating** group than the Massachusetts men. But Virginia destroyed them. Massachusetts tried to kill off the Puritans, but they combined; they set up a communal society which, in the beginning, was little more than an armed camp with an autocratic and very devoted leadership. It was, however, an autocracy by consent, for they were united from top to bottom by a commonly held ideology whose **perpetuation** was the reason and justification for all their sufferings. So their self-denial, their purposefulness, their suspicion of all vain pursuits, their hard-handed justice, were altogether perfect instruments for the conquest of this space so antagonistic to man.

F But the people of Salem in 1692 were not quite the dedicated folk that arrived on the *Mayflower*. A vast differentiation had taken place, and in their own time a revolution had unseated the royal government and substituted a junta which was at this moment in power.[4] The times, to their eyes, must have been out of joint, and to the common folk must have seemed as insoluble and complicated as do ours today. It is not hard to see how easily many could have been led to believe that the time of confusion had been brought upon them by deep and darkling forces. No hint of such speculation appears on the court record, but social disorder in any age breeds such mystical suspicions, and when, as in Salem, wonders are brought forth from below the social surface, it is too much to expect people to hold back very long from laying on the victims with all the force of their frustrations.

---

[4] **a junta . . . power:** *Junta* is a Spanish term meaning "a small, elite ruling council." The reference here is to the group that led England's Glorious Revolution of 1688–1689.

---

ingratiating:
likable,
pleasing

perpetuation:
continuation

The
Massachusetts
colonists unified
under one leader
and ideology.

---

5. **READ ▶** As you read lines 78–105, continue to cite textual evidence.
   - Underline details that describe the Massachusetts colony.
   - Circle text describing the "character" of the Jamestown settlement.
   - In the margin, explain why the Massachusetts colony survived.

6. **◀ REREAD** Reread lines 93–105. According to Miller, what effect does social disorder have on the people of Salem?

Miller suggests that the people of Salem believed that social disorder
comes from "deep and darkling forces," which made them suspicious
of their neighbors.

---

4. **READ AND CITE TEXT EVIDENCE**

D **ASK STUDENTS** to explain why the colonists may not have been totally behind the effort to convert the Indians, according to the author. *The colonists thought it was easier to take land away from heathens than from Christians (lines 62–63).*

FOR ELL STUDENTS Spanish speakers may recognize the word *parochial* (line 61) from its cognate *parroquial*. Explain that *parochial* can mean "related to a parish," but in this context it means "close-minded" or "limited in outlook."

5. **READ AND CITE TEXT EVIDENCE**

E **ASK STUDENTS** what the author implies about the Jamestown colony by calling them "a band of individualists." *The individualists of Jamestown didn't agree and failed; Salem consisted of people who agreed about what is right and wrong.*

6. **REREAD AND CITE TEXT EVIDENCE**

F **ASK STUDENTS** how the author foreshadows the trouble to come to Salem in lines 93–105. *He hints at social disorder and "deep and darkling forces."*

Critical Vocabulary: ingratiating (line 83) The author tells us that the Jamestown men were more "ingratiating" than the Massachusetts men. What does that say about the Massachusetts men? *They were not very likable.*

Critical Vocabulary: perpetuation (line 88) Have students share their definitions of *perpetuation*.

The Salem tragedy, which is about to begin in these pages, developed from a paradox. It is a paradox in whose grip we still live, and there is no prospect yet that we will discover its resolution. Simply, it was this: for good purposes, even high purposes, the people of Salem developed a theocracy, a combine of state and religious power whose function was to keep the community together, and to prevent any kind of disunity that might open it to destruction by material or ideological enemies. It was forged for a necessary purpose and accomplished that purpose. But all organization is and must be grounded on the idea of exclusion and prohibition, just as two objects cannot occupy the same space. Evidently the time came in New England when the repressions of order were heavier than seemed warranted by the dangers against which the order was organized. The witch-hunt was a perverse **manifestation** of the panic which set in among all classes when the balance began to turn toward greater individual freedom.

When one rises above the individual villainy displayed, one can only pity them all, just as we shall be pitied someday. It is still impossible for man to organize his social life without repressions, and the balance has yet to be struck between order and freedom.

The witch-hunt was not, however, a mere repression. It was also, and as importantly, a long overdue opportunity for everyone so inclined to express publicly his guilt and sins, under the cover of accusations against the victims. It suddenly became possible—and patriotic and holy—for a man to say that Martha Corey had come into his bedroom at night, and that, while his wife was sleeping at his side, Martha laid herself down on his chest and "nearly suffocated him." Of course it was her spirit only, but his satisfaction at confessing himself was no lighter than if it had been Martha herself. One could not ordinarily speak such things in public.

manifestation:
a sign

Salem developed a theocracy intending to keep the community together, but instead it was torn apart.

7. **READ ▶** As you read lines 106–140, continue to cite textual evidence.
   - Underline text describing the control the Puritan leaders exerted over the community.
   - In the margin, explain the paradox of the "Salem tragedy" in your own words.

8. **◀ REREAD** Reread lines 124–140. What role did "long-held hatreds of neighbors" have in the witch-hunt? Cite evidence from the text.

The witch-hunt was an "opportunity" for each of the long-repressed people of Salem to accuse their neighbors whom they didn't like.

Long-held hatreds of neighbors could now be openly expressed, and vengeance taken, despite the Bible's charitable **injunctions**. Land-lust which had been expressed before by constant bickering over boundaries and deeds, could now be elevated to the arena of morality; one could cry witch against one's neighbor and feel perfectly justified in the bargain. Old scores could be settled on a plane of heavenly combat between Lucifer and the Lord; suspicions and the envy of the miserable toward the happy could and did burst out in the general revenge.

(Reverend Parris *is praying now, and, though we cannot hear his words, a sense of his confusion hangs about him. He mumbles, then seems about to weep; then he weeps, then prays again; but his daughter does not stir on the bed.*

The door opens, and his Negro slave enters. Tituba is in her forties. Parris brought her with him from Barbados, where he spent some years as a merchant before entering the ministry. She enters as one does who can no longer bear to be barred from the sight of her beloved, but she is also very frightened because her slave sense has warned her that, as always, trouble in this house eventually lands on her back.)

Tituba (*already taking a step backward*). My Betty be hearty soon?
Parris. Out of here!
Tituba (*backing to the door*). My Betty not goin' die . . .
Parris (*scrambling to his feet in a fury*). Out of my sight! (*She is gone.*) Out of my—(*He is overcome with sobs. He clamps his teeth against them and closes the door and leans against it, exhausted.*) Oh, my God! God help me! (*Quaking with fear, mumbling to himself through his sobs, he goes to the bed and gently takes Betty's hand.*) Betty. Child. Dear child. Will you wake, will you open up your eyes! Betty, little one . . .
(*He is bending to kneel again when his niece, Abigail Williams, seventeen, enters—a strikingly beautiful girl, an orphan, with an endless capacity for dissembling. Now she is all worry and apprehension and propriety.*)
Abigail. Uncle? (*He looks to her.*) Susanna Walcott's here from Doctor Griggs.
Parris. Oh? Let her come, let her come.
Abigail (*leaning out the door to call to Susanna, who is down the hall a few steps*). Come in, Susanna.

injunctions:
commands, rulings

A girl lies lifeless on her bed—no one knows why. The suspense builds as her increasingly desperate father is forced to confront the possibility of intervention by "dark forces."

dissembling:
hiding real feelings or intentions

9. **READ ▶** As you read lines 141–180, continue to cite textual evidence.
   - Underline text that helps you understand Reverend Parris.
   - Circle details that describe Abigail.
   - In the margin, explain the initial conflict in this section.

---

7. **READ AND CITE TEXT EVIDENCE**

G **ASK STUDENTS** to discuss the conditions that increase the likelihood of a witch-hunt (lines 117–119). *Students should understand that witch-hunts occur in tightly controlled societies "when the balance began to turn toward greater individual freedom."*

8. **REREAD AND CITE TEXT EVIDENCE**

H **ASK STUDENTS** to identify one of the "sins" that the witch-hunt allowed people to express publicly. What example can they find in lines 127–132? *A woman appeared in a man's bedroom while his wife was sleeping beside him and "nearly suffocated him."*

Critical Vocabulary: manifestation (line 118) Have students share definitions. What caused the "manifestation of the panic" in Salem in 1692? *Students may say that powerful leaders were afraid that their power was slipping.*

9. **READ AND CITE TEXT EVIDENCE** Remind students that lines 9–11 explain that Parris is praying by his daughter's bedside.

I **ASK STUDENTS** to cite evidence describing Parris's reaction when Tituba enters the room. *Students should cite lines 151–153, where he yells at her.*

Critical Vocabulary: injunctions (line 134) After students share definitions, have them paraphrase the sentence. *Possible response: You could express your deepest hatreds without worrying about the Bible's commandments.*

Critical Vocabulary: dissembling (line 161) Have students share definitions. Explain that Abigail has an "endless capacity for dissembling." What are other names for this type of person? *liar, dreamer, fraud, phony*

(Susanna Walcott, *a little younger than* Abigail, *a nervous, hurried girl, enters.*)

Parris (*eagerly*). What does the doctor say, child?

Susanna (*craning around* Parris *to get a look at* Betty). He bid me come and tell you, reverend sir, that he cannot discover no medicine for it in his books.

170 **Parris.** Then he must search on.

Susanna. Aye, sir, he have been searchin' his books since he left you, sir. But he bid me tell you, that you might look to unnatural things for the cause of it.

Parris (*his eyes going wide*). No—no. There be no unnatural cause here. Tell him I have sent for Reverend Hale of Beverly, and Mr. Hale will surely confirm that. Let him look to medicine and put out all thought of unnatural causes here. There be none.

Susanna. Aye, sir. He bid me tell you. (*She turns to go.*)

Abigail. Speak nothin' of it in the village, Susanna.

Parris. Go directly home and speak nothing of unnatural causes.

180 **Susanna.** Aye, sir. I pray for her. (*She goes out.*)

Abigail. Uncle, the rumor of witchcraft is all about; I think you'd best go down and deny it yourself. The parlor's packed with people, sir. I'll sit with her.

Parris (*pressed, turns on her*). And what shall I say to them? That my daughter and my niece I discovered dancing like heathen in the forest?

Abigail. Uncle, we did dance; let you tell them I confessed it—and I'll be whipped if I must. But they're speakin' of witchcraft. Betty's not witched.

(K) **Parris.** Abigail, I cannot go before the congregation when I know you have not opened with me. What did you do with her in the forest?

Abigail. We did dance, uncle, and when you leaped out of the bush so 190 suddenly, Betty was frightened and then she fainted. And there's the whole of it.

Parris. Child. Sit you down.

Abigail (*quavering, as she sits*). I would never hurt Betty. I love her dearly.

---

10. **(◀ REREAD)** Reread lines 166–180. Why do Parris and Abigail tell Susanna to "speak nothing of unnatural causes"? Cite examples from the text.

Parris and Abigail do not want any rumors spread about "unnatural causes" like witchcraft although the doctor says he "cannot discover no medicine for it in his books."

11. **(READ ▶)** As you read lines 181–235, continue to cite textual evidence.

- Underline Parris's references to witchcraft.
- Circle statements Abigail makes about her behavior.
- In the margin, explain Abigail's description of what happened in the forest.

130

> ... the rumor of witchcraft is all about; I think you'd best go down and deny it yourself.

Parris. Now look you, child, your punishment will come in its time. But if you trafficked with⁵ spirits in the forest I must know it now, for surely my enemies will, and they will ruin me with it.

Abigail. But we never **conjured** spirits.

(L) **Parris.** Then why can she not move herself since midnight? This child is desperate! (*Abigail lowers her eyes.*) It must come out—my enemies will bring it 200 out. Let me know what you done there. Abigail, do you understand that I have many enemies?

Abigail. I have heard of it, uncle.

Parris. There is a faction that is sworn to drive me from my pulpit. Do you understand that?

Abigail. I think so, sir.

Parris. Now then, in the midst of such disruption, my own household is discovered to be the very center of some obscene practice. Abominations are done in the forest—

Abigail. It were sport, uncle!

210 **Parris** (*pointing at Betty*). You call this sport? (*She lowers her eyes. He pleads.*) Abigail, if you know something that may help the doctor, for God's sake tell it to me. (*She is silent.*) I saw Tituba waving her arms over the fire when I came on you. Why was she doing that? And I heard a screeching and **gibberish** coming from her mouth. She were swaying like a dumb beast over that fire!

Abigail. She always sings her Barbados songs, and we dance.

Parris. I cannot blink what I saw, Abigail, for my enemies will not blink it. I saw a dress lying on the grass.

Abigail (*innocently*). A dress?

Parris (*It is very hard to say*). Aye, a dress. And I thought I saw—someone 220 naked running through the trees!

Abigail (*in terror*). No one was naked! You mistake yourself, uncle!

⁵ **trafficked with**: met with.

12. **(◀ REREAD AND DISCUSS)** Reread lines 198–208. In a small group, discuss Parris's conflict. Who are his enemies and why is he afraid of them?

131

Abigail, Betty, and Tituba were in the forest dancing. Parris "leaped out of the bush," causing Betty to faint.

conjured: *invented, made up*

gibberish: *nonsense*

---

10. **(REREAD AND CITE TEXT EVIDENCE)** In lines 141–180, Reverend Parris acts as if he's afraid of something.

(J) **ASK STUDENTS** to identify details that convey this fear. *Examples include: "his eyes going wide" (line 173); panic at the mention of the supernatural; his rough manner with Susanna; his obvious defensiveness.*

11. **(READ AND CITE TEXT EVIDENCE)**

(K) **ASK STUDENTS** to explain why Reverend Parris says he cannot "go before the congregation" (lines 187–188). *Abigail has lied to him before and he's afraid she'll lie again, this time in front of the whole town.*

12. **(REREAD AND DISCUSS USING TEXT EVIDENCE)**

(L) **ASK STUDENTS** to recall the description of Parris they read in lines 12–20. What might his mental state have to do with his conviction that "enemies" are out to get him (lines 199–204)? *Since Parris "believed he was being persecuted wherever he went" (line 14), students may conclude that the "enemies" are manifestations of his paranoia.*

Critical Vocabulary: conjured (line 197) Have students share definitions. Have them discuss the difference between conjuring and inventing. *The connotation is that conjuring brings something into existence.*

Critical Vocabulary: gibberish (line 213) Ask students to share definitions. What connotation does *gibberish* have here? *It reflects a condescending attitude.*

abomination:
immoral or shameful act

Parris (*with anger*). I saw it! (*He moves from her. Then, resolved*) Now tell me true, Abigail. And I pray you feel the weight of truth upon you, for now my ministry's at stake, my ministry and perhaps your cousin's life. Whatever **abomination** you have done, give me all of it now, for I dare not be taken unaware when I go before them down there.

Abigail. There is nothin' more. I swear it, uncle.

Parris (*studies her, then nods, half convinced*). Abigail, I have fought here three long years to bend these stiff-necked people to me, and now, just now when
230 some good respect is rising for me in the parish, you compromise my very character. I have given you a home, child, I have put clothes upon your back—now give me upright answer. Your name in the town—it is entirely white, is it not?

Abigail (*with an edge of resentment*). Why, I am sure it is, sir. There be no blush about my name.[6]

Ⓝ **Parris** (*to the point*). Abigail, is there any other cause than you have told me, for your being discharged from Goody[7] Proctor's service? I have heard it said, and I tell you as I heard it, that she comes so rarely to the church this year for she will not sit so close to something soiled. What signified that remark?

240 **Abigail.** She hates me, uncle, she must, for I would not be her slave. It's a bitter woman, a lying, cold, sniveling woman, and I will not work for such a woman!

Parris. She may be. And yet it has troubled me that you are now seven month out of their house, and in all this time no other family has ever called for your service.

Abigail. They want slaves, not such as I. Let them send to Barbados for that. I will not black my face for any of them! (*with ill-concealed resentment at him*) Do you **begrudge** my bed, uncle?

Parris. No—no.

begrudge:
envy (someone) for the possession or enjoyment of (something)

Abigail (*in a temper*). My name is good in the village! I will not have it said my
250 name is soiled! Goody Proctor is a gossiping liar!

(*Enter Mrs. Ann Putnam. She is a twisted soul of forty-five, a death-ridden woman, haunted by dreams.*)

Parris (*as soon as the door begins to open*). No—no, I cannot have anyone. (*He sees her, and a certain deference springs into him, although his worry remains.*) Why, Goody Putnam, come in.

---

[6] **There be . . . my name:** There is nothing wrong with my reputation.
[7] **Goody:** short for *Goodwife*, the Puritan equivalent of *Mrs.*

---

13. **READ ▶** As you read lines 236–293, continue to cite textual evidence.
- Underline statements Abigail and Parris make about Goody Proctor.
- Circle mentions of witchcraft.
- In the margin, tell how Reverend Parris's and Mrs. Putnam's opinions differ.

132

Mrs. Putnam (*full of breath, shiny-eyed*). It is a marvel. It is surely a stroke of hell upon you.

Parris. No, Goody Putnam, it is—

Mrs. Putnam (*glancing at Betty*). How high did she fly, how high?
260 **Parris.** No, no, she never flew—

Mrs. Putnam (*very pleased with it*). Why, it's sure she did. Mr. Collins saw her goin' over Ingersoll's barn, and come down light as bird, he says!

Parris. Now, look you, Goody Putnam, she never—

(*Enter Thomas Putnam, a well-to-do, hard-handed landowner, near fifty.*) Oh, good morning, Mr. Putnam.

Ⓜ **Putnam.** It is a **providence** the thing is out now! It is a providence. (*He goes directly to the bed.*)

Parris. What's out, sir, what's—?

(*Mrs. Putnam goes to the bed.*)
270 **Putnam** (*looking down at Betty*). Why, her eyes are closed! Look you, Ann.

Mrs. Putnam. Why, that's strange. (*to Parris*) Ours are open.

Parris (*shocked*). Your Ruth is sick?

Mrs. Putnam (*with vicious certainty*). I'd not call it sick; the Devil's touch is heavier than sick. It's death, y'know, it's death drivin' into them, forked and hoofed.

Parris. Oh, pray not! Why, how does Ruth ail?

Mrs. Putnam. She ails as she must—she never waked this morning, but her eyes open and she walks, and hears naught, sees naught, and cannot eat. Her soul is taken, surely.
280 (*Parris is struck.*)

Putnam (*as though for further details*). They say you've sent for Reverend Hale of Beverly?

Parris (*with dwindling conviction now*). A precaution only. He has much experience in all demonic arts, and I—

Mrs. Putnam. He has indeed; and found a witch in Beverly last year, and let you remember that.

Parris. Now, Goody Ann, they only thought that were a witch, and I am certain there be no element of witchcraft here.

providence:
destiny, fate

conviction:
certainty, confidence

---

14. **◀ REREAD** Reread lines 236–250. What might the Reverend Parris be insinuating here? Support your answer with explicit textual evidence.

Parris is troubled by the fact that no one wants to hire Abigail. He may be suggesting that Abigail may have caused some trouble when she was in the service of the Proctors.

133

Mrs. Putnam is adamant that witchcraft is at play; Parris advises her not to jump to conclusions.

---

13. **READ AND CITE TEXT EVIDENCE**

Ⓜ **ASK STUDENTS** to consider the new element Mrs. Putnam brings to the discussion. What does she believe caused Betty's symptoms? *She is sure it was witchcraft.* What kind of person is she? *She is gullible, narrow-minded, and mean-spirited.*

Critical Vocabulary: abomination (line 225) Have students share definitions. What is Parris implying by using this word? *He is implying that Abigail has committed crimes against God.*

Critical Vocabulary: begrudge (line 247) Have students share definitions. Ask them to paraphrase Abigail's question to her uncle. *Possible answer: "Would you be so mean as to deny me a bed, uncle?"*

14. **REREAD AND CITE TEXT EVIDENCE**

Ⓝ **ASK STUDENTS** to examine the exchange that takes place between Reverend Parris and Abigail in lines 236–250. How does Abigail's behavior give her away? *Students may suggest: Instead of addressing Parris's points, she lashes out at Goody Proctor and defames her character.*

Critical Vocabulary: providence (line 266) Ask students what they think Putnam means when he says, "It is a providence the thing is out now!" *It is destiny that the real facts have come to light.*

Critical Vocabulary: conviction (line 283) Ask students to share definitions. What issues do they have strong convictions about? *Students may suggest human rights, nuclear disarmament, animal rights, the environment.*

Putnam. No witchcraft! Now look you, Mr. Parris—

290 **Parris.** Thomas, Thomas, I pray you, leap not to witchcraft. I know that you—you least of all, Thomas, would ever wish so disastrous a charge laid upon me. We cannot leap to witchcraft. They will howl me out of Salem for such corruption in my house.

A word about Thomas Putnam. He was a man with many grievances, at least one of which appears justified. Some time before, his wife's brother-in-law, James Bayley, had been turned down as minister of Salem. Bayley had all the qualifications, and a two-thirds vote into the bargain, but a faction stopped his acceptance, for reasons that are not clear.

300 Thomas Putnam was the eldest son of the richest man in the village. He had fought the Indians at Narragansett,⁸ and was deeply interested in parish affairs. He undoubtedly felt it poor payment that the village should so blatantly disregard his candidate for one of its more important offices, especially since he regarded himself as the intellectual superior of most of the people around him.

His **vindictive** nature was demonstrated long before the witchcraft began. Another former Salem minister, George Burroughs, had had to borrow money to pay for his wife's funeral, and, since the parish was remiss in his salary, he was soon bankrupt. Thomas and his brother John had 310 Burroughs jailed for debts the man did not owe. The incident is important only in that Burroughs succeeded in becoming minister where Bayley, Thomas Putnam's brother-in-law, had been rejected; the **motif** of resentment is clear here. Thomas Putnam felt that his own name and the honor of his family had been smirched by the village, and he meant to right matters however he could.

Another reason to believe him a deeply embittered man was his attempt to break his father's will, which left a disproportionate amount to a stepbrother. As with every other public cause in which he tried to force his way, he failed in this.

⁸ **fought the Indians at Narragansett:** The Puritans fought a series of battles against the Narragansett Indians over territory that both groups had settled on.

vindictive:
spiteful, mean, cruel

motif:
theme, pattern

15. **READ** ▶ As you read lines 294–323, continue to cite textual evidence.

- Underline text that describes Thomas Putnam's character.
- Circle text explaining his resentment.
- In the margin, explain the conclusion Miller draws about the effects of Putnam's bitterness (lines 319–323).

134

---

320 So it is not surprising to find that so many accusations against people are in the handwriting of Thomas Putnam, or that his name is so often found as a witness corroborating the supernatural testimony, or that his daughter led the crying-out at the most opportune junctures of the trials, especially when—But we'll speak of that when we come to it.

Putnam (*At the moment he is intent upon getting* Parris, *for whom he has only contempt, to move toward the abyss*). Mr. Parris, I have taken your part in all **contention** here, and I would continue; but I cannot if you hold back in this. There are hurtful, vengeful spirits layin' hands on these children.

Parris. But, Thomas, you cannot—

Putnam. Ann! Tell Mr. Parris what you have done.

330 **Mrs. Putnam.** Reverend Parris, I have laid seven babies unbaptized in the earth. Believe me, sir, you never saw more hearty babies born. And yet, each would wither in my arms the very night of their birth. I have spoke nothin', but my heart has clamored intimations.⁹ And now, this year, my Ruth, my only—I see her turning strange. A secret child she has become this year, and shrivels like a sucking mouth were pullin' on her life too. And so I thought to send her to your Tituba—

Parris. To Tituba! What may Tituba—?

Mrs. Putnam. Tituba knows how to speak to the dead, Mr. Parris.

Parris. Goody Ann, it is a formidable sin to conjure up the dead!

⁹ **clamored intimations:** nagging suspicions.

Putnam's own failures cause him to accuse others of wrongdoing.

contention:
argument, disagreement

16. **◀ REREAD** Reread lines 294–323. After reading this background information, what effect do you think Thomas Putnam will have in the play? Support your answer with explicit textual evidence.

Putnam is "vindictive" and full of "resentment." His desire for vengeance against those he thinks have done him wrong may prompt him to make some false accusations.

17. **READ** ▶ As you read lines 324–379, continue to cite textual evidence.

- Underline events that have caused Mrs. Putnam to believe something wicked is at play.
- Circle the claims the Putnams make about recent events.
- In the margin, tell how the Putnams raise the level of hysteria in the town.

135

---

15. READ AND CITE TEXT EVIDENCE

ASK STUDENTS why they think Miller chooses to use exposition at this point in the play. What is its purpose and what does it bring to light? *It presents a psychological portrait of Thomas Putnam; it presents his life as a series of disappointments and petty grievances.*

Critical Vocabulary: vindictive (line 305) Ask students to cite evidence that explains Thomas Putnam's vindictive nature. *Students may suggest: "Thomas Putnam felt that his own name and the honor of his family had been smirched by the village" (lines 312–313).*

Critical Vocabulary: motif (line 311) Have students share definitions. Tell them that *motif* can also refer to a melodic pattern in a musical composition.

16. REREAD AND CITE TEXT EVIDENCE

ASK STUDENTS to note that Putnam "meant to right matters however he could" (lines 313–314). Have students restate this idea in their own words. *Possible response: He would do anything to get what he wants.*

17. READ AND CITE TEXT EVIDENCE

ASK STUDENTS to explain Mrs. Putnam's involvement in the situation. Why does she bring up her seven dead babies? Why is she interested in Tituba? *She thinks that Tituba can communicate with the dead; she thinks she can find out who murdered her babies (lines 340–341).*

Critical Vocabulary: contention (line 326) Have students share definitions. What is the contention between Mr. Putnam and Reverend Parris? *Mr. Putnam thinks Reverend Parris should confess; Reverend Parris refuses for fear of public scorn.*

117

Q 340 **Mrs. Putnam.** I take it on my soul, but who else may surely tell us what person murdered my babies?

Parris (*horrified*). Woman!

Mrs. Putnam. They were murdered, Mr. Parris! And mark this proof! Mark it! Last night my Ruth were ever so close to their little spirits; I know it, sir. For how else is she struck dumb now except some power of darkness would stop her mouth? It is a marvelous sign, Mr. Parris!

Putnam. Don't you understand it, sir? There is a murdering witch among us, bound to keep herself in the dark. (*Parris turns to Betty, a frantic terror rising in him.*) Let your enemies make of it what they will, you cannot blink it more.

350 **Parris** (*to Abigail*). Then you were conjuring spirits last night.

R **Abigail** (*whispering*). Not I, sir—Tituba and Ruth.

Parris (*turns now, with new fear, and goes to Betty, looks down at her, and then, gazing off*). Oh, Abigail, what proper payment for my charity! Now I am undone.

Putnam. You are not undone! Let you take hold here. Wait for no one to charge you—declare it yourself. You have discovered witchcraft—

Parris. In my house? In my house, Thomas? They will topple me with this! They will make of it a—

(*Enter Mercy Lewis, the Putnams' servant, a fat, sly, merciless girl of eighteen.*)

360 **Mercy.** Your pardons. I only thought to see how Betty is.

Putnam. Why aren't you home? Who's with Ruth?

Mercy. Her grandma come. She's improved a little, I think—she give a powerful sneeze before.

Mrs. Putnam. Ah, there's a sign of life!

Mercy. I'd fear no more, Goody Putnam. It were a grand sneeze; another like it will shake her wits together, I'm sure. (*She goes to the bed to look.*)

Parris. Will you leave me now, Thomas? I would pray a while alone.

Abigail. Uncle, you've prayed since midnight. Why do you not go down and—

Parris. No—no. (*to Putnam*) I have no answer for that crowd. I'll wait till Mr.

370 Hale arrives. (*to get Mrs. Putnam to leave*) If you will, Goody Ann . . .

The Putnams are ready to accuse those who don't agree with them of being the enemy.

18. **REREAD AND DISCUSS** In a small group, discuss the significance of Abigail's whispered line: "Not I, sir—Tituba and Ruth" (line 351).

136

Putnam. Now look you, sir. Let you strike out against the Devil, and the village will bless you for it! Come down, speak to them—pray with them. They're thirsting for your word, Mister! Surely you'll pray with them.

Parris (*swayed*). I'll lead them in a psalm, but let you say nothing of witchcraft yet. I will not discuss it. The cause is yet unknown. I have had enough contention since I came; I want no more.

Mrs. Putnam. Mercy, you go home to Ruth, d'y'hear?

Mercy. Aye, mum.

(*Mrs. Putnam goes out.*)

S 380 **Parris** (*to Abigail*). If she starts for the window, cry for me at once.

Abigail. I will, uncle.

Parris (*to Putnam*). There is a terrible power in her arms today. (*He goes out with Putnam.*)

Abigail (*with hushed trepidation*). How is Ruth sick?

Mercy. It's weirdish, I know not—she seems to walk like a dead one since last night.

Abigail (*turns at once and goes to Betty, and now, with fear in her voice*). Betty? (*Betty doesn't move. She shakes her.*) Now stop this! Betty! Sit up now! (*Betty doesn't stir. Mercy comes over.*)

390 **Mercy.** Have you tried beatin' her? I gave Ruth a good one and it waked her for a minute. Here, let me have her.

Abigail (*holding Mercy back*). No, he'll be comin' up. Listen, now; if they be questioning us, tell them we danced—I told him as much already.

Mercy. Aye. And what more?

Abigail. He knows Tituba conjured Ruth's sisters to come out of the grave.

Mercy. And what more?

Abigail. He saw you naked.

Mercy (*clapping her hands together with a frightened laugh*). Oh, Jesus!

(*Enter Mary Warren, breathless. She is seventeen, a subservient, naive, lonely*

400 *girl.*)

Mary Warren. What'll we do? The village is out! I just come from the farm; the whole country's talkin' witchcraft! They'll be callin' us witches, Abby!

Mercy (*pointing and looking at Mary Warren*). She means to tell, I know it.

Mary Warren. Abby, we've got to tell. Witchery's a hangin' error, a hangin' like they done in Boston two year ago! We must tell the truth, Abby! You'll only be whipped for dancin', and the other things!

trepidation:
anxiety, fear, nervousness

subservient:
obedient, docile, meek

19. **READ** As you read lines 380–442, continue to cite textual evidence.

• Underline new details about what really happened in the woods.

• Circle text that describes the feelings of the girls.

• In the margin, explain why the girls are afraid.

137

---

18. **REREAD AND DISCUSS USING TEXT EVIDENCE**

R **ASK STUDENTS** to discuss what Abigail admits for the first time. *Students should note that she admits for the first time that they were "conjuring spirits" in the forest; previously she had denied this.*

FOR ELL STUDENTS One of the meanings of the verb *to undo* is "to destroy." In this context, *undone* (line 354) means "destroyed."

19. **READ AND CITE TEXT EVIDENCE**

S **ASK STUDENTS** to contrast the positions of Mary Warren, Mercy, and Abigail in this section. What do each of them want to do? *Mary Warren wants to tell all; Abigail wants to stick to the story that they were only dancing; Mercy will go with anything Abigail says.*

Critical Vocabulary: trepidation (line 384) Have students share definitions. Have them take turns saying the line "How sick is Ruth?" with hushed *trepidation*.

Critical Vocabulary: subservient (line 399) Ask students to whom they think Mary is *subservient*. *Students may suggest she is subservient to authority.*

CLOSE READ Notes

The girls are afraid of being hanged as witches.

Abigail. Oh, *we'll be whipped!*

Mary Warren. I never done none of it, Abby. I only looked!

Mercy (*moving menacingly toward* Mary). Oh, you're a great one for lookin', aren't you, Mary Warren? What a grand peeping courage you have! (Betty, *on the bed, whimpers.* Abigail *turns to her at once.*)

Abigail. Betty? (*She goes to* Betty.) Now, Betty, dear, wake up now. It's Abigail. (*She sits* Betty *up and furiously shakes her.*) I'll beat you, Betty! (Betty *whimpers.*) My, you seem improving. I talked to your papa and I told him everything to—

Betty (*darts off the bed, frightened of* Abigail, *and flattens herself against the wall*). I want my mama!

Abigail (*with alarm, as she cautiously approaches* Betty). What ails you, Betty? Your mama's dead and buried.

Betty. I'll fly to Mama. Let me fly! (*She raises her arms as though to fly, and streaks for the window, gets one leg out.*)

Abigail (*pulling her away from the window*). I told him everything; he knows now, he knows everything we—

Betty. You drank blood, Abby! You didn't tell him that!

Abigail. Betty, you never say that again! You will never—

Betty. You did, you did! You drank a charm to kill John Proctor's wife! You drank a charm to kill Goody Proctor!

Abigail (*smashes her across the face*). Shut it! Now shut it!

Betty (*collapsing on the bed*). Mama, Mama! (*She* **dissolves** *into sobs.*)

Abigail. Now look you. All of you. We danced. And Tituba conjured Ruth Putnam's dead sisters. And that is all. And mark this. Let either of you breathe a word, or the edge of a word, about the other things, and I will come to you in the black of some terrible night and I will bring a pointy reckoning that will shudder you.[10] And you know I can do it; I saw Indians smash my dear parents' heads on the pillow next to mine, and I have seen some reddish work done at night, and I can make you wish you had never seen the sun go down! (*She goes to* Betty *and roughly sits her up.*) Now, you—sit up and stop this! (*But* Betty *collapses in her hands and lies* **inert** *on the bed.*)

Mary Warren (*with hysterical fright*) What's got her? (Abigail *stares in fright* at Betty.) Abby, she's going to die! It's a sin to conjure, and we—

Abigail (*starting for* Mary). I say shut it, Mary Warren!

(*Enter* John Proctor. *On seeing him,* Mary Warren *leaps in fright.*)

---

[10]**bring . . . shudder you:** inflict a terrifying punishment on you.

dissolves: melts; fades away

inert: lifeless, not moving

20. ◀ **REREAD AND DISCUSS** Reread lines 428–437. In a small group, discuss what you find out about Abigail. In what way does she affect the other girls?

138

Proctor was a farmer in his middle thirties. He need not have been a **partisan** of any faction in the town, but there is evidence to suggest that he had a sharp and biting way with hypocrites. He was the kind of man—powerful of body, even-tempered, and not easily led—who cannot refuse support to partisans without drawing their deepest resentment. In Proctor's presence a fool felt his foolishness instantly—and a Proctor is always marked for calumny[11] therefore.

But as we shall see, the steady manner he displays does not spring from an untroubled soul. He is a sinner, a sinner not only against the moral fashion of the time, but against his own vision of decent conduct. These people had no ritual for the washing away of sins. It is another trait we inherited from them, and it has helped to discipline us as well as to breed **hypocrisy** among us. Proctor, respected and even feared in Salem, has come to regard himself as a kind of fraud. But no hint of this has yet appeared on the surface, and as he enters from the crowded parlor below it is a man in his prime we see, with a quiet confidence and an unexpressed, hidden force. Mary Warren, his servant, can barely speak for embarrassment and fear.

---

[11]**marked for calumny:** singled out to have lies told about him.

partisan: member, follower

hypocrisy: insincerity

21. **READ ▶** As you read lines 443–459, continue to cite textual evidence.
- Underline details that describe John Proctor's best qualities.
- Circle details that show Proctor's worst qualities.

22. ◀ **REREAD AND DISCUSS** Reread lines 443–459. In a small group, discuss John Proctor's inner struggle.

139

---

20. REREAD AND DISCUSS USING TEXT EVIDENCE

T **ASK STUDENTS** to think about Abigail's tone in lines 431–437. What approach does she use to get them to see things her way? *Abigail bullies and threatens them; she makes them understand that if they don't do as she says, she will "bring a pointy reckoning that will shudder you."*

Critical Vocabulary: dissolves (line 429) Have students share definitions of *dissolve*. Then ask them to explain what it means when used in other contexts, such as chemistry and film production.

Critical Vocabulary: inert (line 438) Ask students why they think the author chose the word *inert* to describe Betty's state. *The word has a scientific connotation; it suggests that she is non-reactive.*

21. READ AND CITE TEXT EVIDENCE

U **ASK STUDENTS** how they can tell Proctor plays an important part in the play. *Upon seeing Proctor, Mary "leaps in fright"; the author breaks into the story with a long commentary on his character; he is a tortured soul with inner demons.*

22. REREAD AND DISCUSS USING TEXT EVIDENCE

V **ASK STUDENTS** to discuss the main difference between Proctor and the other characters. *Students may say he is principled.*

Critical Vocabulary: partisan (line 444) Ask students to share definitions. What do they think a bipartisan decision in Congress is? *It is the decision made by two political parties—the Republicans and Democrats.*

Critical Vocabulary: hypocrisy (line 455) Have students discuss which character in the play is the worst hypocrite.

Mary Warren. Oh! I'm just going home, Mr. Proctor. 460

Proctor. Be you foolish, Mary Warren? Be you deaf? I forbid you leave the house, did I not? Why shall I pay you? I am looking for you more often than my cows!

Mary Warren. I only come to see the great doings in the world.

Proctor. I'll show you a great doin' on your arse one of these days. Now get you home; my wife is waitin' with your work! (*Trying to retain a shred of dignity, she goes slowly out.*)

Mercy Lewis (*both afraid of him and strangely* **titillated**). I'd best be off. I have my Ruth to watch. Good morning, Mr. Proctor.

titillated:
excited

(*Mercy sidles out. Since Proctor's entrance, Abigail has stood as though on tiptoe, absorbing his presence, wide-eyed. He glances at her, then goes to Betty on the bed.*) 470

Abigail. Gah! I'd almost forgot how strong you are, John Proctor!

Proctor (*looking at Abigail now, the faintest suggestion of a knowing smile on his face*). What's this mischief here?

Abigail (*with a nervous laugh*). Oh, she's only gone silly somehow.

Proctor. The road past my house is a pilgrimage to Salem all morning. The town's mumbling witchcraft.

Abigail. Oh, posh! (*Winningly she comes a little closer, with a confidential, wicked air.*) We were dancin' in the woods last night, and my uncle leaped in on us. She took fright, is all. 480

winningly:
believably,
convincingly

Proctor (*his smile widening*). Ah, you're wicked yet, aren't y'! (*A trill of expectant laughter escapes her, and she dares come closer, feverishly looking into his eyes.*) You'll be clapped in the stocks before you're twenty.

(*He takes a step to go, and she springs into his path.*)

Abigail. Give me a word, John. A soft word. (*Her concentrated desire destroys his smile.*)

Abigail and Proctor had a brief but passionate affair that ended when his wife fired her.

Proctor. No, no, Abby. That's done with.

Abigail (*tauntingly*). You come five mile to see a silly girl fly? I know you better. 490

Proctor (*setting her firmly out of his path*). I come to see what mischief your uncle's brewin' now. (*with final emphasis*) Put it out of mind, Abby.

---

23. **READ ▶** As you read lines 460–523, continue to cite textual evidence.
   • Underline details that show Abigail's true feelings for John Proctor.
   • In the margin, make an inference about what happened between them.

Abigail (*grasping his hand before he can release her*). John—I am waitin' for you every night.

Proctor. Abby, I never give you hope to wait for me.

Abigail (*now beginning to anger—she can't believe it*). I have something better than hope, I think!

Proctor. Abby, you'll put it out of mind. I'll not be comin' for you more.

Abigail. You're surely sportin' with me.

Proctor. You know me better. 500

Abigail. I know how you clutched my back behind your house and sweated like a stallion whenever I come near! Or did I dream that? It's she put me out, you cannot pretend it were you. I saw your face when she put me out, and you loved me then and you do now!

Proctor. Abby, that's a wild thing to say—

Abigail. A wild thing may say wild things. But not so wild, I think. I have seen you since she put me out; I have seen you nights.

Proctor. I have hardly stepped off my farm this sevenmonth.

Abigail. I have a sense for heat, John, and yours has drawn me to my window, and I have seen you looking up, burning in your loneliness. Do you tell me you've never looked up at my window? 510

Proctor. I may have looked up.

Abigail (*now softening*). And you must. You are no wintry man. I know you, John. I know you. (*She is weeping*) I cannot sleep for dreamin'; I cannot dream but I wake and walk about the house as though I'd find you comin' through some door.
(*She clutches him desperately.*)

---

24. **◀ REREAD** Reread lines 460–523. What angers Abigail most about Proctor's refusal to see her? Why do you think she drank a charm to kill Goody Proctor?

She thinks he is denying his true feelings for her. She wanted to get rid of Goody Proctor so she could continue her affair with John.

---

23. **READ AND CITE TEXT EVIDENCE**   Have students look at the author's stage notes in lines 460–480 for words that convey the nature of the relationship between Abigail and Proctor.

W **ASK STUDENTS** to cite examples of suggestive words. *Examples: Mercy Lewis is "strangely titillated" by Proctor's presence (line 468); Abigail is "absorbing his presence, wide-eyed" (line 471); she gives a "nervous laugh" (line 476); "a trill of expectant laughter escapes her," "feverishly looking into his eyes" (lines 482–484); she has a "confidential, wicked air" (lines 479–480).*

Critical Vocabulary: titillated (line 468) Ask students why they think the author chose this word to describe Mercy's reaction to Proctor's entrance. *She suspects something illicit is going on.*

Critical Vocabulary: winningly (line 479) Ask students why they think the author chose this word to describe Abigail's behavior. What is its connotation? *She is being flirtatious.*

24. **REREAD AND CITE TEXT EVIDENCE**

X **ASK STUDENTS** to cite evidence showing why Abigail can't accept the fact that Proctor has cooled toward her. *Abigail is convinced he still loves her. Students should cite lines 510–511: "I have seen you looking up, burning in your loneliness. Do you tell me you've never looked up at my window?"*

Left page (142)

CLOSE READ Notes

Proctor (*gently pressing her from him, with great sympathy but firmly*). Child—

520 **Abigail** (*with a flash of anger*). How do you call me child!

Proctor. Abby, I may think of you softly from time to time. But I will cut off my hand before I'll ever reach for you again. Wipe it out of mind. We never touched, Abby.

Abigail. Aye, but we did.

Proctor. Aye, but we did not.

Abigail (*with a bitter anger*). Oh, I marvel how such a strong man may let such a sickly wife be—

Proctor (*angered—at himself as well*). You'll speak nothin' of Elizabeth!

Abigail. She is blackening my name in the village! She is telling lies about me!

530 She is a cold, sniveling woman, and you bend to her! Let her turn you like a—

Proctor (*shaking her*). Do you look for whippin'?

(*A psalm is heard being sung below.*)

Abigail (*in tears*). I look for John Proctor that took me from my sleep and put

pretense: knowledge in my heart! I never knew what **pretense** Salem was, I never knew

deception; the lying lessons I was taught by all these Christian women and their

sham covenanted[12] men! And now you bid me tear the light out of my eyes? I will not,

I cannot! You loved me, John Proctor, and whatever sin it is, you love me yet!

(*He turns abruptly to go out. She rushes to him.*) John, pity me, pity me!

(*The words "going up to Jesus" are heard in the psalm, and Betty claps her ears*

540 *suddenly and whines loudly.*)

Abigail. Betty? (*She hurries to Betty, who is now sitting up and screaming.*

Proctor goes to Betty as Abigail *is trying to pull her hands down, calling*

"Betty!")

unnerved: **Proctor** (*growing* **unnerved**). What's she doing? Girl, what ails you? Stop that

panicky, wailing!

anxious

12**covenanted:** In Puritan religious practice, the men of a congregation would make an agreement, or covenant, to govern the community and abide by its beliefs and practices.

---

25. **READ** ▶ As you read lines 524–573, continue to cite textual evidence.
    • Underline details that show a change in Betty's condition.
    • Circle details that describe the other characters' reactions.
    • In the margin, explain what Mrs. Putnam thinks is happening to Betty.

142

Right page (143)

> She is blackening my name in the village! She is telling lies about me!

(*The singing has stopped in the midst of this, and now* Parris *rushes in.*)

Parris. What happened? What are you doing to her? Betty! (*He rushes to the bed, crying, "Betty, Betty!"* Mrs. Putnam *enters, feverish with curiosity, and with her* Thomas Putnam *and* Mercy Lewis. Parris, *at the bed, keeps lightly slapping*

550 Betty's face, *while she moans and tries to get up.*)

Abigail. She heard you singin' and suddenly she's up and screamin'.

Mrs. Putnam. The psalm! The psalm! She cannot bear to hear the Lord's name!

Parris. No. God forbid. Mercy, run to the doctor! Tell him what's happened here! (Mercy Lewis *rushes out.*)

Mrs. Putnam. Mark it for a sign, mark it!

(Rebecca Nurse, *seventy-two, enters. She is white-haired, leaning upon her walking-stick.*)

Putnam (*pointing at the whimpering* Betty). That is a notorious sign of

560 witchcraft afoot, Goody Nurse, a **prodigious** sign!

Mrs. Putnam. My mother told me that! When they cannot bear to hear the name of—

Parris (*trembling*). Rebecca, Rebecca, go to her, we're lost. She suddenly cannot bear to hear the Lord's—

(Giles Corey, *eighty-three, enters. He is knotted with muscle, canny, inquisitive, and still powerful.*)

She thinks Betty is having a bad reaction to hearing a psalm.

prodigious: *extraordinary; exceptional*

---

26. **◀ REREAD** Reread lines 524–538. As Proctor responds to Abigail's insults about Elizabeth, what do his words and the stage directions suggest about his view of his marriage?

Proctor orders Abigail to be quiet and threatens to whip her. He wants to protect Elizabeth and his marriage. The stage directions make his anger toward Abigail clear.

143

---

25. **READ AND CITE TEXT EVIDENCE**

Y ASK STUDENTS to tell what causes Betty to suddenly clap her ears and whine loudly. *She has heard the words "going up to Jesus" in a psalm.* What does this tell them about the nature of her malady? *It suggests that there is a religious component.*

Critical Vocabulary: pretense (line 534) Have students share definitions. Have them explain what makes a person pretentious. *Pretentious people try to impress others by presenting themselves as something other than what they are.*

Critical Vocabulary: unnerved (line 544) Ask students to describe what unnerves Proctor in lines 541–545. *He sees Betty sitting up and screaming and doesn't know why.*

26. **REREAD AND CITE TEXT EVIDENCE** In line 531, Proctor threatens to whip Abigail.

Z ASK STUDENTS what Abigail has just said that might explain his violent reaction. *She has just insulted his wife, called her a liar and a "cold, sniveling woman"; she says that "you bend to her."*

Critical Vocabulary: prodigious (line 560) Point out that *prodigious* usually has a positive connotation. Why would Mr. Putnam say that Betty's reaction was a "prodigious sign" of witchcraft? *He is thrilled that finally there is proof.*

CLOSE READ Notes

Rebecca. There is hard sickness here, Giles Corey, so please to keep the quiet.

Giles. I've not said a word. No one here can testify I've said a word. Is she going to fly again? I hear she flies.

570 **Putnam.** Man, be quiet now!

(*Everything is quiet. Rebecca walks across the room to the bed. Gentleness exudes from her.* Betty *is quietly whimpering, eyes shut.* Rebecca *simply stands over the child, who gradually quiets.*)

SHORT RESPONSE

Cite Text Evidence The plot of *The Crucible* slowly becomes more and more complicated. Why do you think Miller chooses to reveal information gradually rather than all at once? Look back at your reading notes and be sure to support your ideas by **citing evidence from the text.**

Miller weaves together narrative and drama to present a taut, historically accurate, and morally complex story about a town taken over by paranoia, mass hysteria, and religious intolerance. Miller reveals the plot gradually in order to build suspense. Little by little, we learn details about the characters and events in the forest. By revealing details slowly, he creates intrigue and allows his readers to understand how rumors spread. At the same time Parris is trying to figure out what he has seen, we as readers, are piecing together details from the text about what happened. Miller also uses other characters to spread rumors, using Mrs. Putnam to claim that Betty "cannot bear to hear the Lord's name" and Giles who asks if Betty is going to fly.

144

SHORT RESPONSE

Cite Text Evidence Students should:

- explain how the author provides in-depth information about the characters and setting.
- explain how the author uses text structure to gradually reveal the plot and create suspense.
- analyze the characters' interactions and development through the use of dialogue.

TO CHALLENGE STUDENTS . . .

It is no accident that the Salem witch trials of the 1690s bear a striking resemblance to events that happened a quarter-century later in the United States, known as the McCarthy hearings. Miller drew his inspiration for *The Crucible* from this bleak period in the history of our country. It was a time when a U.S. Senator named Joseph McCarthy waged a one-man campaign against "Communists" who he believed were trying to take over the government—a belief stemming from his own paranoia and inner demons. Even though McCarthy was stopped in his tracks, he succeeded in destroying the lives of many people. In addition, the entire country was enveloped in fear and dread. Neighbors turned each other in and no one was to be trusted.

ASK STUDENTS to research the period of history known as the "Red Scare," and the role of Senator Joseph McCarthy. Have them look online for a speech McCarthy gave to the Irish Fellowship Club in Chicago in 1954 defending his "war on Communism." Have students look for parallels between the nation in McCarthy 's time and the Salem community.

Have students form groups and discuss similarities between the McCarthy hearings and *The Crucible*. Ask them to consider questions such as:

- What can they tell about McCarthy's character from his speech in 1954? What do his words suggest? What is conveyed by his demeanor?
- Why was he obsessed with the "threat" of Communism? What did Communism represent to him?
- How did he get his information?
- What percentage of the witnesses turned in their friends or coworkers? How many refused?
- How and when was McCarthy finally disabled?

DIG DEEPER

1. With the class, return to Question 16, Reread. Have students share the results of their discussion.

   ASK STUDENTS to recall the author's characterization of Thomas Putnam. Given what students know about Putnam, have them address the following:

   - How far would Putnam go in order to "right matters"? What "matters" might he have to right? *Students should recognize that Putnam will to go to any lengths to prove the existence of witchcraft. He is quick to target others as he feels he has been targeted.*

   - What has happened to Putnam that might explain his bitterness? *Students may mention the incident in which his father willed his stepbrother a disproportionate amount of money.*

   - Have students give evidence of Putnam's vindictive nature. *He put someone in jail he knew was innocent out of resentment.*

   - Have students discuss why Putnam always feels slighted. What makes him feel superior to other men? *He was born the eldest son of the richest man in the village; he believes he is "the intellectual superior of most of the people around him."*

2. With the class, return to Question 18, Reread and Discuss.

   ASK STUDENTS to share their responses to Question 18.

   - Have students review what Abigail finally admits to Reverend Parris. How does she implicate Tituba? *She tells him that they were in the woods but that only Tituba and Ruth conjured spirits.*

   - Do students believe her story? Why or why not? *Students may say they do not believe her; she acts guilty and the author describes her as a dissembler.*

   - What does Tituba represent? *Students may say that Tituba represents wildness, chaos, magic, sensuality—and the forest, the site of all things dark and dangerous.*

   - Why is Tituba a subject of contention between Mrs. Putnam and Reverend Parris? *Mrs. Putnam thinks Tituba can conjure up the dead and seeks her help; Reverend Parris is scandalized—he thinks conjuring is a sin and wants nothing to do with it.*

   ASK STUDENTS to return to their Short Response answer and revise it based on the class discussion.

CLOSE READING NOTES

Science, Guided by Ethics

Essay by Freeman Dyson

Why This Text

Students may leave the text of an argument without a thorough understanding of the writer's point of view. Arguments such as this one, addressed in a persuasive essay by Freeman Dyson, may use complex reasoning and persuasive rhetoric that become clear only with careful study. With the help of the close-reading questions, students will evaluate Dyson's argument that technology must be guided by ethics in order to benefit both rich and poor.

Background Have students read the background information about Freeman Dyson. Introduce the essay by telling students that Dyson, a quantum physicist, astrophysicist, and mathematician, owes his interest in science to the famous astronomer Frank Watson Dyson. Though they were not related, the author claims that as a boy, it was not so much Frank Watson Dyson's work in astronomy that first intrigued him, but the fact that they shared the same last name.

AS YOU READ Ask students to pay attention to the reasons Dyson gives to support his position that technology "must be guided and driven by ethics" if it is to benefit both rich and poor. How soon into his essay can students begin to identify his point of view?

Common Core Support

- cite multiple pieces of textual evidence
- determine two or more central ideas of a text and analyze their development
- assess an author's claims and reasoning
- determine an author's point of view, analyzing how style and content contribute to the persuasiveness of the text

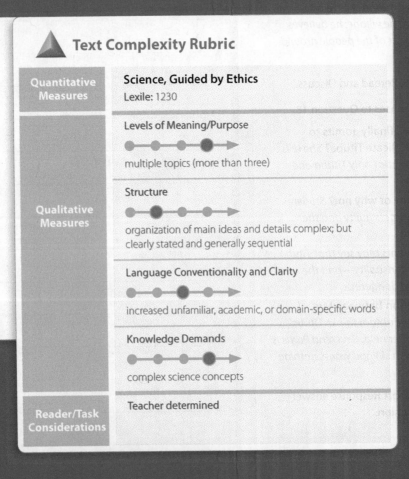

Text Complexity Rubric

Quantitative Measures	Science, Guided by Ethics Lexile: 1230
Qualitative Measures	**Levels of Meaning/Purpose** multiple topics (more than three)
	Structure organization of main ideas and details complex; but clearly stated and generally sequential
	Language Conventionality and Clarity increased unfamiliar, academic, or domain-specific words
	Knowledge Demands complex science concepts
Reader/Task Considerations	Teacher determined

Strategies for CLOSE READING

Analyze Author's Point of View

Students should read this essay carefully all the way through. Close-reading questions at the bottom of the page will help them focus on a thorough analysis of the argument. As they read, students should record comments or questions about the text in the side margins.

WHEN STUDENTS STRUGGLE...

To help students follow the reasons Dyson cites to support his claim that we need ethics to guide our use of green technology, have students work in a small group to complete a chart such as the one below.

CITE TEXT EVIDENCE For practice in analyzing an author's point of view, ask students to evaluate the content and style of Dyson's essay.

Author's Purpose	New green technology must be guided by ethics for the benefit of all, not the few.
Content	Dyson provides enough examples to support his purpose.
Tone	The author's tone is serious but not condescending—he presents his points in a friendly, confident manner.
Word Choice	Dyson uses everyday language that is no more complex than the subject demands.
Sentence Structure	The sentences are concise and straightforward and clearly present the author's case.
Overall Structure	Dyson alternates his presentation of possible benefits and downfalls of green technology, leading the reader to accept his premise that science should be guided by ethics.

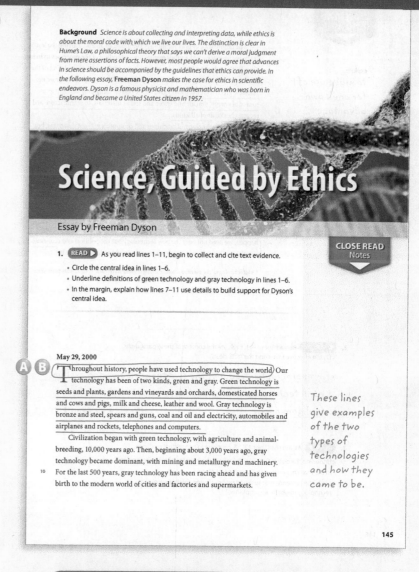

Background *Science is about collecting and interpreting data, while ethics is about the moral code with which we live our lives. The distinction is clear in Hume's Law, a philosophical theory that says we can't derive a moral judgment from mere assertions of facts. However, most people would agree that advances in science should be accompanied by the guidelines that ethics can provide. In the following essay,* **Freeman Dyson** *makes the case for ethics in scientific endeavors. Dyson is a famous physicist and mathematician who was born in England and became a United States citizen in 1957.*

Science, Guided by Ethics

Essay by Freeman Dyson

CLOSE READ
Notes

1. **READh** As you read lines 1–11, begin to collect and cite text evidence.

• Circle the central idea in lines 1–6.
• Underline definitions of green technology and gray technology in lines 1–6.
• In the margin, explain how lines 7–11 use details to build support for Dyson's central idea.

May 29, 2000

Throughout history, people have used technology to change the world. Our technology has been of two kinds, green and gray. Green technology is seeds and plants, gardens and vineyards and orchards, domesticated horses and cows and pigs, milk and cheese, leather and wool. Gray technology is bronze and steel, spears and guns, coal and oil and electricity, automobiles and airplanes and rockets, telephones and computers.

Civilization began with green technology, with agriculture and animal-breeding, 10,000 years ago. Then, beginning about 3,000 years ago, gray technology became dominant, with mining and metallurgy and machinery. For the last 500 years, gray technology has been racing ahead and has given birth to the modern world of cities and factories and supermarkets.

These lines give examples of the two types of technologies and how they came to be.

145

1. **READ AND CITE TEXT EVIDENCE** Explain that Dyson divides technology into two types: green and gray.

A **ASK STUDENTS** to cite evidence that explains how Dyson bolsters his central idea that for thousands of years, people have used technology to change the world. *Students should cite specific textual evidence in lines 7–11 to list the details about green technology (lines 7–8) and gray technology (lines 8–11) that Dyson cites to support his central idea.*

FOR ELL STUDENTS Spanish speakers will probably recognize the word *technology* from its cognate, *tecnología*. The word is formed from the Greek *techne*, meaning "art" or "skill," and *logia*, meaning "knowledge of." Ask students to use the word parts to define *automobile* (line 5) and *telephone* (line 6).

exploit:

to make use of for one's own advantage

Dyson believes that green technology can change the world for the better.

The dominance of gray technology is coming to an end. During the last 50 years, we have achieved a fundamental understanding of the processes in living cells. With understanding comes the ability to **exploit** and control. Out of the knowledge acquired by modern biology, modern biotechnology¹ is growing. The new green technology will give us the power, using only sunlight as a source of energy, and air and water and soil as materials, to manufacture and recycle chemicals of all kinds.

20 Our gray technology of machines and computers will not disappear, but green technology will be moving ahead even faster. Green technology can be cleaner, more flexible and less wasteful than our existing chemical industries. A great variety of manufactured objects could be grown instead of made. Green technology could supply human needs with far less damage to the natural environment. And green technology could be a great equalizer, bringing wealth to the tropical areas, of the planet, which have most of the world's sunshine, people and poverty.

I am saying that green technology could do all these good things, not that green technology will do all these good things. To make these good things happen, we need not only the new technology but the political and economic 30 conditions that will give people all over the world a chance to use it.

¹ **biotechnology:** the manipulation of living organisms or their components to produce useful products (such as pest resistant crops).

2. ◀ REREAD Reread lines 1–11. Evaluate the content of these paragraphs. Is Dyson effective in making the facts clear?

The first paragraph introduces the two technologies and explains what each technology is. The second paragraph explains the historical dominance of each technology, supported by examples.

3. READ ▶ As you read lines 12–36, continue to cite textual evidence.

• Underline the claims Dyson makes about the benefits of green technology.
• In the margin, paraphrase Dyson's point of view.
• Circle the sentence that summarizes how Dyson thinks new green technology might be accomplished.

146

We all know that green technology has a dark side, just as gray technology has a dark side.

To make these things happen, we need a powerful push from ethics. We need a consensus of public opinion around the world that the existing gross inequalities in the distribution of wealth are intolerable. In reaching such a consensus, religions must play an essential role. Neither technology alone nor religion alone is powerful enough to bring social justice to human societies, but technology and religion working together might do the job.

We all know that green technology has a dark side, just as gray technology has a dark side. Gray technology brought us hydrogen bombs as well as telephones. Green technology brought us anthrax bombs as well as antibiotics. Besides the dangers of biological weapons, green technology brings other 40 dangers having nothing to do with weapons. The ultimate danger of green technology comes from its power to change the nature of human beings by the application of genetic engineering² to human **embryos**.

hydrogen bombs, biological weapons

² **genetic engineering:** the development and application of science and technology that allows direct manipulation of genes in order to change the hereditary traits of a cell, organism, or population.

embryo:

an organism in early stages of development

4. ◀ REREAD Reread lines 31–36. How does Dyson define social justice? What does he say we need in order for green technology to become a "great equalizer?"

He defines social justice as a society in which there are no longer "gross inequalities in the distribution of wealth." He says we need ethics to help guide our use of technologies.

5. READ ▶ As you read lines 37–58, continue to cite textual evidence.

• In the margin, note one danger of gray technology and one danger of green technology.
• Underline the summary statement Dyson makes in lines 51–58 about the possible benefits of biotechnology and of green technology.
• Circle the summary statement he makes in lines 51–58 about the possible evils of green technology.

147

---

2. **REREAD AND CITE TEXT EVIDENCE**

B **ASK STUDENTS** to explain the two types of technology Dyson describes in their own words. *Students should understand that green technology has to do with agriculture and farming while gray technology is manufacturing and industry.*

3. **READ AND CITE TEXT EVIDENCE**

C **ASK STUDENTS** to cite evidence that best states Dyson's point of view. *Students should cite specific textual evidence from lines 20–26, 28–30, and 34–36 to paraphrase Dyson's viewpoint that green technology must work together with ethics (or religion) to make the world a better place.*

Critical Vocabulary: exploit (line 14) Have students explain *exploit* as Dyson uses it in his argument.

4. **REREAD AND CITE TEXT EVIDENCE**

D **ASK STUDENTS** to cite evidence explaining how Dyson defines *social justice* and what he means when he says that green technology could become a "great equalizer." *He defines social justice as a society in which there is a fair "distribution of wealth" (lines 32–33), and he implies that for green technology to become a "great equalizer," it will need a "push from ethics" (line 31).*

5. **READ AND CITE TEXT EVIDENCE**

E **ASK STUDENTS** what Dyson believes is the greatest peril of green technology. *He worries about the "power to change the nature of human beings" (line 42) through genetic engineering.*

Critical Vocabulary: embryo (line 43) Have students share their definitions of *embryo*.

> Science and religion should work together to abolish the gross inequalities that prevail in the modern world.

If we allow a free market in human genes, wealthy parents will be able to buy what they consider superior genes for their babies. This could cause a splitting of humanity into hereditary castes. Within a few generations, the children of rich and poor could become separate species. Humanity would then have regressed all the way back to a society of masters and slaves. No matter how strongly we believe in the virtues of a free market economy, the free
50 market must not extend to human genes.

I see two tremendous goods coming from biotechnology: first, the alleviation of human misery through progress in medicine, and second, the transformation of the global economy through green technology spreading wealth more **equitably** around the world.

equitably: *fairly*

6. ◀ REREAD Reread lines 37–50. What does Dyson say is the "ultimate danger" he sees in green technology? In what way does he support his claim? Support your answer with explicit textual evidence.

He claims that there is a danger in genetic engineering. He supports his claim by positing that "If we allow a free market in human genes, wealthy parents will be able to buy . . . superior genes for their babies," creating "hereditary castes," and perhaps "separate species." Humans could revert to "a society of masters and slaves."

148

The two great evils to be avoided are the use of biological weapons and the corruption of human nature by buying and selling genes. I see no scientific reason why we should not achieve the good and avoid the evil. The obstacles to achieving the good are political rather than technical.

G
60 Unfortunately a large number of people in many countries are strongly opposed to green technology, for reasons having little to do with the real dangers. It is important to treat the opponents with respect, to pay attention to their fears, to go gently into the new world of green technology so that neither

H human dignity nor religious conviction is violated. If we can go gently, we have a good chance of achieving within a hundred years the goals of ecological sustainability and social justice that green technology brings within our reach.

The great question for our time is how to make sure that the continuing scientific revolution brings benefits to everybody rather than widening the gap between rich and poor.

To lift up poor countries, and poor people in rich countries, from poverty,
70 technology is not enough. Technology must be guided and driven by ethics if it is to do more than provide new toys for the rich. Scientists and business leaders who care about social justice should join forces with environmental and religious organizations to give political clout to ethics.

7. READ ▶ As you read lines 59–77, continue to cite textual evidence.
- Circle Dyson's recommendation for dealing with opponents of green technology.
- Underline what he sees as "the great question for our time."
- In the margin, summarize the position Dyson states in lines 74–77.

149

6. REREAD AND CITE TEXT EVIDENCE

F **ASK STUDENTS** to cite explicit textual evidence to support Dyson's claim that genetic engineering is the greatest danger in green technology. *Students should cite evidence from lines 40–43 and 44–50 to support his claim that the "ultimate danger" he sees is a "free market in human genes," in which rich parents could buy "superior genes for their babies," separating "humanity into hereditary castes."*

Critical Vocabulary: equitably (line 54) Have students share their definitions of *equitably*. How does Dyson use the word to support his claim about a huge benefit of green technology? *He uses the word to bolster his position that by transforming the global economy, green technology will promote a more just distribution of wealth around the world.*

7. READ AND CITE TEXT EVIDENCE

G **ASK STUDENTS** to explain how Dyson uses rhetoric, style, and content to make his argument more convincing. *Students should cite specific textual evidence to emphasize that his use of persuasive rhetoric—must (line 70) and should (line 74)—compelling content, and a powerful writing style (the use of the alliterative p in poor, poor people, and poverty in line 69), contribute to the power and persuasion of his claim that "the great question for our time"(line 66) is how we can ensure that the "continuing scientific revolution" will benefit both rich and poor without "widening the gap" between them (lines 66–68).*

FOR ELL STUDENTS Point out the phrase *political clout* in line 73. Explain that in this context *clout* means "influence." Have a volunteer explain the term *political clout*. *It means "having the power to affect political decisions."*

127

CLOSE READ
Notes

Science and religion should work together to guide technology.

Science and religion should work together to abolish the gross inequalities that prevail in the modern world. That is my vision, and it is the same vision that inspired Francis Bacon[3] 400 years ago, when he prayed that through science God would "endow the human family with new mercies."

[3] **Francis Bacon:** a natural philosopher, scientist, judge, statesman, and writer, Bacon (1561–1626) pondered questions of ethics in his writing, even in his works of natural philosophy.

8. **◀ REREAD** Reread lines 59–77. What is Dyson's point of view about the future of green technology? Support your answer with explicit textual evidence.

In the future, green technology will benefit both rich and poor if it is guided by ethics: "If we can go gently, we have a good chance of achieving within a hundred years the goals of ecological sustainability and social justice that green technology brings within our reach."

SHORT RESPONSE

Cite Text Evidence Do you think Dyson offers a convincing argument that green technology must be guided by ethics? Review your reading notes, and evaluate the merit of his claim and evidence offered. **Cite textual evidence** in your response.

Dyson offers a reasonable claim and strong evidence to support his position and point of view. He supports his position with rhetoric ("the existing gross inequalities in the distribution of wealth are intolerable"; "provide new toys for the rich") and with the valid argument that "a powerful push from ethics" is needed to restrain the pursuit of technology having as its only purpose "widening the gap between rich and poor." Dyson recognizes a "dark side" to green technology, but uses that understanding to further his case.

150

8. **REREAD AND CITE TEXT EVIDENCE**

Ⓗ ASK STUDENTS to reread lines 61–65 and note the phrase Dyson repeats in these lines. What does he mean by urging us "to go gently"? *Dyson urges us to "go gently" into the new world of green technology by using ethics as a guide and to use technology as a way to benefit everyone rather than a select few.*

SHORT RESPONSE

Cite Text Evidence Students should cite evidence from the text to support their positions. They should:

- explain whether or not they agree with Dyson's argument.
- give reasons for their point of view.
- cite specific evidence from the text to support their reasons.

TO CHALLENGE STUDENTS . . .

For more context and a deeper understanding of Dyson's argument about the need for green technology and ethics to work together to bring about social justice, students can research green technology online.

ASK STUDENTS why green technology is at the forefront of scientific research. *Students should note that Dyson and many other scientists believe that green technology is likely to be used on a wide scale to solve some of Earth's most challenging problems.*

Encourage students to work in small groups and research one aspect of green technology. Then, have them write a persuasive essay about an environmental topic such as the need for green technology (e.g., solar or wind power) to provide us with a clean source of energy. Explain that the essay should state the group's point of view and attempt to persuade an audience. Remind groups to use convincing reasons to support their argument, guiding them to employ effective rhetoric, style, and content, and to use the writing process to draft their essay. Alternatively, they could present their opinion as an oral argument.

DIG DEEPER

With the class, return to Question 7, Read. Have students share their responses.

ASK STUDENTS whether they agree or disagree with Dyson's point of view. Then, ask students to form two groups according to their responses. (If students are unsure, they may wait to join a group.) Have each group cite explicit evidence to support their point of view about green technology.

- Guide students to tell whether there was any compelling evidence cited by group members holding a different opinion. If so, was that evidence powerful enough to change the group's opinion?
- Did everyone in the group agree as to what evidence best supported the group's position. Were there any differences of opinion the group needed to resolve?
- After the opposing groups have spoken, ask if any students changed their personal opinions and if so, why.

ASK STUDENTS to return to their Short Response answer and to revise it based on the class discussion.

CLOSE READING NOTES

Acknowledgments

Excerpt from "Abigail Adams' Last Act of Defiance" by Woody Holton from *American History* Magazine, April 2010. Text copyright © 2010 by Woody Holton. Reprinted by permission of Weider History Group.

"Ambush" from *The Things They Carried* by Tim O'Brien. Text copyright © 1990 by Tim O'Brien. Reprinted by permission of Houghton Mifflin Harcourt Publishing Company, Harper Collins Publishers, Ltd. and Tim O'Brien.

"Bonding Over a Mascot" by Joe La Pointe from *The New York Times*, December 29, 2006, *www.nytimes.com*. Text copyright © 2006 by The New York Times Company. Reprinted by permission of PARS International, on behalf of The New York Times.

Excerpt from "Act 1" from *The Crucible* by Arthur Miller. Text copyright © 1952, 1953, 1954, renewed 1980, 1981, 1982 by Arthur Miller. Reprinted by permission of Viking Penguin, a division of Penguin Group (USA) Inc. and The Wylie Agency, Inc.

Excerpt from "The General History of Virginia" by John Smith from *The Complete Works on Captain John Smith, 1580–1631,* edited by Philip L. Barbour. Text copyright © 1986 by The University of North Carolina Press. Reprinted by permission of The University of North Carolina Press.

"Indian Boy Love Song (#2)" from *The Business of Fancydancing* by Sherman Alexie. Text copyright © 1992 by Sherman Alexie. Reprinted by permission of Hanging Loose Press.

"Mother Tongue" from *The Opposite of Fate* by Amy Tan. Text copyright © 1989 by Amy Tan. First appeared in Threepenny Review. Reprinted by permission of the Sandra Djikstra Literary Agency and the author.

"Ode to a Large Tuna in the Market" by Pablo Neruda, translated by Robin Robertson from *Poetry* Magazine. Text copyright © 2011 by the Fundacion Pablo Neruda. Reprinted by permission of the University of California Press and the Agencia Literaria Carmen Balcells.

Excerpt from "Reflection on the Atomic Bomb" by Gertrude Stein. Text copyright © 1946 by Gertrude Stein. Reprinted by permission of David Higham Associates Ltd.

"Science, Guided by Ethics, Can Lift Up the Poor" (Retitled: "Science, Guided by Ethics") by Freeman Dyson from *The New York Times,* May 29, 2000, www.nytimes.com. Text copyright © 2000 by The New York Times Company. Reprinted by permission of PARS International, on behalf of The New York Times.

"Spoiling Walden: Or How I Learned to Stop Worrying and Love Cape Wind" by David Gessner from *ONEARTH* Magazine, December 12, 2011, *www.onearth.com*. Text copyright © 2011 by David Gessner. Reprinted by permission of the National Resources Defense Council.

"The Weary Blues" from *The Collected Poems of Langston Hughes* by Langston Hughes, edited by Arnold Rampersad with David Roessel, Associate Editor. Text copyright © 1994 by the Estate of Langston Hughes. Reprinted by permission of Alfred A. Knopf, a division of Random House, Inc., and Harold Ober Associates, Inc. Any third party use of this material, outside of this publication, is prohibited. Interested parties must apply directly to Random House, Inc. for permission.

"The Yuckiest Food in the Amazon" by Mary Roach from *Salon,* December 15, 1998, *www.salon.com*. Text copyright © 2012 by Salon Media Group, Inc. Reprinted by permission of Salon Media Group, Inc.

Index of Titles & Authors

A

Abigail Adams' Last Act of Defiance, 28
Alexie, Sherman, 14
Ambush, 100

B

Bonding Over a Mascot, 62

C

Crane, Stephen, 70
Crucible, from *The,* 110

D

Dekanawida, 58
Dyson, Freeman, 124

E

Emancipation Proclamation, The, 54
Emerson, Ralph Waldo, 40

G

General History of Virginia, from *The,* 2
Gessner, David, 46

H

Hall, Prince, 24
Holton, Woody, 28
How It Feels to Be Colored Me, 104
Hughes, Langston, 104
Hurston, Zora Neale, 104

I

I Hear America Singing, 36
Indian Boy Love Song (#2), 14
Iroquois Constitution, from *The,* 58

J

Journey, A, 84

L

Lapointe, Joe, 62
Lincoln, Abraham, 54

M

Men in the Storm, The, 70
Miller, Arthur, 110
Mother Tongue, 8

N

Nature, from, 40
Neruda, Pablo, 94
Noiseless Patient Spider, A, 36

O

O'Brien, Tim, 100
Ode to a Large Tuna in the Market, 94

P

Petition to the Massachusetts General Assembly, 24

R

Roach, Mary, 78

S

Science, Guided by Ethics, 124
Self-Reliance, from, 40
Smith, John, 2
Spoiling Walden, 46

T

Tan, Amy, 8

U

United States Constitution, from *The,* 20

W

Weary Blues, The, 104
Wharton, Edith, 84
Whitman, Walt, 36

Y

Yuckiest Food in the Amazon, The, 78